JUSTICE AND DESERT-BASED EMOTIONS

The clear message proposed in this book is that justice matters for morality and desert matters for justice – and that emotions matter for desert, justice and morality. Moreover, and no less importantly, justice education needs to take all those facts into consideration.

Kristján Kristjánsson's new book falls on the cutting edge of the latest developments in justice discourse, both in philosophy and in the social sciences. Written from a philosophical perspective, it gives an accessible but penetrating exploration of various interlocking and interdisciplinary themes relating to justice. Kristjánsson justifies the necessary interplay between philosophers and social scientists dealing with justice, probes the role of desert in justice and explains the rising interest in the emotionality of justice. He then analyses the main desert-based emotions, connects his discussion to recent trends in developmental and social psychology, offers a moral justification of desert and desert-based emotions, and concludes by applying all those ideas in a close study of how justice and desert should be handled in moral education at school.

Kristjánsson deftly weaves together insights from disparate academic areas relevant for justice, in general, and desert, in particular. This is an engaging, eye-opening and provocative book that should excite anyone interested in justice discourse and help generate debate in different areas related to justice: philosophical, psychological and educational.

This book is dedicated to the most important people in my life:
my wife, son and mother, and to the memory of my father

Justice and Desert-Based Emotions

KRISTJÁN KRISTJÁNSSON
University of Akureyri, Iceland

ASHGATE

Published by
Ashgate Publishing Limited
Gower House
Croft Road
Aldershot
Hants GU11 3HR
England

Ashgate Publishing Company
Suite 420
101 Cherry Street
Burlington, VT 05401-4405
USA

Ashgate website: http://www.ashgate.com

British Library Cataloguing in Publication Data
Kristján Kristjánsson.
Justice and desert-based emotions: a philosophical exploration
1. Justice (Philosophy) 2. Affect (Psychology)
I. Title
172.2

Library of Congress Cataloging-in-Publication Data
Kristján Kristjánsson.
Justice and desert-based emotions : a philosophical exploration / Kristján Kristjánsson.
p. cm.
Includes bibliographical references and index.
ISBN 0-7546-5199-1 (hardcover : alk. paper)
1. Justice. 2. Justice–Psychological aspects. I. Title.
BJ1533.J9K75 2006
172′.2–dc22 2004029550

ISBN 0 7546 5199 1

Typeset by CPI Tradespools, Chippenham, Wilts
Printed and bound in Great Britain by CPI Antony Rowe, Chippenham, Wilts

Contents

List of Figures

Preface

I started out as a political philosopher with a special interest in conceptual issues; my first book in English, *Social Freedom: The Responsibility View* (Cambridge University Press, 1996), had, accordingly, a somewhat narrow focus. After becoming disillusioned with much of what nowadays dresses up as political philosophy – an endeavour that blissfully ignores any conceptual foundational work and denies the notion of a common underlying humanity – I turned in my second book, *Justifying Emotions: Pride and Jealousy* (Routledge, 2002), to questions concerning some of our common emotions and their moral justification. Noting that many of these were based on a deep-seated belief in just deserts – the yearning for a 'tailored fit' between certain outcomes and certain actions and characteristics of individuals – and becoming, in the process, enamoured of Aristotle's treatment of such emotions, I decided to move on to the emotionality of justice itself and to some of the specific emotions that our sense of justice elicits. The product of that decision can be seen here, in a work that has helped me pool my various interests and resources and travel, so to speak, full circle from political philosophy, through philosophical psychology, to the relocation of questions that are germane to essentially political and moral concerns.

It is well known that philosophical and psychological explorations of human values and emotions have tended to run on parallel tracks without much mutual engagement. I do not believe that deep insights about justice can any longer (if they ever could) be obtained by wearing academic blinders and fixing one's attention upon the books on a single library shelf. If we are to reach out to the perplexities of justice, we need to take account of work done in fields as distinct as philosophy, psychology, sociology, education and even law. In this present book, I have tried to forge a link between concepts originating in different research fields, and to span, in my exploration, a number of disparate disciplines. My main expository aim throughout the book has been to write about justice and desert in a way that is tough-minded but fair to adversarial positions, and which, while essentially philosophical in orientation, is informed as far as possible by the host of research already carried out in other areas, invoked for purposes of confirmation or confrontation. All in all, my intention has been to write an engaging and provocative book that should excite anyone interested in justice discourse and help generate debate in different areas related to justice. Whether I have achieved that goal is for the reader to judge.

As can be divined from the foregoing paragraph, this book is meant for a wide readership. I hope it will be of interest to anyone concerned with the intersection between moral philosophy, psychology and education in the field of justice research. That should include philosophers, psychologists and educationists, as well as students of those subjects. The utility of my book for philosophy students lies, I dare to hope, in its detailed, deductive line of argument about justice and desert, giving emotions their proper place in helping us address socio-moral questions and make sense of the world. Psychology students should gain from the philosophical critique of psychological concepts and theories, and education students will find here a work that addresses specifically the topic of justice education as part of moral education.

In what follows, which represents the results of several years' work on justice, desert and the emotions, I borrow liberally from my own published articles and papers on the subject: 'In Defence of "Non-Expansive" Character Education', *Journal of Philosophy of Education*, **36**, 2002; 'Values Education at School: A Taxonomy of Some Recent Trends', in *Philosophieren in schwieriger Zeit*, ed. M. Bolz (Münster: LIT Verlag, 2003); 'Fortunes-of-Others Emotions and Justice', *Journal of Philosophical Research*, **28**, 2003; 'The Development of Justice Conceptions and the Unavoidability of the Normative', *Journal of Moral Education*, **32**, 2003; 'Justice, Desert, and Virtue Revisited', *Social Theory and Practice*, **29**, 2003; 'On the Very Idea of "Negative Emotions"', *Journal for the Theory of Social Behaviour*, **33**, 2003; 'Children and the Belief in a Just World', *Studies in Philosophy and Education*, **23**, 2004; 'Review of Susan L. Hurley, *Justice, Luck, and Knowledge*', *Mind*, **113**, 2004; 'Beyond Democratic Justice: A Further Misgiving about Citizenship Education', *Journal of Philosophy of Education*, **38**, 2004; 'Empathy, Sympathy, Justice, and the Child', *Journal of Moral Education*, **33**, 2004; 'Justice and Desert-Based Emotions', *Philosophical Explorations*, **8**, 2005; 'A Utilitarian Justification of Desert in Distributive Justice', *Journal of Moral Philosophy*, **2**, 2005. Although I have incorporated material from all these sources in my book (for the specific permissions to which I am grateful), I hope it will read as a cumulative, thoroughly composed monograph, rather than as an amalgam of vaguely connected papers.

I thank all the editors and anonymous referees in question for their comments on initial versions of those papers, and the audiences at various university conferences and seminars (in Reykjavík, Akureyri, Cambridge, Oxford, London, Lillehammer and Oslo), to whom earlier versions of some portions of the book were read, for valuable insights that prompted numerous improvements. My thanks go to a number of friends and colleagues who read portions of the manuscript at different stages and offered salutary criticisms, without benefit of which the final version would have been markedly inferior: Aaron Ben-Ze'ev, Haraldur Bessason, Guðmundur Heiðar Frímannsson, Sigurður J. Grétarsson, Logi Gunnarsson, Atli Harðarson, Terry Irwin, Mikael M. Karlsson, Terry McLaughlin, Serena Olsaretti and Stefán Snævarr. The positive encouragement I received from Robert C. Solomon (on the foundation of whose groundbreaking work much of my research has constructively attempted to build), Peter Goldie and

Samuel S. Scheffler should not go unmentioned here either. Barbara B. Nelson deserves special thanks for carefully copy-editing the whole manuscript; any remaining infelicities of style or language are not her fault. I am also grateful to Paul Coulam, the Philosophy Editor at Ashgate Publishing, for the confidence he had in my project from the very beginning, and to him and his colleagues there who followed the book with such care through the publishing process.

I would like to thank the Philosophy Department at Cornell University, in particular Terry Irwin, for inviting me as a Fulbright Fellow in the spring of 2001 and for providing me with the facilities which enabled me to begin my research on this book. I am grateful to the Iceland–US Educational Commission (Fulbright Visiting Scholar Program) for financial assistance. Most of the book was written during two sabbatical semesters (the spring semesters of 2002 and 2004) as a Visiting Scholar in the Faculty of Education, Cambridge University, and as a Visiting Fellow at St Edmund's College. I am eternally indebted to Terry McLaughlin for being by main host on both occasions, and to the College, in particular its Master, Sir Brian Heap, for providing me with a social environment congenial to interdisciplinary discussions and self-improvement. All of this facilitated my work on the book immeasurably. The financial help I have received from my own university, while on sabbatical in the USA and in Britain, is gratefully acknowledged, as is the efficient service of the Akureyri University Library.

My heartiest thanks must, however, go to my wife for her constant encouragement and care, and to my son and my mother for being there for me.

Chapter 1

Introduction

1.1 Mapping the Field

'I experienced profound joy when I heard about the dot-com bankruptcy'; 'I felt so happy about Anne's promotion; she really deserved a break after all her tough luck'; 'I was genuinely sorry for John when he was diagnosed with lung cancer although I suppose he had it coming to him after all his crazy smoking'; 'I feel kind of guilty about my recent stroke of luck; my poor brother would really have deserved some of it'; 'Don't you feel, like me, that Bill has had more than his fair share of good fortune recently?'; 'Why does my brother always get a bigger birthday cake than me? I know he's three years older than me, but it still isn't fair'; 'I cannot honestly complain about my recent set-backs, I probably deserved them the way I behaved'; 'I admit that Beth is talented, but I hate the way she seems to think this gives her a moral claim to an extra share of the good things in life'; 'I know it is wrong, but when my colleague went to have her teeth bleached this morning and they turned a putrid yellow colour, boy, did I get a kick out of that!'

From an early age, our emotions take up a substantial part of everyday conversation. If we consider the judgements passed at the dinner table or while doing the washing-up – at the times when the tongue speaks what the heart thinks – many of those will, I believe, turn out to be of the kind exemplified above: that is, having to do with the good or bad fortunes, just or unjust, deserved or undeserved, of ourselves and of our relatives, friends, colleagues and neighbours, and how we react emotionally to our lot and theirs. Where do such emotions stem from? What beliefs and desires do they incorporate? What is their relationship to ideals of justice, and where does the notion of desert fit into the picture? Are desert-based emotions morally justifiable under some circumstances and if so, how should we cultivate them in moral education? The present book is precisely about such emotions: their genesis, nature, moral standing and schooling. The key terms to highlight here, as we initiate our discussion, are 'emotions', 'justice', 'desert' and 'schooling', and this is the place for a few prefatory remarks about each of those in turn.

There has been a burgeoning of interest in the *emotions* in recent years. After decades, even centuries, of relative neglect, empirical and evaluative research on the emotions has gradually been coming into its own as an established discipline – or, perhaps more aptly put, as a series of established sub-disciplines – in the fields of psychology, philosophy, sociology and education. The phoenix-like rise of academic interest in the emotions, in general, and in their moral implications, in particular, is surely long overdue, given the fact, amply illustrated through history in countless intriguing novels and other works of art, that most of what is interesting about human life – at least from a moral point of view – is played out in the field of the emotions (cf. de Sousa, 1987, p. 17). Some of the academic interest has also percolated through to the public. The fundamental message of the prevailing cognitive theories of late, that emotions are in principle educable and regulatable, has, indeed, struck such a chord with the ordinary person that academic buzzwords such as 'emotional intelligence' have suddenly become topics of spirited discussion in the workplace and at the dinner table. I will assume here, from the beginning, that in order to make sense of the good life, the life worth living, we need to implicate emotions in our moral explorations, and to consider, for example, the moral basis on which the emotionally driven everyday statements of my opening paragraph above, about deserved and undeserved fortunes, could rest.

There has never been a dearth of interest in *justice* in academic circles. Since the ancient Greeks, questions of justice have riveted the attention of almost every major philosopher. It may be asked how many strings justice has to its bow. While a fair diversity of scholarly opinion continues to be generated on that question, the days are gone when the idea of *desert* as a possible string in the justice-bow could be dismissed with a few peremptory remarks. Indeed, as critical attention has shifted away from the Rawlsian (1973) and Nozickean (1971) accounts of institutional justice, which dominated the debate in the 1970s and 1980s, towards a Feinbergian (see originally Feinberg, 1970) discursive tradition that accommodates desert-based pre-institutional concerns as one consideration among others in a *pluralistic* account of justice, the notion of desert or deservingness – one systematically overlooked and maligned since Enlightenment times – has undergone a revival. This revival is not only evident among moral and political philosophers (see, for example, Olsaretti, 2003a), but also among social scientists (see, for example, Ross and Miller, 2002). Some have focused on what people mean by 'desert' (for example, Feather, 1999), others on what they ought to mean in order to advance the debate (for example, Sher, 1987), and yet others on children's alleged acquisition of a 'natural' belief in a world where people get what they deserve (see various articles in Ross and Miller, 2002); lurking in the background have been deeper normative questions about what role, if any, desert should play in a sound moral outlook (see, for example, Miller, 1999).

In contrast to the *desert-ignoring* theories of a quarter of a century ago, the pluralistic philosophical justice theories of late tend to be either *desert-sensitive* – that is, they accept pre-institutional desert as a salient, if somewhat easily defeasible, ingredient in overall justice (for example, ibid.; this also seems to have been Feinberg's view in his groundbreaking essay of 1970) or *desert-prioritizing* – that is, they consider desert the most important single ingredient in justice although it can sometimes be morally outweighed by other considerations (taken collectively), for example those of institutional entitlements (for an early formulation, see Sadurski, 1985). *Desert-monistic* accounts of justice – that is, attempts to couch justice solely in terms of desert – notably remain as scarce as before; rare exceptions to the rule are Feldman (1995a: 'My conception of justice is based on the ancient and plausible idea that justice is done when people receive goods and evils according to desert', p. 573), Pojman (2001) and McLeod (2003). Nevertheless, the recent drift towards accommodating desert concerns in justice signifies a major change of academic emphasis, particularly so when viewed in conjunction with another, largely simultaneous, trend, namely one which heralds the return to an Aristotelian conception of justice as primarily, psychologically and logically a personal virtue, rather than, as Rawls held, essentially a 'virtue of social institutions' (1973, p. 3).

Most of the recent accounts of justice are, in fact, triply *pluralistic*. In the first place, they suggest various ingredients in justice, including desert, which need to be weighed against one another; in the second, they argue that desert claims are traceable to a variety of irreducibly different desert bases (a view which I, incidentally, do not share); and in the third, they accept that justice may need to be weighed against other values in overall judgements of morally right distributions of benefits and burdens. Notably, even desert-monistic theories of justice can be pluralistic in the second and third of these three senses.

Now some would argue that the reintroduction of desert in justice theories has created more problems than it has solved. For instance, the question of what constitutes the basis or bases of desert, the grounds in virtue of which a person can be said to deserve some treatment or outcome, opens up a 'new' source of controversy. While public opinion seems to prioritize moral virtue as the most important – or even the single all-embracing – desert basis, many philosophers disagree. Even though I happen to be more sympathetic to such a single-basis view of desert than the philosophical majority, I would be getting ahead of my argument (in Chapter 2) to press that point here. Let me, rather, at this juncture, highlight the fact that the revival of desert in academic discourse typically represents more than just a conceptual thesis about the meaning of justice. It also tends to imply a psychological thesis about the origin, development and nature of justice concerns in human beings – and, additionally, a sympathetic view of the potential relevance of the latter for the former.

What has fuelled this new-found interest in desert in philosophical circles? One reason may be the widely heard call of a leading liberal thinker who fears that the failure of liberals to take sufficient account of desert-based 'reactive attitudes' – attitudes that are an ingrained part of the common person's moral sense – could be leading liberalism into political isolation (Scheffler, 1992; cf. Strawson, 1962, on 'reactive attitudes' as essentially natural, morally ineliminable, human reactions). Whatever liberal politicians profess, there seems to be a broad consensus among the general public that desert should carry considerable weight in the distribution of benefits and burdens (see, for example, Galston, 1991, pp. 159–62). Another is probably the recent cautious venture of a number of philosophers across the barricades traditionally separating philosophy from the social sciences. Academics working in the latter domain have never considered justice to be primarily about a set of theoretical principles, but rather about a set of powerful personal feelings – that is, a deeply emotional matter. In the philosophical, as well as in the psychological, literature, insights have been resurfacing about the essential emotionality of justice itself: namely, that justice is – as the ancients realized – not primarily a lofty intellectual virtue, grounded in abstract, detached beliefs, but rather, at bottom, an earthbound, if complex, emotional virtue, grounded in certain compelling beliefs and desires which are deeply embedded in human nature (Scheffler, 1992; Solomon, 1995). As a complex emotional virtue, justice seems to encompass certain desert-based emotions that are certainly important developmentally – and perhaps also morally – for an understanding of this virtue. Interestingly, the trend away from justice as a grand political blueprint towards its personalization, emotionalization and (by implication) depoliticization takes us right back to the familiar and ancient territory of Aristotle's *nemesis*: an emotional and moral disposition towards pain felt at fortune, either good or bad, if undeserved, and towards pleasure if deserved: a disposition which forms an inseparable part of Aristotle's overall conception of justice (cf. Curzer, 1995; see further in Chapter 3 of the present book).

However much we might welcome the recent philosophical trend towards exploring justice via desert-based emotions and through a productive, if still somewhat cautious, intercourse with the social sciences, it would be premature to assert here that the virtue of justice necessarily requires a disposition toward desert-based emotions. *Qua* particular emotions, the desert-based ones must pass the same test of moral justifiability as other emotions: they must be deemed both rational and morally fitting in the given circumstances (see Kristjánsson, 2002, chs 1–2). Questions still linger as to whether the desert-based emotions pass this test, as well as to what extent they should be allowed to shape our actions and allocation decisions. In other words, we cannot conclude from the assumptions that (a) justice is a virtue, (b) desert is an ingredient in justice and (c) desert-based emotions express desert claims, that the desert-based emotions are themselves virtuous and that desert claims express (other things being equal) a virtue. It could well be that these are morally neutral, or even immoral, and that there are other, perhaps institutional, aspects of justice which make it all-in-all virtuous. We still need, therefore, an independent moral justification of desert and desert-based emotions. After all, Strawson did not morally justify 'reactive attitudes', although he posited them as 'essentially natural human reactions', the absence of which would be practically inconceivable in this world (1962, pp. 195–7). In light, however, of the wide historic consensus on justice as a virtue and the recently growing consensus on the relevance of desert, in general, and desert-based emotions, in particular, for this virtue, it might seem reasonable to predict that the emotions in question will on many occasions pass the test of moral justifiability and, hence, be thought of as virtuous. But again, let us not get ahead of our argument here; this is another point that I will revisit and argue for later in the present book (Section 4.3).

Our final 'key term' was that of *schooling*. Recently, educationists have joined in the enthusiasm for justice with two major trends in values education extolling justice as a fundamental virtue to be transmitted to students. Thus proponents of 'citizenship education' highlight justice as a public, democratic virtue, whilst followers of 'character education' champion the virtuosity of justice as a personal, pre-institutional character trait. Once again, there is ample room for disagreement about which ingredients of justice should be emphasized and through what means as we explain this virtue to, and attempt to cultivate it in, our students.

Earlier I mentioned a recent venture across traditional academic lines. It is a commonplace that *philosophical* research on moral concepts, virtues and emotions, on the one hand, and *social-science* research into the same moral issues, on the other, have tended to run on parallel tracks without significant mutual acknowledgement. This familiar polarization, and its resulting lack of integrative work, is a lamentable state of affairs, not least so in the field of justice research where it often leads to the denial of insights that could have helped us to think productively about the issues at hand. One can, indeed, hardly think of another field where the combined efforts of describing the evaluative and evaluating the descriptive are as urgently called for.

One side of the coin has been the woeful lack of awareness among philosophers of the empirical research that has been conducted by social scientists concerning people's justice-based intuitions, beliefs and emotions. When mentioned at all in philosophical writings, these tend to be dismissed out of hand as unconsidered and irrelevant: what matters is what people *should* think, not what they *do* think. The reverse side of the coin has been the corollary reluctance of social scientists to take account of work done by philosophers. In the following section, I argue for the indispensability of interdisciplinary work on justice. We should refuse the gambit offered to us by a strict descriptive–evaluative dichotomy and engage each other in debate on issues that are of relevance to both social scientists and philosophers exploring justice. Ideas of the natural origin and development of desert and other justice concerns, to take one example, are not merely *psychologically* interesting; they can also have important *moral* ramifications, especially for naturalist theories of morality such as utilitarianism and virtue ethics. These theories assume that moral theory construction must take full account of empirical research and that we need to know a lot about how human beings are before we can construct a moral code which will help them to function and flourish. Furthermore, a developmental account of justice concerns appears to be the natural starting point for the construction of *educational* perspectives on justice, since educational interventions – for example in values education classes at school – aimed at stimulating or stifling certain intuitions students might have about just states of affairs would, I submit, have to rely on psychological facts about the nature and origin of such intuitions. Conversely, psychologists and educators urgently need to enlist the aid of philosophers in clarifying and analysing the concepts and issues that form the objects of social-scientific inquiry into justice.

Fortunately, as already noted, the age-old disdain that philosophers and social scientists have had for each others' work seems now gradually to be subsiding and attempts at mutual engagement in critical, interdisciplinary debates on justice are slowly gathering pace. Once the myth of the mutual irrelevance of these two academic fields to one another has been buried, we can – as I plan to do in this book – proceed on a more extended front and make capital of research carried out in otherwise distinct scholarly areas. Although my main focus will inevitably be that of a philosopher, as I am educated as one and cannot claim equal competence in the field of social science, I will make the effort at least to step across the 'imaginary barbed wire' (Solomon, 2002b, p. 119) between philosophy and social science and to rely as much as I can upon both foci.

Plan and Summary

The cardinal aim of this book is to fall on the cutting edge of the latest developments in discourse about distributive justice, in both philosophy and the social sciences. More specifically, I plan to (a) justify the necessary interplay between philosophers and social scientists dealing with justice, (b) probe the role of desert in justice, (c) explain the rising interest in the emotionality of justice and explore the main desert-based emotions, (d) connect my discussion to recent trends in developmental and social psychology, (e) morally justify desert and desert-based emotions and (f) provide advice as to how justice and desert should be handled in moral education at school.

In furtherance of those ambitions, I set out in the remainder of this chapter to explore the historical lack of interest in interdisciplinary work on justice. That exploration takes shape in a series of arguments for the necessity of integrative justice research which bridges the gap between insights and research findings in developmental and social psychology, education, political science, moral as well as political philosophy and philosophy of mind. I then rehearse briefly, in the final section of this chapter, some relevant points from recent debates about the nature of emotions in general, and gauge their pertinence for desert-based emotions in particular. I zero in specifically on the notion of so-called negative emotions, as some of the desert-based emotions are likely to be categorized as such. I argue that the invocation of the term 'negative emotion' cannot be done without cost to our understanding since it obscures all sorts of relevant complexities. There are thus no emotions to which we can helpfully refer collectively as 'negative', although there are of course painful emotions, emotions that evaluate states of affairs negatively, emotions that are negatively morally evaluated and so forth. Furthermore, while attempts are under way to reappraise various (commonly) negatively evaluated emotions, those attempts involve different kinds of arguments that cannot and should not be collected together as 'defences of negative emotions'. My discussion here points to various topics that receive more sustained scrutiny in subsequent chapters.

Chapter 2 is about the concept of desert: its contours and implications, as well as its role in justice. I argue that desert claims have a single basis, moral virtue, and offer four main reasons for this being the most philosophically illuminating and serviceable account of desert: (1) it has strong intuitive appeal; (2) it helps to account for the sense in which need is, and also the sense in which need is not, relevant for justice; (3) it sheds light on the controversial issue of if and how responsibility is required for desert attribution; and (4) it best accords with social-science research on what people actually think desert is. This account is set in the context of post-Feinbergian analyses of the ingredients of justice, and it is compared to other accounts of the basis or bases of desert.

Despite the resurgence of interest in the emotions, which goes back all the way to the 1970s, not much attention has been focused, until quite recently, on those emotions that relate to the deserved or undeserved fortunes of ourselves and others. In Chapter 3, I ponder the reasons for this increased attention and offer a logical and moral overview of some common emotions of this particular sort. I argue that when Aristotle's treatment of the family of *other-reactive* desert-based emotions is stripped of certain anomalies, it gives a logically satisfying and morally suggestive, if perhaps overly rigid, account of such emotions and their relations. I use those insights, *inter alia*, to challenge some recent accounts of *Schadenfreude* and to characterize instead pleasure at deserved bad fortune as *satisfied indignation*. Subsequently, I suggest that an analogous general account can be given, along Aristotelian lines, of *self-reactive* desert-based emotions. The proper experience of desert-based emotions, in the Aristotelian model, lays the ground for justice as a personal virtue, a virtue that, in turn, is required for full-scale social justice. All in all, Chapter 3 helps to refine and amplify my account of the inevitable emotionality of justice concerns. Although it does not give a definitive answer to the question of whether the desert-based other-reactive and self-reactive emotions really are virtuous (the answer to that emerges at a later juncture), it aims at enriching our understanding of what kind of virtue they might possibly represent.

Chapter 4 shifts the scrutiny first to psychological concerns and then to questions of moral justification. I start out with a survey and critique of insights from contemporary research in developmental psychology on 'justice internalization'. I spell out the way in which normative concerns enter unavoidably into the design and interpretation of empirical research on children's development of justice conceptions, with special emphasis on

William Damon's well-known stage theory of such development. Normative considerations provide assumptions not only about what counts as a conception of justice in the first place but also about what counts as a better or worse conception. Damon, for one, relies on the questionable normative premise that all distributive choices are choices about justice. An alternative research programme is suggested, based on piecemeal mutual adjustments between the normative and the empirical, a programme that would focus on children's desert-based emotions. Martin Hoffman's empathy theory is germane to this debate since it gives an essentially emotion-oriented account of moral development in general, as well as an explanation of the gradual bonding of empathy/sympathy with justice. Hoffman's theory explains in detail how all moral concerns, including justice concerns, depend upon the child's original capacity for empathy, but, on the other hand, it seems to underestimate the emotionality of justice itself. This unnecessarily weakens, as we see at a later stage, the thrust of Hoffman's educational suggestions about induction as the most productive method of pro-social stimulation. I also subject, in Chapter 4, to philosophical scrutiny a well-known theory in social psychology, the theory of a belief in a just world (BJW theory). Should parents and teachers discourage or encourage children to believe in a just world, in the sense given to such a belief in this theory? The intricacies of BJW theory are explored, with special emphasis on the strange case of 'victim derogation'. I conclude that the theory remains, for various reasons, unilluminating, both morally and educationally, unless supplemented by normative and factual interpretative conditions. Some such conditions are then suggested and discussed. The marshalling of arguments relating to psychological findings turns, as I go on to contend, to be crucial to the question of the moral justification of desert and desert-based emotions. In the final section of Chapter 4, I take on the challenge of articulating and defending a utilitarian justification of desert in distributive justice. I argue, first, that while there may be ways of accommodating desert concerns in liberal theory, this cannot, in the view of liberals themselves, be done without considerable cost to the ideals that are closest to their hearts. Conversely, I suggest that a deceptively simple classical utilitarian (Millian) defence of desert can be made to work. As I seek to gain a receptive hearing for my suggestion, I parry various possible objections that might be raised against such a utilitarian justification and conclude that none of them confutes it.

Finally, for those readers who persevere that far, in Chapter 5 I seek to pin down some of the educational implications of my foregoing discussion. While avoiding committing myself to any single narrow conception of exactly what justice education should comprise, I offer a conceptual schema for identifying and categorizing different positions on values education and their take on justice. I analyse and attempt to surmount a handful of objections that have been raised against the idea of so-called non-expansive character education, and contrast such character education with the teachings of citizenship education on justice. In keeping with the broader Aristotelian tenor which animates the whole book, I try to clarify – and to some extent rectify – an Aristotle-inspired, character-based and emotion-driven justice pedagogy.

This book is not tied to any cluster of political aspirations. Yet, while not promoting any particular political agenda, my discussion carries a strong moral and educational message: justice matters for morality and desert matters for justice. Emotions matter for desert, justice and morality. Moreover, and no less importantly, justice education needs to take all those facts into consideration.

1.2 Crossing the Barbed Wire

Philosophers theorizing about justice have historically, with rare exception, turned a blind eye to empirical evidence gathered by social scientists about prevailing justice beliefs: what the public thinks justice is. A corollary fault on the part of social scientists, which I go on to consider later in this section, is their disregard for the conceptual work done by philosophers. So while philosophers have tended to pursue justice at the level of upper-case abstractions, social scientists have commonly treated justice beliefs as if springing from an intellectual vacuum. This mutual lack of engagement forms part of a larger picture: the general reluctance of both philosophers and social scientists to take into account insights from each others' work. Arguably, the resulting 'great divide' is caused by the (mostly unreasonable) fear, on the part of both philosophers and social scientists, of importing 'impure' elements into their studies: in the case of the former, the 'petty ideas' of the *ignobile vulgus*; in the case of the latter, normative, and hence 'unscientific', considerations.

A change of compass might have been expected with the post-1980s upsurge of naturalist moral theory, particularly in the form of virtue ethics, and the continuing popularity of Rawls's 'reflective equilibrium' (1973) as a methodology for conceptual studies in moral and political philosophy. After all, what ultimately distinguishes moral naturalism from rationalism and other forms of non-naturalism is the belief that all moral propositions are, in principle, empirically defeasible, and the method of 'reflective equilibrium' is concerned primarily with achieving coherence and congruence between abstract theory and people's considered everyday (recordable) intuitions. One would thus not only have expected books espousing virtue ethics to abound in references to the testimony of psychologists, educators and health professionals about what is, in fact, conducive to our flourishing – what makes us tick – but also have expected books employing Rawls's methodology to be keenly aware of empirical evidence, gathered by social scientists, about people's intuitions.

That this is, alas, not the case does not need much elaboration. Leading virtue ethicists (for example, Hursthouse, 1999; Foot, 2001) seem to think that we have more to learn about human virtues from zoologists studying the behaviour of bees and wolves than from social scientists; and explorations of political concepts through the Rawlsian method of 'reflective equilibrium' typically consider only what rational agents might think after due reflection in artificially conceived choice situations rather than exploring what ordinary people think here and now. The elision of desert from considerations of justice should have been a potential source of embarrassment for Rawlsians, given the fact that empirical evidence about what the public takes justice to mean invariably indicates the importance of desert concerns (see, for example, Miller, 1999, ch. 4). Not that this seems to worry the Rawlsians overly much, however; they seem not even to have been much disturbed by the fact that repeated studies, both in the USA and in Europe (Frolich and Oppenheimer, 1992), have failed to record any substantial public support for Rawls's famous 'difference principle' of justice (maximizing the minimum income). To explain away such findings, Rawlsians have tended to embrace the assumption that only the intuitions of a certain stock set of philosophers can be seen as 'considered' enough to merit investigation. The resulting danger, however, is that the reflective equilibrium being sought then collapses into a transference of bones between philosophical graveyards.

All in all, when philosophers have invoked empirical considerations in inquiries into conceptual or substantive topics, those considerations have typically been of the armchair-empiricism kind, based on anecdotal evidence derived from their own experiences – from then on referred to as 'our intuitions' – or on contrived science-fiction scenarios. Although there are recent notable exceptions (for example, as already mentioned, Miller, 1999), much of this 'evidence' tends to be uninformed by any public-view, social-system or human-nature constraints. Aristotle's counsel, later echoed by Mill, for consulting the opinions of the 'many and the wise' is not even heeded; what end up on the table are, at best, the opinions of the 'few and the wise'.

Let us focus our attention for the moment on *conceptual* inquiries. After all, in order to understand the nature and salience of desert in general, as well as the nature and salience of the desert-based emotions in particular, in justice talk, we must first establish a proper understanding of the concepts of desert and justice and of the emotion concepts in question. Notably, all of these concepts are open-textured ('semi-open'), in contrast to the 'closed' concepts of logic and mathematics where strict rules prescribing the necessary and sufficient properties of the relevant concept, rectangularity for example, can be given, settling definitively every question of usage – as well as to the 'wide-open' concepts of mere subjective preferences where the conditions for a particular item falling under a concept, such as beauty, may be simply a matter of taste. The proper understanding of a semi-open concept – the search for the best conception – should, in my view, rely neither on stipulation nor mere reference to prevailing intuitions, but should rather be backed up by various distinct arguments showing why the suggested specification is the most theoretically serviceable one available. My preferred method is thus one of *critical conceptual revision* (see Kristjánsson, 1996, ch. 7). As our starting point, we need to collocate people's common conceptions about the given concept, then work through the puzzles of contradictions in usage and beliefs, and finally formulate a new account which we bring back to the conceptions, trying to retain the truth of the greatest number and, in particular, the most authoritative of these. In the end, we may be doing more than just tidying up ordinary usage: it does happen that common usage fails to honour distinctions which themselves emerge from an analysis of common usage; or, possibly, we find that distinctions entrenched in ordinary language are in fact redundant. This is in no way mysterious: definitions are created to serve a purpose; they do not fall into our lap by chance. Nevertheless, there is no other way to proceed rationally *at the outset* than by taking our cue from common conceptions. What we *then* need to show, for instance for concepts such as justice, desert and the particular desert-based emotions, are their point or role in human relations and, furthermore, to argue critically for characterizations of the given concepts that best convey these points. In the end, what we hope emerges are definitions that are not essentially contestable or irredeemably relative, but rather objective in the sense of being objectively useful to those interested in certain relations between human beings, the reference being fixed by our universal human sphere of experience (see further in Kristjánsson, 2002, s. 1.3).

I do not claim any special originality for this method of conceptual inquiry and the aspirations associated with it. I chose the title 'critical conceptual revision', rather than simply 'conceptual analysis' or 'philosophical analysis', merely in order to distinguish it from abuses of such analysis which have tended to give it a bad name: analyses where either the 'terminological regimentation' has so tightened everyday usage as to squeeze all the juice out of it, leaving us with obscurantist, trivial definitions that, despite their analytical precision, are little more than philosophical playthings (see, for example, the radical departure from everyday intuitions in Kramer's account of freedom, 2003) or, alternatively, where the supposedly respectful reference to ordinary intuitions is actually but a veneer for a declaration of the writer's own idiosyncratic conception, swamping any real everyday beliefs (witness the worst excesses of the so-called ordinary-language analysis of the 1960s). By contrast, all good 'conceptual analyses', such as the one preached as well as practised in Robert C. Roberts's recent book on the emotions (2003, s. 1.5), follow more or less the course outlined above as 'critical conceptual revision'. Indeed, I fully agree with Roberts that conceptual analysis of this (proper) sort is a method eminently suited for revealing the structure of human beings' experiences in a common natural and social world.

Now, if recourse to common intuitions is the natural springboard for conceptual inquiries – and thus for the substantive theorizing which rests on the foundation of such inquiries – what explains the numbing silence of most philosophers in respect of those intuitions? Why are philosophical justice theorists, for instance, not actively engaged in a study of people's intuitions and experiences relating to justice and desert, intuitions that have been duly recorded in the social-science literature? Why does their focus so rarely stray from the ideas of their own philosophical colleagues? Three main reasons come to mind.

First, those philosophers engaged in constructing formalist (for example rationalist) theories of justice, based on the tenets of pure reason and applicable in all possible worlds, may rightly have supposed that they had little to learn from common intuitions. However, even with the decline of rationalist, and the resurgence of naturalist, approaches to justice, the focus has not so much (as noted earlier) shifted to human beings as to the behaviour of bees and wolves! Second, philosophers have long suspected that on issues as complex as those of justice, the intuitions of the general public are simply too confused and incoherent to be taken seriously. As Brian Barry puts it, 'not only do different people have different ideas' but the 'different and incompatible ideas jostle one another within a single psyche, one coming out on top in one context and another in a different context' (1995, p. 5). Such assumptions, that people do not really know what they think about justice or even how to decide what the possibilities for thinking about it are, have led many philosophers to either eschew completely any empirical evidence or, at best, revert to some kind of armchair empiricism. Third, and most important, the received philosophical wisdom has long been that what matters morally is not what people currently (and perhaps even momentarily) *do* think about justice but rather what they *should* think. Thus empirical findings of public opinion have tended to be dismissed in the philosophical literature as 'mere quirks' since the opinions recorded are *historically unsophisticated* (having been hastily arrived at and uninformed by knowledge of philosophical ideas), leading to their being both *formally indeterminate*, that is, not having satisfied any established formal criteria to qualify as justice judgements, and *substantively indeterminate*, that is, not having been based on moral principles as opposed to, say, mere personal preferences (see, for example, Liebig, 2001). Since the empirical evidence is not considered to exemplify rigorous moral points of view, this is thought to reflect negatively on the prospect of utilizing it as grist for the mill of moral and political theorizing.

Why Philosophical Justice Theories need Social Science, and Vice Versa

I do not think that any of the reasons typically given by philosophers for disregarding the social-science evidence about justice beliefs is a particularly good one. The first reason given above may appeal to writers of a formalist persuasion, but rationalist and other formalist accounts of justice no longer hold the field in philosophical justice discourse, and for the growing number of philosophers who are interested in justice as a personal virtue, the appeal to the non-naturalist nature of the virtue will seem alien. Also misdirected for the most part are the second and third reasons: concerning people's alleged conceptual confusions and inconsistencies, and concerning the lack of historical sophistication, leading to formally and substantively indeterminate research designs. Even if this were, indeed, a faithful description of a large proportion of existing research, then it would simply be the job of the social scientists to overcome such problems, by making clear to their respondents, in advance, the relevant conceptual grounds and asking more searching questions that elicit not only unconsidered and/or self-interested justice intuitions but morally informed justice judgements. This can be achieved and has been achieved through better designed questionnaires and research scenarios as well as through careful correlations of respondents' appraisals of just or unjust situations with other appraisal criteria (see, for example, Liebig, 2001; Mikula et al., 1998). If the respondents need to be taught some philosophy into the bargain, then so much the better for them! In other words, philosophers do not have good reasons for ignoring all social-science findings about people's justice beliefs; they only have a reason for ignoring the results of badly conducted research and, at the same time, a duty to encourage and help social scientists improve their work.

So far, Adam Swift (1995, 1999), the author who has written most astutely on the relation between philosophical justice theories and social-science research into popular beliefs about distributive justice, would probably agree with my line of argument. He thinks that empirical research into such beliefs and their causal determinants provides invaluable food for thought, and that the beliefs themselves constitute important feasibility constraints on the realization of philosophical justice theories. He refuses, however, to go further and grant that the justice beliefs can be constitutive – in any significant sense – of the rationale of justice and, hence, that they can play a role in the justification of particular justice principles. The reason given by Swift is that even after the necessary pruning of conceptual inconsistencies and the amendment of research designs undertaken by the philosopher (or by the social scientist under philosophical supervision), there is no guarantee that the informed results of public opinion on justice will coincide with the well-argued justice theory of the philosopher. It may still be the case that public opinion rests upon faulty inference that can be demonstrated through subtle philosophical argument (1999, esp. pp. 356–7, 361).

As a thorough-going naturalist, I would be inclined to go further than Swift allows, and I will do so in Section 4.3 when I tender my arguments for the justification of desert. Let it suffice to remind the reader here of the Millian insight that the best reason we can give for something being morally desirable lies in its actually being desired by competent (wise and experienced) judges. Now, this is obviously not tantamount to saying that the actuality of a large number of people having converged upon the same view of justice provides a reason for giving this view a constitutive role in the justification of justice principles – for we cannot assume that those people constitute wise and experienced judges. Nevertheless, if we advisedly follow Miller in rejecting the view that philosophers can discover truth by means which are, in principle, not available to lay people (1999, pp. 52–3; for a discussion, see Mason, 2002), then the actuality of a large number of people having converged upon the same view of justice, *combined* with the fact that the research into their views was carried out in accordance with the best available standards (sufficient formal and substantive determination of research design and so forth), provided good reason for giving this evidence a justificatory role as the evidence of competent judges. It may still be the case that their particular view is wrong, as shown after further scrutiny by philosophers or lay people, but then again the essential fallibility of *all* theories (moral, political or otherwise) is no novelty in post-Popperian times.

Swift's defence of the philosophical salience of social-science findings on justice is thus, in my view, an unduly limited one. I fully agree with Miller that 'empirical evidence should play a significant role in justifying a normative theory of justice', with such a theory being tested, in part, by its correspondence with considered everyday intuitions about justice (1999, p. 51). I also agree with Simmons, who claims that the obvious starting point for the construction of philosophical perspectives on justice lies in the 'origin and development of social justice principles' (1981, p. 41) – both, I would hasten to add, their historical development (through the history of moral ideas) and their psychological one (through the development of the relevant conceptions in the individual person). I will, however, suspend further exploration of those developmental and justificatory issues until Chapter 4.

Let us now bestow some attention upon the other side of the coin: the reluctance of social scientists to pay heed to philosophical insights on justice. While there are important exceptions there also of theorists trying to forge links and span disciplines (for example Feather, 1999), the general tendency has been to try to advance and test hypotheses – for example about people's conceptions of this or that situation as just or unjust, deserved or undeserved – without recourse to philosophical theory. The social scientist is likely to point out that there is an endless array of conflicting philosophical justice theories, that the disputes between them are rationally irresolvable, and that such theories are, in any case, irrelevant to empirical studies as the theories incorporate evaluative concerns. This position is, as Miller correctly points out, a legacy of the (unsustainable) positivist view that empirical and evaluative questions are radically distinct and that answers to the latter are beyond the scope of objective justification (1999, p. 42).

Let me briefly explain here why I think that this particular exclusion of insights 'from the other side' may be even more academically debilitating than the previously described flip side. The crux of the matter is this: while philosophers' lack of interest in empirical evidence leads, at worst, to conclusions that are irreducibly relative or hopelessly trivial, the corollary defect fosters psychological self-deceptions and logical errors. First, social scientists frequently deceive themselves (and their readers) into thinking that they have come up with results that are completely 'unbiased' by any normative concerns, when such concerns have actually informed their research design and questions from the very beginning. A case in point is Parrott and Smith's (1993) examination of the qualitative differences in the experiences of envy and jealousy, which was supposed to confirm one specific assumption of the conceptual distinction between these two emotions; the research questions, however, already presupposed the assumption that the experiment was meant to confirm, thus leaving us with the foregone conclusion of a self-fulfilling prophecy (for a critique, see Kristjánsson, 2002, s. 5.2). Second, there are areas where, logically speaking, no empirical research can take place except against the background of normative theory, for the simple reason that the very terms which denote the objects of research are themselves unavoidably normative. A good example here, recently explored and underscored by Carr (2002), is the notion of *moral development*. Social scientists, including Kohlberg, interested in children's moral development have normally gone about their business in the conviction that they are merely trading in empirically discernible facts about human growth. As Carr, however, immediately and correctly points out, 'any such facts are entirely fictions': there are no developmental facts, in the purely descriptive sense, lying there unproblematically before our gaze, to which developmental norms can then later be related, because 'the very idea of moral development is itself exhausted by its normative … content' (ibid., p. 17). In other words, the very notion of moral development is an inherently normative one; otherwise, we would have no guidelines for what counts as progress – or, for that matter, regress – in the moral domain.

I will pick up Carr's general thread in due course (Section 4.1), in order to spell out the way in which normative concerns unavoidably enter into empirical research on children's development of justice conceptions. The specific question of why social scientists investigating justice need input from philosophers will be largely shelved until Chapter 4, where a myriad of concrete examples unfolds. A general point which can, however, already be pressed is this: an important reason why social scientists need philosophy is the converse of one of the reasons, discussed above, concerning why philosophers need social science. Social scientists need philosophy in order to make their research designs more formally and substantively determinate and thus to guarantee less haphazard results. Some social scientists seem to equate conceptual determination with over-determination, but as will become apparent later, laying bare a reasonable conceptual ground is not the same as over-determining the research design, and in any case, under-determination is a more typical problem marring social-science research on justice than over-determination.

I have so far written in this section as if the mutual ignorance of social scientists and philosophers exploring justice, and their lack of interest in each other's work, is – with rare exception – an enduring affliction without a cure in sight. This may have been a somewhat pessimistic presentation, at least in light of certain more sanguine remarks made in the foregoing section about a gradually emerging, if circumspect, shift to interdisciplinary work. Indeed, both sympathizers and critics of integrative work on justice have noticed some 'crossing-over' between philosophical and social-scientific approaches to justice in recent years (cf. Birnbacher, 1999, pp. 319–20). Perhaps it signals the beginning of a peacemaking, fence-crossing process, where it is at once acknowledged that there cannot be a 'value-free' social-science theory of justice or of its constitutive emotions, any more than there can be a reasonably developed philosophical theory of justice without a grounding in the empirical knowledge of how people actually feel and think about justice (cf. Solomon, 1994, p. 309). The present work is meant as a contribution to this (it is hoped) evolving process.

1.3 Emotional Virtues

This book ponders the role of desert and desert-based emotions in justice and also sheds some light, I hope, on the role of justice in an account of the morally right. As we gauge the moral pertinence of desert, we should not forget that desert concerns typically manifest themselves through vivid emotions: what I have already termed 'desert-based emotions'. In order to understand and evaluate the *desert* part of those concerns, we must first learn to understand them as *emotions*.

Since the 1970s, a cognitive theory of the emotions has dominated the field of emotion studies, in both psychology and philosophy. Perhaps it would be more apposite to talk about 'cognitive theories' than a single theory, for a cognitive account of the emotions appears in many guises and is (still) beset by a number of problems, the different approaches to the resolution of which divide cognitive theorists markedly among themselves as well as, collectively, from their remaining antagonists. I will try to overlook the 'internal' differences as far as possible in the following. However, for those not well versed in the intricacies of cognitive theories of late, I presume that a brief overview of some of their main features will be helpful. I have had occasion to explore this topic in considerable detail elsewhere (Kristjánsson, 2002, chs 1–2), and cannot here reiterate the whole discussion. Rather, I will offer some brief and sundry observations, (a)–(e) below, on the emotions. The choice of those observations relies primarily on the extent to which I think they may aid the reader in understanding the nature of desert-based concerns *qua* (cognitively structured) emotions; and secondarily on the extent to which something new has been added to the relevant discursive field since my earlier exploration. Of special interest, for our present purposes, is the role of the emotions in a morally well-rounded life: that is, the way in which emotions can be considered virtues (or vices). That is why I finish the present section – and thereby close this introductory chapter – with a more in-depth discussion of the possible objection that because many of the desert-based emotions would normally be termed 'negative', in one sense of the term or another, they cannot be considered potential candidates for an emotional virtue.

(a) The first thing to observe is that emotions can be *episodic* (occurent states with determinate durations), such as my indignation at my colleague's undeserved good fortune here and now, or *dispositional*, such as my strong tendency to experience indignation in various situations. It may be helpful further to distinguish dispositional emotions from *background* emotions which, so to speak, persist in the back seat of our psyche and influence our whole psychological make-up but go unnoticed unless something brings them into consciousness. Related to, but distinguishable from, emotions in all their forms, are our (objectless) *moods*, to which I return briefly later. Desert-based emotions can and do, of course, occur as immediate short-term responses. They are more morally interesting, however, as long-term commitments: as dispositions or even as background emotions. If taken together, along Aristotelian lines, as forming collectively a person's 'sense of justice' (see later in Sections 3.2–3.3), the desert-based emotions are best understood not as mere episodes, nor even as mere isolated dispositions, but rather as an ingrained part of a person's way of life (cf. Solomon, 1994, p. 294).

(b) There is a long tradition in emotion research of trying to identify a group of 'basic' emotions, which underlie more complex or 'non-basic' ones. This search has not yielded any unanimous results, partly – no doubt – because of the disparate search criteria invoked and applied, relating to diverse domains: evolutionary history, developmental priority, universality, prevalence, forcefulness, uniqueness, moral significance and so forth. Indeed, there are ample grounds for siding with Solomon's recent conclusion that the search for those alleged 'building-block' emotions has distorted, rather than furthered, our understanding of the emotional landscape, by obscuring all sorts of important complexities (2002b, p. 118). It may, nevertheless, be salutary to invoke the notion of basicness in a sense relative either to a given *domain* or to a given *complex emotion*. As an example of the former, we can say with a considerable degree of certainty that at least some of the desert-based emotions that I explore in subsequent chapters are *developmentally* prior to various other emotions, which perhaps require a more developed – but not necessarily more morally significant – view of one's self and its place in the social environment (I am thinking here, for instance, of some subtle experiences of social embarrassment). Furthermore, we could say that Aristotle's emotion of *eleos* (which I will call 'compassion' rather than 'pity', as typically translated, see Section 3.2) is more basic than, for instance, disgust, in being of greater *moral significance* for the human good – without implying that the latter emotion could ideally be eliminable from our lives.

As well as being basic relative to a given domain, a particular emotion can be basic relative to another emotion. Good examples here relate to the so-called compound emotions, which are made up of other emotions, basic relative to the former, without the compound ones simply being a combination of those more basic emotions and reducible to them. Jealousy is a case in point, constituting a unique compound of (1) *envy* at the recipient (*R*) of a favour that the jealous person (*J*) believes he or she deserves as much as, or more than, *R* and from whom *J* would ideally want the favour to be removed, (2) *anger* at the provider (*P*) of the favour and (3) *indignation* over *R*'s undeserved favouring by *P*. While the envy, anger and indignation are here basic relative to jealousy, jealousy could itself be basic relative to some other complex or compound emotion, for instance racial hatred (Kristjánsson, 2002, pp. 24–6 and ch. 5; cf. Roberts, 2003, pp. 185–92).

(c) What are the necessary ingredients of an emotion? In the cognitive theories, of course, the linchpin of an emotion is a *cognition*, that which gives the emotion a direction, its focus on a (propositional) object. The cognition underlying sympathy is, for instance, that a person has suffered or is suffering. Again, however, there is ample room for disagreement. The remaining heirs of the positivist separation of facts and values believe that the cognition must have a factual part as well as a (logically distinguishable) evaluative part or, alternatively, that the evaluation is an add-on to the cognition (see, for example, Ben-Ze'ev, 2000, ch. 3). Those who have parted with the positivist tradition will insist that evaluation is simply one form of description, a description of evaluative facts, and that no add-on is necessary (for example, Kristjánsson, 2002, pp. 26–8). However, this does not exhaust the variety of cognitive accounts of cognition. For even if we view cognition as a single element – an appraisal – there remains the raging debate between *phenomenalists*, who understand the appraisal in terms of a perception of a state of affairs (say, the perception that someone is suffering), and *judgementalists*, who understand it as involving a belief or a judgement (about the person's suffering). In favour of the former view is the well-known fact of so-called recalcitrant emotions: emotions that seem to be experienced in default of, or even in open contrast to, an existing belief. Fear of cockroaches is possible without any (conscious) belief of their being dangerous; anger at a person does frequently occur although we do not judge the person to have done anything wrong. Also cited in favour of the phenomenological variant is the alleged fact of animal emotions, which are supposed to occur without any associated beliefs or judgements in the ordinary sense. A difficulty endemic to emotional phenomenology of this sort is, however, the loss of the propositional content, the very element that seems to be at the heart of a cognitivist theory; mere perceptions do not have such content. Moreover, those who are reluctant to attribute emotions to animals will claim that the fact that phenomenologists allow for such emotions places them in a precarious logical position.

The clash between phenomenologists and judgementalists in the cognitive camp has unleashed a number of intermediary positions: positions that we can, following D'Arms and Jacobson (2003), term *quasi-judgementalism*. According to quasi-judgementalism, the cognitive element of emotions comprises 'thoughts', 'passive-assent judgements' or 'concern-based construals' (for a general explication of those suggestions and a defence of the last variant, see Roberts, 2003). Solomon, in a recent article (2003b), neatly sums up the history of his own considerations of this matter and concurrently the trajectory of theoretical approaches to the nature of the cognitive element in emotion during the last three decades or so. Appearing in his earlier works as the prototypical judgementalist, Solomon still persists in referring to the cognitive element in emotion as *judgement*, but he now modifies his earlier use of the term in various ways so as to allow for reflective as well as non-reflective judgements: both knowing how (as bodily skills and practices) and knowing that (as propositional knowledge).

While I find much to sympathize with in Solomon's account and have previously rejected both emotional phenomenologism and quasi-judgementalism (Kristjánsson, 2002, pp. 30–36), I also stick unflinchingly to my earlier position and refer to the cognitive element in emotions as 'belief'. I would, however, be ready to make many corollary concessions regarding 'belief' just as Solomon does regarding 'judgement': beliefs can be reflective and unreflective, conscious, semi-conscious, subconscious and so forth. Such considerations solve, I think – or at least go a considerable distance toward solving – the problem of emotional recalcitrance (see ibid., pp. 31–3). Solomon claims that belief is not the 'right sort of psychological entity to *constitute* emotion' (2003b, p. 4). While I agree that beliefs do not *constitute* emotions – if only because emotions are essentially motivational whereas beliefs do not normally incorporate motivation – I do not consider rejecting belief altogether as a fundamental element in emotion for something potentially more elusive to be the right response; rather, our response should be to acknowledge that an emotion involves, in addition to a belief, a *desire* for a certain state of affairs. Sympathy involves, in addition to the belief that a person is suffering, the desire that the suffering be alleviated; *Schadenfreude* involves, in addition to the belief that someone has been undeservedly unfortunate, a desire for a certain state of affairs to obtain involving this undeserved misfortune. The desire element in emotions aptly explains their *affectional* side. Sympathy is painful because your desire for the non-suffering of the relevant person is frustrated; *Schadenfreude* is pleasant (if immoral, which is another matter) because your desire for a certain state of affairs involving undeserved misfortune is satisfied. The desire element also holds the key to the association of emotions with certain *actions* and *behaviour patterns*: a person pained because of someone else's suffering is, for example, likely (other things being equal) to do something in order to relieve the suffering (see further in Kristjánsson, 2002, pp. 28–30). However, an emotion can easily have motivational moral force in default of the required circumstances for taking action; the motivational force is then merely one that guides reaction, not action – an important issue to which I will return in Sections 2.1 and 4.3.

(d) One further feature of cognitive theories of emotions, which many theorists find unsettling, is their potential for endless, uncontrollable proliferation of kinds of emotion, or – put in different terms – their lack of rigour in individuating 'real' emotions. It does not matter here whether we understand the cognitive element of emotion to constitute a judgement, a belief or a construal; there seems at first glance no limit to the kinds of emotions we can posit by combining a judgement, belief or construal with a desire/concern and affect (see, for example, D'Arms and Jacobson, 2003, p. 133). What distinguishes those cognitive elements that can form the basis of an emotion from those which cannot, and how can we distinguish clearly between different emotions? Is 'angling indignation' (the indignation of an unlucky angler who sees other, less qualified, anglers catching fish all around him), for instance, a specific emotion?

I used to consider this a serious problem in cognitive theories of emotion, and perhaps in any known emotion theory (Kristjánsson, 2002, pp. 17–18), but I am no longer so concerned about it. First, there exists remarkable agreement, across centuries and cultures, in the identification of the most common kinds of emotion, such as anger, fear, hope, envy, jealousy, indignation, joy, pride, shame and so forth (see, for example, Roberts, 2003, pp. 185–92); this is precisely why we can so easily appreciate works of art from distant cultures. Second, many of the examples typically given of the endless multiplicity of emotions are simply examples of 'cognitive sharpenings' (D'Arms and Jacobson, 2003, p. 137) of well-known emotions: namely, their applications in particular contexts. This would, for instance, explain the alleged emotion of 'angling indignation' posited above: it is not a specific, 'new' emotion, but merely ordinary indignation set in the context of an angling competition. Third, while the possibility of compound emotions (see earlier) does tend to the proliferation of emotion concepts, it hardly does so to any 'uncontrollable' degree. Most cases of emotion combinations are simply cases of two or more co-occurring emotions without their being uniquely combined into a single whole. A simple test to check whether we have a case of emotional compound or mere coexistence is to ask whether (each of) the remaining emotion(s) would still be the same if the other(s) were removed. For instance, John may feel indignant towards Paul's undeserved promotion and envy him his new post. Provided that John still envied Paul his post even if he did not believe (or, if you like, judge or construe) Paul to have got it undeservedly, or alternatively still considered him to have got it undeservedly even if not envying him, we would, in the original example, have a case of simple envy combined with simple indignation. If, however, John's envy were inseparably tied up with his indignation of Paul's having undeservedly got the post, and would cease to exist as soon as he stopped feeling indignant (and vice versa), we would have a case of the compound emotion *indignant envy* (cf. Kristjánsson, 2002, s. 5.1).

It is true that emotion concepts do not carve nature as neatly at its joints as do concepts of such quintessential natural kinds as *gold* or *water*. Nevertheless, such concepts fit well into an account which could – following Nussbaum (1992, p. 208) – be termed 'empirical essentialism' about human beings: as a natural species living in a pretty homogeneous natural environment and sharing a set of pretty similar concerns about life, health, interactions with other human beings and the environment, and ultimate death. The notion of a 'narrative structure' may helpfully be invoked here (cf. Snævarr, 2004). A narrative describes changes that occur to permanent objects. Furthermore, it has a beginning, middle and an end. These three elements are tied together by the plot, which makes the narrative a meaningful entity by simultaneously describing and explaining the given course of events (see Danto's famous characterizations, 1985, pp. 234, 251–2). Peter Goldie explains how emotions fit the remit of a narrative structure by comprising an unfolding, structured sequence of thoughts, feelings, perceptions and bodily changes (2000, esp. pp. 4 and 14). Our presupposition is, broadly, that another person's paradigmatic narrative structure for an emotion is the same as ours (ibid., pp. 133–4), and although, as Goldie admits, we can and do step back from this presupposition in proportion to a person's (or a person's background) remoteness from ours, that retreat is, I submit, limited by the person's belonging to the same natural species as us. As long as we consider the other person human, the narrative structure into which we fit his life, including the 'stories' we tell about his emotions in order to explain and evaluate his doings and non-doings, is necessarily guided by questions of objectively evaluable human fulfilment and well-being: of what the Greeks called *eudaimonia* (cf. Roberts, 2003, p. 190).

The notion of a 'narrative structure' of emotions helps us dispense with another potentially thorny problem for cognitive theories of emotion: that of 'mixed emotions' or 'emotional ambivalence'. While the idea of contrasting beliefs underlying contrasting *co-occurring* emotions seems, for conceptual reasons, detrimental to a cognitive theory, some developmental psychologists assume that children's realization of the possibility of emotional ambivalence, namely the acknowledgement that a single situation or episode can elicit contrasting emotions, marks an important step in emotional development, normally not reached until about the age of ten (see Harris, 1989, pp. 109–25). This assumption, however, is somewhat misleading. What is true in it is that when telling the story of a person's emotional life, we will consider more subtle awareness of emotional nuances and possibilities as progress: 'The child had previously thought that one would be bound to rejoice at a friend's deserved good luck; now it has started to realize that some people might be filled with invidious envy at such an occurrence and would rather hope that the friend came to grief.' We would not, however, consider true emotional ambivalence, that is the simultaneous focusing of opposed emotions, in the same person, on the very same feature of the same thing (Pugmire, 1996, pp. 32–3), as progress, for narrative explanations are undermined by such conceptual inconsistencies. The protagonist in a well-ordered story cannot rejoice at a friend's good fortune and at the same time and in the same respect also hope that the friend comes to grief (although his emotions may, of course, vary from one to the other at different times or through different perspective-taking) if we are to continue considering the narrative structure of his emotions to be the same as – that is, as fully human and understandable as – our own.

(e) Most philosophers who have written about the emotions during the recent renascence of emotion research have been chiefly interested, just as I am in the present book, in their applicability to ethics, a fact correctly noted by Roberts (2003, p. 36). To talk of emotions as moral virtues might have sounded outlandish some time ago; it does not, however, since the powerful resurgence of an Aristotelian approach that views emotions precisely as potential virtues or ingredients in virtues, sound that way any more. The received wisdom of the day is that emotions chart an important terrain of moral inquiry: they record our moral values, convey such values to others, establish our values in novel situations and supply us with motives for action (see, for example, Sherman, 1999). Emotions are also, importantly, constitutive of a good life, a life worth living – or as Roberts puts it: 'certain patterns of emotional response are characteristic of the flourishing, mature, and "happy" human life, while alternative patterns constitute ill-function and immaturity and tend to misery' (2003, p. 2). At least from a developmental, if not also a justificatory, point of view, the basis of morality is to be found in our disposition to experience certain emotions.

Such emotional foundationalism – as a kind of moral naturalism (see de Sousa, 2001) – is part of the moral baggage carried by the reigning Aristotelian view of the moral salience of the emotions, a view to which I fully subscribe. In the Aristotelian model, all emotions are intrinsically relevant to ethics, but for an emotion to be morally justified in a particular context, it must be felt towards the right person, for the right reason, in the right proportion, at the right time. And persons can only be fully virtuous if they are disposed to experience emotions in this way on a regular basis. In other words, virtuousness not only requires regularly choosing the right *actions* but regularly feeling the right *passions*. Roberts (1989) has introduced some useful distinctions between the different kinds of virtues that are, in an Aristotelian model, connected to emotions. He divides them into (a) 'emotion-virtues', (b) 'virtues of will power', (c) 'passional virtues', (d) 'virtues of proper affect' and (e) 'detachment virtues'. In my view, the distinctions between some of these groups seem somewhat overworked, especially those between (b), (d) and (e). To suggest an alternative classification, we might distinguish between emotion virtues, emotion-regulating virtues and emotion-combining virtues.

Emotion virtues are themselves particular dispositional emotions, either simple, such as compassion, or complex, such as (proper) jealousy (Kristjánsson, 2002, ch. 5). These emotions, in their proper form, constitute a golden mean of feeling: that is, the feeling of the right emotion, towards the right person, in the right amount, at the right time and so on. *Emotion-regulating virtues* are dispositions to regulate emotions so that the latter are properly felt, although these virtues are not themselves emotions. Good Aristotelian examples here are courage (which regulates fear) and good temper (which regulates anger). *Emotion-combining virtues* are emotional dispositions to experience a number of particular emotions; the emotional disposition of pridefulness, for instance, disposes one to feel shame and pride at the appropriate times, although it may itself also appear as an independent emotion (see ibid., chs 3–4). The relevance of this latest group of virtues to our present inquiry will become apparent in Chapter 3.

Notwithstanding the credibility of the Aristotelian moral-relevance account of the virtues, we should avoid a moralistic conceptual account of the rationality of emotions, as D'Arms and Jacobson (2000) have done well to remind us. An emotion can be rationally fitting although it is not morally proper and, hence, not morally justifiable. For instance, a person is not necessarily experiencing a rationally unfitting emotion when feeling pain at another person's (say, an enemy's) deserved good fortune. However, such an emotion is (other things being equal) not morally proper and hence not morally justifiable. While sympathetic to the main thrust of D'Arms and Jacobson's argumentation, I think that they commit some missteps along the way. For one thing, they consider the rational unfittingness of an emotion to concern not only the emotion's *shape* (the way it presents its object with evaluative features which the object, in fact, lacks), but also its *size* or *proportionality*, for example in cases of emotional overreactions (ibid., pp. 74–5). I do, by contrast, concur with Goldie, who holds that proportionality has 'ethical dimensions' which go beyond mere questions of rationality (2000, p. 3). The paediatric nurse who is a 'soft touch' and is driven to extreme compassion by every weeping child in her ward can hardly be called irrational; on the other hand, the lack of proportionality in her reaction may be indicative of moral failings *qua* nurse. For another thing, D'Arms and Jacobson accuse a utilitarian, who holds that *Y* is the fitting attitude for us to take toward *X* if our taking that attitude toward *X* will maximize the general happiness, of a conflation of a moral concern with the question of emotional correctness: of whether the emotion fits the object (2000, p. 78). This may be true if the utilitarian understands 'fittingness' (as D'Arms and Jacobson exclusively do) to mean *rational* fittingness. If, however, we understand the utilitarian to be making a judgement about *moral* fittingness, he seems not to be committing the 'moralistic fallacy'.

On the Very Idea of 'Negative Emotions'

In this book, I will be concerned with the possible moral justification (rational fittingness *and* moral propriety) of certain desert-based emotions. Can a moral justification of such emotions possibly be sustained in light of the fact that some of them would evidently be termed 'negative'? This sceptical question requires more thorough attention than that given to other issues briefly touched upon in the present section.

As both scholarly and public attention has shifted towards the emotions in general, the so-called *negative emotions* have recently come in for renewed interest. Just as every family has its skeleton in the cupboard, every academic subject has its own pathology: in this case it is the despised emotions typically referred to as 'negative' (for an enlightening historical overview, see Solomon and Stone, 2002). But what, precisely, does 'negative emotion' denote? Is there such a thing as a negative emotion? Does the term 'negative emotion' – as opposed to 'positive emotion' – serve a useful theoretical purpose, or should we perhaps consider it an unwelcome visitor in the field of emotion research? These are the kinds of questions that I propose to take on in this closing subsection, and I will be aiming at brief, but definitive, answers to at least some of them.

A *Google* search in May 2003 revealed 13,700 web entries for the search term 'negative emotion'. A quick glance at the first 100 web sites (in the search engine's order of relevance) did not produce a single specification of the term in question. Those 100 web sites could be divided roughly into three categories. The first comprised pages espousing various kinds of Eastern philosophies and ideologies (broadly conceived), in particular Buddhist ones. The emphasis there was on the eradication of those 'unwholesome and destructive' negative emotions 'on which Western society runs'. Nowhere were those emotions identified or listed. We must bear in mind, however, that in traditional Buddhism, one of the fundamental goals is to empty the mind of the clatter of agitations, and although there is a distinction there between those emotions which are counted as agitations and those which are not, the latter have, more or less, lost the conative and affective components that characterize the corresponding emotions in the Western philosophical sense, having become rather manifestations of universal reason or cosmic benevolence. The absence of any clear distinction between negative and positive emotions in those popular Buddhist web sites can, thus, be partly condoned by the fact that their most salient point of emphasis was the general negativity of emotions in the Western sense (for a popular but somewhat more rigorous account of the Buddhist position than found on the web, see Revel and Ricard's 1998 bestseller.) In any case, I will leave Eastern accounts of 'negative emotions' out of consideration in the following.

The second category of web sites concerning the negative emotions turned out to be one which many academic philosophers and psychologists would, I presume, refer to dismissively as 'psychobabble'. A couple of citations will give the reader a fair glimpse of the standard of discussion: 'As long as you hold a negative emotion about someone, you are emotionally tied to that person. When you love someone, you are tied to them. When you are angry at someone or afraid of them, you are also tied to them. Being tied to them keeps you from growing and moving on emotionally.' (Fortunately, this web site offered a cassette tape with complete visualization exercises to help us release our negative emotions and 'feel good again'.) A second web site provided the insight that negative emotions 'express an attempt or intention to Exclude' while positive emotions 'express an attempt or intention to Include', adding a list of typical positive emotions that boasted, among other things, laughter, boredom, interest and action! There was, obviously, not much philosophical illumination to be gained there.

Within the third category were of a number of academic or semi-academic (popularized) explorations of negative emotions, often compiled by psychotherapists of various persuasions. The most promising of those sites set out with the uncharacteristically salient question 'What is a negative emotion?', but unfortunately this turned out to be a mere rhetorical question, never to be answered, perhaps in order to avoid disturbing the flow of revolutionary advice about how to 'better manage' all those enervating 'uncomfortable experiences'.

This quick look at 100 'relevant' web sites might give one the impression that scant consideration has generally been given to the core notion at stake, namely what a 'negative emotion' really is. But, as someone could plausibly observe, is this not simply typical of the web, with all of its slipshod banalities: much ado about nothing? Surely, as soon as one delves into the scholarly literature, one will become more enlightened. To test that hypothesis, I conducted a search of recent articles listed in the database *PsycINFO* where the search term 'negative emotion' appeared in the relevant abstracts. When browsing through a dozen or so of those, chosen at random from the years 2000–2002 – most of which had been published in respected social-science periodicals – I was dismayed to learn that not only was there scarcely more attention paid there to underlying conceptual issues concerning emotional 'negativity' and 'positivity' than in the web-based material, but the use of the very term 'emotion' also seemed to depart radically from what I had taken to be a relatively stable consensus in recent emotion research.

To take a couple of examples, one essay aims to give an overview of various research findings relating negative emotions to a range of immune-system diseases (Kiecolt-Glaser et al., 2002). The notion of negative emotion is given short shrift in the introduction; the authors simply report their intention of highlighting the medical consequences of 'depression, anxiety, and hostility' (ibid., p. 84). No consideration is given to the question of whether those are emotions in the first place, let alone negative emotions. In default of such considerations, the authors seem to be rather premature, after producing their findings, in drawing the conclusion that *negative emotions* can intensify a variety of health threats – unless they, counter-intuitively, consider it a *logical* truth (as may have been the view of some medieval physiologists) that any psychological condition which leads to illness is a 'negative emotion', as distinct from the more common view that negative emotions can *in fact* lead to illness. Otherwise, what the authors could, at most, have reasonably concluded is that *depression, anxiety* and *hostility* seem to have such an effect. Another paper examines 'the structure of negative emotions in a sample of nonclinical adolescents'. After a large sample of adolescents completed certain standard self-report questionnaires measuring symptoms of 'fear, anxiety, and depression' and those questionnaires had been factor-analysed, we are told that the results support the idea that 'fear, anxiety, and depression are reasonably distinct but correlated components of negative emotions' (Muris et al., 2001). At what point in the research design or the interpretation of the given data the notion of negative emotion entered in is, however, left unexplained.

Notice that in both these papers, *depression* and *anxiety* are, evidently, taken as prototypical examples of negative emotions. The problem here is that the dominant cognitive-theory accounts of emotion, old and new, would not consider these as *emotions* at all but rather as *moods*. First, emotions have intentional objects (I am sad at some particular loss; about some misfortune); moods, such as depression, do not. The latter are, so to speak, directed at everything and anything, which is why Solomon refers to them as 'metaphysical generalizations' of emotions (1983, p. 133). Second, emotions are propositional (structured by and articulable in declarative sentences); moods, however, are not differentiated by any propositional content. Third, emotions have reasons; moods have causes – and the list goes on (see, for example, ibid., pp. 132–3; de Sousa, 1987, p. 7; Roberts, 2003, pp. 112–15). This is not to say that there is no connection between emotions and moods – moods predispose to certain emotions and emotions beget moods, which is quite another, if no less interesting, story – nor is it to say that emotion theorists share a common view of the individuation of emotions; quite the contrary, there is no consensus in that area, as I have already admitted. Conceding all that, it nevertheless remains odd that so many academics describe as emotions – and even take as representative of the subset of negative emotions – precisely those psychological states which the emotion literature tends to classify as examples of non-emotions.

Philosophers often accuse social scientists of conceptual sloppiness. Are the papers I have mentioned not simply cases in point? That may well be, but for the present line of inquiry we should be aware of the danger of the pot calling the kettle black. For despite what Solomon correctly calls 'increasingly sophisticated debates' (2002b, p. 115) about emotions in the philosophical literature, precise characterizations of the elusive term 'negative emotion' (no less frequently invoked there than in psychological circles) are rare. The closest we come to a systematic, carefully crafted account is in Ben-Ze'ev's (2000) extensive interdisciplinary study of the emotions. Yet even in his account something is, I submit, amiss.

Ben-Ze'ev claims that the division of emotions into positive and negative is a 'basic' one, expressing the centrality of the evaluative component in emotions. He also notes, as others have done before him, that there are more emotion words available to describe negative than positive emotions and that the former seem to be more subtly differentiated (ibid., p. 99). 'Essentially', Ben-Ze'ev remarks, 'positive emotions incorporate a positive evaluation, pleasant feelings, and the desire to maintain the situation; negative emotions incorporate a negative evaluation, unpleasant feelings and the desire to change the situation' (ibid., p. 68). (In what follows, let me, for brevity's sake, refer to emotions that incorporate a negative evaluation of a state of affairs as 'negatively evaluating' emotions, and emotions that incorporate a positive evaluation of a state of affairs as 'positively evaluating' emotions.) Ben-Ze'ev's characterizations are consistently followed in his analyses of different emotions and seem theoretically useful, at least for his own line of inquiry.

There are some apparent snags, however, the first one being that these characterizations have arguably little to do with the way in which the terms 'negative emotion' and 'positive emotion' are used in everyday language. For instance, in Ben-Ze'ev's analysis, compassion and sympathy, traditionally praised as positive and virtuous, become negative emotions, while *Schadenfreude* and pride – the former, when understood in the traditional way (see later in Section 3.2) as pleasure at another's undeserved misfortune, universally condemned, and the latter commonly viewed askance – become 'positive'. Now, there may be good reasons for departing from ordinary language. Sometimes distinctions deeply embedded in ordinary language turn out to be useless; alternatively, there may be good arguments for invoking new distinctions which cut across ordinary usage (see my earlier discussion in Section 1.2). I will not get involved in the tangled thicket of conceptual methodology except to reiterate that while any satisfactory inquiries into the nature of open-textured concepts (such as emotion concepts) will be critical and revisionary, involving the trimming of the 'ragged edges' of ordinary language where necessary, such trimming must be done *respectfully*, by providing good arguments for their necessity. However, Ben-Ze'ev does not provide any such arguments except simply to state the obvious, namely that apart from the psychological criterion (chosen by him) for distinguishing between negative and positive emotions, there also exists a moral criterion, according to which a negative emotion would, for instance, count as one negatively evaluated in light of moral values, criteria which may easily conflict (ibid., p. 103; see also Ben-Ze'ev, 2003). But why choose the psychological one if the other seems closer to everyday usage (at least, as I have pointed out, for emotions such as compassion and *Schadenfreude*) – unless, that is, one is in the grip of a flawed and outdated fact–value distinction about evaluation necessarily supervening on value-free description (see my observations marked (c) in the foregoing subsection)?

Ben-Ze'ev is not the only one who seems undermotivated in dealing with these two potentially conflicting criteria: the plethora of words used as substitutes for 'negative' emotion in the emotion literature, such as 'malign', 'antisocial', 'hostile', 'antipathetic' and even 'nasty', may betray an inadequate grasp of the underlying conceptual conflict, if not a covert or overt attempt at evading it. The official newsletter of the International Society for Research on Emotions recently devoted a whole issue to the topic of 'nasty emotions'. The editors manage to equivocate, saying that the emotions in question got to be considered nasty 'at least partly' through their close association with morality and moral condemnation (Cornelius and Fischer, 2002, p. 2). The Society's President is a little less ambiguous in his opening column, where he characterizes nasty emotions as 'for the most part a subset of the negative affects' (Solomon, 2002a, p. 3; for a more nuanced exposition of Solomon's view, see Solomon and Stone, 2002). 'For the most part' must be considered an important caveat here: an emotion such as, say, Aristotle's morally maligned 'pleasure at someone else's undeserved fortune' is – at least in Aristotle's schema of fortunes-of-others emotions – a nasty one (further analysis awaits Section 3.2), although it does not involve any negative affects; quite the opposite obviously. Incidentally, it is altogether unclear whether the remaining authors in this issue of the newsletter share their President's conception of what constitutes a nasty emotion; none of them engages directly with the specification of the term.

Blissfully unaware of those conceptual difficulties – or so it seems – writers continue to speak of 'negative and unpleasant emotions' (La Caze, 2002, p. 155) as if those fall unproblematically into line. If we understand 'negative' in this particular citation to mean 'psychologically negative' in Ben-Ze'ev's sense above, and 'unpleasant' to mean 'painful for the experiencing subject', we realize, however, that even within the psychological criterion of negativity, there may lurk sub-criteria which are at odds with one another. Here we come to the second snag in Ben-Ze'ev's position, the position according to which – as we recall – negative emotions essentially incorporate a negative evaluation *and* unpleasant feelings. The snag is this: anger, which incorporates a negative evaluation, can be pleasant for the subject; love or gratitude, which incorporate positive evaluations, are often painful, and so forth. Ben-Ze'ev's response to this observation is that love is, nevertheless, 'basically a positive emotion', meaning that 'the positive evaluation and its associated positive motivational component and pleasant feelings are more essential in love than are the negative elements'. So even for emotions as complex or ambivalent as the above-mentioned trio of anger, love and gratitude, 'we can nevertheless characterize their typical cases as either positive or negative' (2000, p. 72). Let it suffice here to say that this response seems to offer a somewhat *ad hoc*, if not a Procrustean, solution to the problem at hand. Ben-Ze'ev would, of course, not agree. He provides, for example, a lengthy and somewhat complex explanation of the centrality of the evaluative element in emotion in his book (ibid., pp. 67–73). Given that evaluation is more central here than feeling, we may ask, however, why Ben-Ze'ev does not simply drop the reference to feelings in his categorization of 'negative emotion'. It may well be that unpleasant feelings are more essential (at least in the sense of being more common) in anger than pleasant ones, but this does not change the simple fact that there is no necessary connection between an emotion's evaluative pattern and its affective component.

We have already seen how the term 'negative emotion' has, in the emotion literature, become a grab-bag of ill-assorted, and often internally conflicting, elements. Which precise senses could reasonably underlie uses of this term in different contexts and why is it perhaps not so helpful to saddle those senses with the label 'negative emotion'? Let me distinguish between six senses, most of which are commonly encountered, the first three broadly *moral* and the last three broadly *psychological*.

(a) Morally unjustifiable emotion Picking up a thread from Aristotle, many theorists have ruminated over the moral evaluation of emotional episodes in specific contexts: whether these are, first, *rational* and, second, *morally proper* within the given circumstances, that is, experienced at the right time, in the right proportion, towards the right person and so forth, as I have already explained. From a moral point of view, this is a perfectly valid enterprise, but equating it with the search for 'negative' as opposed to 'positive' emotions obscures rather than illuminates, for the terms 'negative' and 'positive' are surely more at home when engaging with emotions in a dispositional, rather than an episodic, sense.

(b) Morally unjustifiable emotional disposition Moral philosophers have long been interested in delineating vicious traits of character, traits that dispose the agent to immoral deeds or emotions; witness the compilation and subsequent vilification of the 'seven deadly sins'. Referring to morally unjustifiable emotional dispositions as 'negative emotions', however, invites both a moral and a practical problem. The moral one is that, owing to the context-dependence of moral appraisals, most emotions would, *qua* dispositions, be difficult to categorize as exclusively unjustifiable, or exclusively justifiable, from a moral perspective. Even the most 'positive' emotion according to common opinion, such as compassion, would count as morally unjustified in cases where it is felt out of proportion by, say, a health professional. Few emotions would remain unambiguously within the present category except perhaps invidious envy and motiveless malice, making the term 'negative emotion' a rather unproductive label. Furthermore, practically speaking, the blatant value-ladenness of this category would make it ill suited to typical psychological research into people's 'negative emotions'.

(c) Emotion which is generally evaluated negatively Judging from my – admittedly unscientific – investigations of what the general public means by 'negative emotion', this category probably comes closest to it. When references to compassion as a 'positive emotion', or *Schadenfreude* as a 'negative emotion', crop up in everyday conversation, this is, I presume, what people typically mean, namely emotions that are generally evaluated positively or negatively. Psychologists might be interested in 'negative emotions' in this sense, in the context of recording people's prevailing opinions, but philosophers would probably soon lose interest, since for them what matters in the end is not what happens to be generally evaluated morally this way or another, but rather what is so evaluated by informed, experienced and competent judges (namely here senses *(a)* and *(b)*).

(d) Painful emotion This is evidently also a sense in which an emotion is labelled negative, but it takes us back to a problem noted earlier concerning Ben-Ze'ev's conception: a painful emotion need not be negatively evaluating, which Ben-Ze'ev thinks of as the central aspect of a negative emotion. Nor of

course need it be negatively evaluated – not to mention the more subtle problem that the seemingly straightforward criterion of pain may be shot through with ambiguities; witness some good old Millian insights about the complexity, multi-dimensionality and contextuality of pain and pleasure (see, for example, Solomon and Stone, 2002, pp. 423–5).

(e) Negatively evaluating emotion This refers to an emotion evaluating the object or the object's situation as negative. It forms the core of Ben-Ze'ev's characterization of 'negative emotion' and is no doubt useful for various theoretical purposes in psychology. But as already pointed out, it bears scant resemblance to the ordinary-language understanding of 'negative emotion', since it includes, for instance, compassion under its rubric. Moreover, a similar problem of ambiguity as that mentioned in *(d)* could crop up here regarding the criterion of pain: an evaluation of 'the object or the object's situation' need not constitute a simple or single evaluation.

(f) Emotion which negatively evaluates a state of affairs which is positive for the object, or positively evaluates a state of affairs which is negative for the object I suggest this as a serviceable operational definition for possible use in some psychological experiments. It goes some distance towards capturing the moral dimension of senses *(b)* and *(c)* (although an emotion such as righteous indignation – pain at someone else's undeserved fortune – would constitute an obvious exception in this respect since the object would presumably in most cases evaluative his fortune positively; but indignation is not, from the moral point of view of senses *(b)* and *(c)*, a negative emotion) and hence is more in line with ordinary intuitions than conceptions *(d)* and *(e)*, which most psychologists opt for when examining what they call 'negative emotions'. Yet this definition is non-normative: a treat for old-fashioned social scientists! The defects of this suggestion, however, are that it invokes an understanding of the so-called negative emotions which no researcher has to my knowledge held, and, additionally, it would only be applicable in the case of other-regarding emotions, that is emotions where the subject and the object of the emotion are not the same person.

Let us notice two things about these six possible senses of 'negative emotion'. The first is that all except *(f)* have been utilized, at one time or another, for theoretical or practical purposes. Much of the current emotion literature, in so far as it is morally inspired, deals with sense *(a)*. Some of the infamous seven 'deadly sins' are negative emotions in sense *(b)*, and when Calhoun and Solomon discuss the possible meanings of the labels 'positive' and 'negative' in their often-cited introduction to *What Is an Emotion?*, their first suggestion seems to be that a negative emotion is one which is 'hostile' in a moral sense (1984, p. 33). The public's choice for the meaning of 'negative emotion' would probably be *(c)*, and that conception has also usefully entered into some of the psychology literature (see, for example, Karasawa, 1995). Michael Stocker (1996) has, for one, made some intriguing observations about painful emotions *(d)* as non-negative (see more later). Finally, *(e)* seems to be the preferred alternative of many philosophers (for example, Ben-Ze'ev, 2000, even if somewhat strangely mixed with *(d)*) and most psychologists (for example Stein and Jewett, 1986).

The second thing to note is that *(a)–(f)* all delineate important categories of emotion. None of these categories is arbitrary or trivial. Almost all have been referred to productively in philosophical explorations and/or psychological experiments. But why not simply call them by their respective names rather than forcing them into the Procrustean bed of 'negative emotion'?

In the end, I want to claim something similar about the pursuit of 'negative emotions' as Solomon said concerning the pursuit of 'basic emotions' (see foregoing subsection): namely that it has historically distorted rather than furthered our understanding of emotions. We can say everything that we need to say about *negatively evaluated* emotions, *negatively evaluating* emotions, *painful* emotions and so on without recourse to any fuzzy notion of 'negative emotion'. Moreover, invoking that notion cannot be done without cost to our understanding since it obscures all sorts of relevant nuances. 'Negative emotion' is not even applicable as a general umbrella term to cover all the phenomena described by *(a)–(f)*, for while an emotion may belong under the umbrella according to the criteria for inclusion in one category (for instance, 'compassion' in *(e)*), it may be specifically forced out from under the umbrella according to the criteria for inclusion in another category (for instance, compassion as not belonging to *(c)*).

In a more recent article than the one about 'basic emotions', Solomon (along with Stone, 2002) has argued, in a similar vein, that facile uses of 'positive' and 'negative' characterizations of emotions are simple-minded and detrimental to serious emotion research. While I agree with many of the substantial points made by the authors, I do not fully share their 'deconstructionist' suspicions concerning polarities and 'oppositional thinking' (ibid., pp. 432–3). I do believe that important and interesting contrasts can be drawn between painful versus pleasant emotions, negatively evaluating versus positively evaluating emotions, morally justifiable versus morally unjustifiable emotions and so on. My criticisms of the term 'negative emotion' are, as can be seen from the above argumentation, more *internal to* that notion (concerning how it is used in a lot of different senses which are not in accord), rather than having to do with ways in which 'negative emotion' is falsely contrasted with 'positive emotion' through an 'insistence on oppositional thinking' (ibid., p. 432).

In any case, the term 'negative emotion' stands revealed as a red herring in emotion research: one which should be discarded as soon as possible or, perhaps better still, sent down to Doctor Leon's useful web glossary of useless psychobabble (http://www.drleons.com/babble.htm). Incidentally, I think that much the same applies, *mutatis mutandis*, to the term 'positive emotion', although an exploration of that issue is not as relevant for our present purposes. I would, thus, fully concur with Solomon's point that it adds, as such, nothing to an analysis of pride to say that it is 'positive' (Solomon, 2003a, p. 10). For a number of reasons 'positive emotions' have not formed as lively a topic of debate as 'negative emotions'. Fewer 'positive' emotions have been differentiated and named, they rarely give rise to health problems and they do not as typically produce specific urges to action (see Solomon and Stone, 2002, p. 421, citing research by Barbara Fredrickson). Still, interest in 'positive' emotions may be rising; just a few months before writing these words, a new issue of the *Emotion Researcher* (vol. 18, no. 2, 2003), devoted to the 'nice' emotions, appeared in my mailbox.

Finally, let us move on to the recent so-called moral reappraisals of 'negative emotions'. It is a commonplace in recent emotion literature that, as Ben-Ze'ev puts it, 'certain emotions that have traditionally been considered as negative' are now being defended or even elevated to the status of the morally commendable (2002, p. 148). Given my earlier conclusion that there is, as a matter of fact, no category of emotions which can helpfully be referred to as 'negative', we need to take this commonplace with a grain of salt. What should be observed first is that 'negative' must here be used in a moral sense: it is plainly not the case, for instance, that emotions which have hitherto been considered as incorporating negative evaluations of certain states of affairs (see category *(e)* above which formed the core of Ben-Ze'ev's [2000] sense of 'negative emotion') have now been miraculously discovered to be positively evaluating. The claim must rather be understood in such a way that certain emotions which have traditionally been evaluated negatively from a moral perspective are now being given a more sympathetic hearing. In my view, however, even this formulation of the above-mentioned commonplace invites confusion by obscuring salient differences between these recent 'reappraisals'. Different strands of argument are described as if they belong to a uniform fabric, when it is clearly in the service of conceptual clarity to keep them separated. In order to do justice to those recent efforts to re-evaluate certain emotions, let me try to separate and clarify various distinct arguments abroad in the literature, listed here in ascending order of radicality, starting with the more modest ones.

(i) Instrumental-value argument A number of recent studies argue that particular stigmatized emotions, such as envy and jealousy, have some redeeming features: that they are not as black as they have been painted, do not deserve their 'unqualified opprobrium' and so on (for example Farrell, 1989, p. 262, on jealousy). The idea here is that while we would generally be better off without those emotions, there are some factual or conceptual considerations which force us to accept them, however cautiously and conditionally, because of their instrumental value. One of two approaches is then usually taken. One is to argue that the emotions in question can bring about positive moral consequences in particular (marginal, inessential) cases (for example, Ben-

Ze'ev, 2000, p. 262). The other is to emphasize the contrast value of those emotions: they offer a kind of testimonial or guarantee of authenticity to the moral emotions by making the latter stand out in sharp relief to the former (for example de Sousa, 1987, p. 321, citing a view expressed by Laurence Thomas).

(ii) Value-of-the-painful argument A less guarded defence is suggested, for instance, by Michael Stocker's justification of 'painful emotions' such as regret and grief. These are not merely instrumental means for the development of a good moral life. Rather, the painful emotions are said to be intrinsically valuable because they are necessary ways of experiencing, dealing with and resolving the conflicts and ambivalences of daily life as we know it, and that 'not to have these problems is not to be a person like us'. The ideal of wholly pleasant emotions is, by contrast, a 'fantasy-ideal'. A life where we could only experience those 'might well not be a life at all' and 'most certainly … not … anything even approaching a good life' (1996, pp. 235–7). This argument constitutes a variation on an old theme, expressed in such proverbial sayings as 'He is a fool that is not melancholy once a day.' Given the state of the world as it is, reactions of cheerlessness, if not downright agony, are often natural moral reactions.

(iii) One-term-many-emotions argument The crux here is that certain emotion terms, such as 'envy' and 'pride', wrongly give the impression that only a single emotion is at issue – and a morally flawed one at that. However, once we disentangle various uses of a given term in various locutions, we realize that it refers to a number of distinguishable emotions – generally left undistinguished in everyday speech – where some are, admittedly, morally reproachable and avoidable, but others are morally defensible and even morally required in certain contexts (for example La Caze, 2001, on kinds of envy; Kristjánsson, 2002, chs 3–4, on kinds of pride).

(iv) Proper-focus argument The argument here goes something like this. With various emotions, such as jealousy, contempt or vengeance, we have been systematically misled by philosophers and moralists to concentrate on their extreme forms (typically: the defects of excess) as their only possible manifestations, and these, then, are correctly written off as morally flawed beyond redemption. The truth, however, is that there are properly focused intermediate forms of these emotions where the emotion is both rational (appropriate to its target) and morally proper in the given circumstances. This argument usually draws heavily on Aristotle's notion of a morally justifiable emotion as one experienced in the right way, at the right time and so forth (as discussed earlier), as well as his architectonic of the golden mean, in particular his defence of proper anger as a mean between the extremes of deficiency (inirascibility) and excess (irascibility): 'This form of the passion [righteous anger] has always been considered as not unbecoming in the greatest and

most high-minded of men, being justified by the occasion that called it forth' (Bain, 1899, p. 190). In other words, many (if plainly not all) commonly negatively evaluated emotions can, in their proper dosage, be seen as virtues or as ingredients in virtues: as parts of a good human life. That these can also be improperly (excessively or deficiently) experienced does not, as such, tell against the plausibility of their moral justification, for, as the Latin has it, *abusus non tollit usum*: abuse is no argument against proper use (see, for example, Mason, 2003, on the propriety of properly focused contempt; Kristjánsson, 2002, ch. 5, on jealousy; Solomon, 1994, on vengeance). This argument is sometimes used in conjunction with *(iii)*: for instance, I have used it to defend jealousy *after* characterizing jealousy as a specific form of envy (Kristjánsson, 2002, ch. 5). Moreover, it can sometimes be difficult to distinguish between *(iii)* and *(iv)* in certain writings as there is, admittedly, a thin line between claiming, on the one hand, that the term '*x*' refers to distinct emotions and, on the other, that emotion *x* can assume distinct forms with respect to its focus and fittingness. Nevertheless, this distinction is not a negligible one since it indicates a significantly different conceptual and moral approach.

(v) Misdescription argument This is, in a sense, the most radical argument. Emotion term '*x*', which people have generally considered to refer to a particular (unsavoury) combination of emotion-forming ingredients (cognition, desire, affect and so on), can actually be shown by good arguments (linguistic, psychological, conceptual or moral) to refer to another and more acceptable combination. For example, John Portmann argued, in a book which caught the attention of the public media in the wake of the dot-com crash, that *Schadenfreude* should not be understood as pleasure at another's undeserved misfortune, but rather as pleasure at another's deserved misfortune, with the former emotion being better captured by the term 'malicious glee' (Portmann, 2000; for a further analysis and critique, see Section 3.2 in the following).

What these different arguments have in common is the assumption that we have been too hard on emotions which we have not properly understood and that these are not really (for various reasons) ignoble or eliminable from moral life. To refer collectively to those arguments as 'recent defences of negative emotions' is, however, misleading not only because of the fuzziness of the term 'negative emotion', but also because it involves an avoidable oversimplification of arguments which differ essentially in radicality, employ different tactics and draw on different philosophical persuasions. To be sure, there may be something to Mason's claim that in order to see anything like 'properly focused contempt' – or other emotions of that ilk – required for the moral life, one must have become dissatisfied with the idea that 'an enlightened morality must be a gentle morality' (2003, p. 236), dissatisfied with the indiscriminate rejection of various emotional responses to the experience of which human beings seem to have a natural faculty but an acquired difficulty. Most of the writers mentioned in this subsection share broadly Aristotelian naturalist sympathies and are not antagonistic to the view that people can be of unequal moral worth as persons depending on their demonstrated level of moral attainment (see, for example, Kristjánsson, 2002, pp. 130–35). Most seem to favour a moral society where proper pride is considered a more wholesome character trait than sheepish humility (cf. also some related final thoughts at the very end of the present book). But these are little more than the most general of similarities. The view that morality can properly countenance some commonly stigmatized emotions does not require an Aristotelian grounding in the strict sense; it can be defended along Humean or Millian lines or even along the lines of contemporary virtue ethics. Moreover, as already noted, the scope and force of the arguments themselves are diverse enough to defy any generalization, with each one of those having to be analysed and judged on its own merit.

I said at the beginning of this discussion of 'negative emotions' that I would be aiming at definitive answers to at least some of the questions posed. Enough has, I hope, been said to fulfil that promise. To recapitulate, there are no emotions to which we can helpfully refer collectively as 'negative', although there are of course painful emotions, emotions that incorporate negative evaluations of states of affairs, emotions that are negatively morally evaluated and so forth. To put it bluntly, there is no such thing as a *negative emotion*. Furthermore, while genuine attempts are under way to reappraise various (commonly) negatively evaluated emotions, those attempts involve different kinds of strategies which cannot and should not, either logically or morally, be collected together under a single label. We will thus proceed, in Chapter 3, to explore and evaluate the desert-based emotions without worrying that the fact that some of them might be termed 'negative' makes them, from the word go, morally irredeemable. But before that, we must turn our attention to the very notion of desert and its connection to justice.

Chapter 2

The Nature of Desert

2.1 Justice and Desert

An old Chinese parable tells us of the recruitment of a country magistrate and of a military officer in the province of Nanyang. On both occasions, the wise old Qi Huangyang was consulted. As for the first vacancy, he advised that Xie Hu be given the post, for although Xie happened to be his personal enemy, Xie was undoubtedly, according to Qi, the best qualified candidate. As for the second post, Qi recommended that it be given to his son, Qi Wu. When eyebrows were raised about the appropriateness of this advice, given the tie of consanguinity between old Qi and the candidate, the former replied: 'You asked me who would be suitable for the post, not who my son was.' Upon hearing this story, Confucius is said to have remarked: 'Qi Huangyang's judgement is commendable indeed. When recommending one outside his family, he did not discriminate against his enemy. When recommending a member of his family, he had no scruples about choosing his own son. This is indeed a just and impartial man.'

This last comment by Confucius, as well as similar statements that an ordinary person would be tempted to make about King Solomon having been a 'just arbitrator' in the affairs of his subjects, for instance, or a particular teacher having been 'ever so just' in all dealings with his students, might sound somewhat archaic to the average contemporary philosopher – if less so, perhaps, to a layperson. The tide of mainstream philosophy turned against the notion of justice as a *personal virtue* some time ago, with such a notion being considered at best irrelevant and old-fashioned, at worst incoherent and confusing. While the standard formal textbook definition of justice as 'a state of affairs in which just decisions are taken' does not, by itself, undermine the commonplace idea that justice is a *virtue* and an important one at that, modern philosophers have tended to view justice solely as a virtue of *social institutions*, and thus as relating to institutional decisions and public policy, rather than as a virtue of *individual persons* and their decision-making. What brought about this erosion of the deeply ingrained conviction of most pre-modern philosophers that justice is, first and foremost, a virtue pertaining to a person's reactions and actions? Why has Aristotle's general conception of justice, for example, seemed to many to be of such dubious modern appositeness, namely his conception of justice as primarily a character trait (*hexis*) of individuals, while only derivatively of institutions, and, conversely, of injustice as, at bottom, a result of intrapersonal rather than interpersonal misorientation (see, for example, O'Connor, 1988, pp. 417–37)? At least three explanations quickly suggest themselves.

First, there is a strong intuition that the virtue of justice is, by its very nature, more 'social' than most of the other virtues. One can easily fail to hit the 'golden mean' of a typical moral virtue such as *temperance* in private: through, for instance, gluttony (*qua* excess) or inappropriate indifference towards food (*qua* deficiency). It is, by contrast, difficult to imagine Robinson Crusoe doing anything that could be called just or unjust on his desert island before Man Friday came along. If one is to be properly called just or unjust, it must be with regard to other persons, not to oneself, let alone to inanimate objects or even animals. As Aristotle himself insisted, 'what is just or unjust must always involve more than one person' (1985, pp. 145–6 [1138a]). What this intuition shows, however, is only that justice (and perhaps some other related virtues) needs a social context for its actualization; it does not show that justice cannot, primarily, be the virtue of an individual person.

Second, justice talk may, at first, seem more appropriate to issues relating to large-scale social interaction and public policy than to the small-scale family affairs and personal relationships where many of our moral virtues are typically played out. Would it not be odd to say that a husband acts *justly* towards his wife and children, in addition to simply acting well, or correctly, towards them? This semblance of oddness may, however, be illusory. For instance, the compound emotion of jealousy, so common in close personal relationships, requires, as I have already noted, the justice-based emotion of righteous indignation as one of its ingredients. If the eight-year-old Betsy feels bothered because her teacher chose only Kate's poster to hang in the hall at the school fair, we cannot describe Betsy's emotion as one of jealousy, as distinguished from, for example, invidious envy, unless we add to Betsy's belief the indignation-grounding conviction that she deserved to be favoured more than, or at least as much as, Kate (Kristjánsson, 2002, ch. 5). Or, to take a less complex and controversial example, justice issues of the most prototypical distributive kind are involved in many family conflicts, for example those having to do with the extent to which different siblings should get involved in the care of an ageing, non-institutionalized parent (for a vivid personal example, see Lerner, 2002, pp. 23–5). So it does make perfect sense to talk about justice or lack of justice in small-scale personal interactions.

Third, and perhaps most important historically, the notion of justice as a personal virtue has not fared well within the theoretical province of liberalism, the theory that dominated, for many years at least, modern discussions of the moral and political salience of justice. Liberals fear that consideration of justice as a personal virtue inexorably entails the notion of more or less 'deserving' individuals, getting or not getting 'their due', in justice talk, and this they find unacceptable. The reasons behind the liberal antipathy to desert are well known and need only be rehearsed briefly here. They can be summarized in three theses.

1 *The plurality-of-the-good thesis* Desert implies a thick, substantive ideal of the good life. Liberalism, by contrast, is about 'thin' (formal or procedural) rules, and must remain neutral toward all 'thick' substantive conceptions of the good and competing individually chosen life-plans.
2 *The non-responsibility thesis* Desert implies a strict sense of personal responsibility. But we are not really responsible for our positions in life, in respect to either nature (the distribution of natural endowments) or nurture (home environment, socio-economic class), nor for various events which befall us during our lifetime. Desert thus demands distribution based on factors over which the recipients have no control, which is truly unjust.
3 *The equal-worth thesis* Desert requires the allocation of benefits and burdens according to (proportional) differences in merit. It is thus incompatible with the liberal (and Christian) presupposition of the equal moral worth of individuals.

Such accounts as liberals are typically able or willing to give of justice discount its status as a personal virtue. Thus, in order to gain a view of justice as anything other than a characteristic of social institutions, one must have become dissatisfied with the general framework of liberal theory. Such dissatisfaction is, however, common nowadays. Liberals have, after all, taken a lot of flak in recent years from 'communitarians' (such as Sandel, 1982) and 'empirical essentialists' about human nature (such as Nussbaum, 1992), with respect to the disembeddedness and thinness of liberal accounts of the self and the good. There may even be strong reasons for claiming that it is precisely the liberal neutralized account of the good required, *inter alia*, for warding off concerns about desert that will in the end make liberalism collapse into a much more radically relativized theory of value than it was ever made out to be, consigning coherent liberals to a postmodern slide into unreason (see Kristjánsson, 2002, s. 2.1). Besides, if liberalism does not accommodate a correct understanding of justice, an understanding which is provided by a rival moral theory, we may have a better reason for rejecting liberalism and opting for the other theory than for revising substantially our understanding of the virtue.

None of the explanations canvassed so far turns out to constitute a compelling justification for the deletion of justice as a personal virtue from philosophical vocabularies. Quite the reverse in fact: the more we engage with it, the more plausible the old idea seems of justice as a social virtue being parasitic on justice as a personal virtue. From a *logical* point of view, there appears to be good reason for saying that, just as freedom talk is parasitic on talk about individual free action (see Kristjánsson, 1998a; 1998b), so justice talk is parasitic on talk about individual action and reaction. Can we think of a just society without just persons? A society where decisions of public policy happened, for instance, to be just because persons lacking justice simply stumbled upon just institutional arrangements through some weird stroke of luck, or deliberately chose to implement such arrangements in virtue of some detached calculated rationality *à la* Mr Spock, would – I submit – be better described as one of pseudo-justice. The society would look from the outside as if it were just without really being so, in any profitable sense of the term in question, just like a society where music was played day in, day out without anyone actually relishing it would only seem to be, but not really be, a musical society. Needless to say, justice as a personal virtue, however widespread and entrenched it may be, will not guarantee a just society; people will after all need considerable practical wisdom (Aristotle's *phronesis)* and political know-how to put the virtue into public practice. But this does not mean that justice at the system level and justice at the individual level 'belong to different categories', as Chung-ying Cheng for one thinks (2001, p. 341); it merely indicates that personal justice is not *sufficient* for justice at the system level, although it may well be, as I have suggested, *necessary* for it.

This becomes even clearer if we look at the issue from a *psychological* point of view. It is hard to imagine what could induce people, in our world as it is, to establish and sustain just institutions if they were not driven by personal justice as a motive. The just person is, as Roberts notes, a 'person with a passion for just states of affairs' (1989, p. 294). While that claim still leaves it open which states of affairs are just – in other words, precisely to what kind of states of affairs the person with a passion for justice aspires, a question to which I soon turn – the reasonable recognition that 'passions' (emotions) and their development play an important role in our understanding of justice only becomes intelligible against the background of an understanding of justice as a personal virtue. This notion of justice as primarily residing in persons and rooted in their emotional make-up does conceptually depoliticize justice discourse to a certain extent; nevertheless, considering injustice, in an Aristotelian way, as 'the interpersonal result of an intrapersonal misorientation' (O'Connor, 1988, p. 422) still leaves open to debate all the familiar substantive (political) questions about how to cope with injustices at the societal level.

Apart from what seems to be an unreasonable reluctance to understand justice as a personal virtue – a fairly recent obstacle in the justice literature – there is another, much older and more pervasive, bar to our understanding of the nature and salience of this virtue. By this I mean the common view that justice is of a different and higher order than the other moral virtues or, alternatively, while on the same level as the other virtues, it somehow automatically overrides them, carrying more moral weight. When taken to its extreme, this view, which I will henceforth refer to as the 'primacy-of-justice thesis', collapses all claims about moral rightness into claims about justice. Although this thesis may be motivated by an understandable, and even admirable, quest for a single moral currency – a set of terms in which all moral issues can be couched and, it is hoped, resolved – it tends to obscure important issues at stake in moral and political decision-making. The conceptual cost of monistic simplicity here is simply too high as it makes us, among other things, unable to make sense of conflicts between justice and other moral values in cases where we might reasonably ask whether distribution *D*, although falling foul of justice principles, might not still be, for reasons external to justice, the best overall moral option.

Plato's is, of course, if not the earliest then at least the most famous statement of the thesis in question. Justice is, in Platonic philosophy, the superior harmonizing and organizing element holding together not only the conflicting elements of the soul (reason, spirit and desire) but also the conflicting classes in society (philosophers, warriors and commoners) and, in the end, the other three cardinal virtues (wisdom, courage and temperance). In modernity, the primacy-of-justice thesis resounds with fullest force in Kantian-inspired deontological theories of morality, culminating perhaps in Kohlberg's (1981) view of moral development, where justice has simply replaced morality as the central concept. In the political arena, another Kantian-inspired thinker, Rawls, placed justice on a pedestal, from which it has not yet fully descended, with his proverbial claim that 'justice is the first virtue of social institutions, as truth is of systems of thought' (1973, p. 3). While the primacy-of-justice thesis seems, for obvious reasons, less at home in moral theories of a naturalist rather than a formalist kind, it is an indicator of its grand appeal than even there it has its followers. The virtue ethicists *par excellence*, Anscombe and Foot, have thus both posited the superiority of justice over the other virtues (Anscombe, 1981b, p. 39; Foot, 1985, p. 206; 2001, p. 78) – although that position must rank as external rather than internal to virtue ethics – and the avowed consequentialist Fred Feldman proposed, at a time when he still couched his view in utilitarian terms, a version of utilitarianism, 'justicized act utilitarianism', according to which an act is morally right if and only if it maximizes universal justice levels (1992, p. 185; I say more about Feldman's view in Section 4.3). Unsurprisingly, other utilitarians accused him of taking justice promotion too seriously at the expense of welfare promotion (for example Vallentyne, 1995). Most shockingly, even some leading postmodernists, of all people, have been caught reifying justice as a solitary grand rock, rising above the sea of otherwise incommensurable values. These examples show the attraction of the primacy-of-justice thesis to be such as to induce theorists to sacrifice central tenets of their theories (virtue ethics' assumption of the non-cardinality of the virtues; utilitarianism's welfare/happiness as a monistic intrinsic good; postmodernism's radical value relativism) in order to accommodate it.

The primacy-of-justice thesis has tended to mar social-scientific research on justice, both on ordinary people's conceptions of justice and the development of justice concerns in children. Exemplifying in different ways the unavoidability of normative theory in social-science research (see Section 1.2) – pernicious as it essentially is only to the extent that the theory is covert and un-argued for by the researcher – the primacy-of-justice thesis is, typically, either covertly presupposed, as in Kohlberg's research on moral development where the research design slants the evidence right from the start in favour of a certain view of the nature and salience of justice, or covertly smuggled in at the interpretative stage, such as in Damon's theory of the development of justice conceptions in children. I confront Kohlberg and Damon at later stages in this book (Sections 2.2 and 4.1, respectively), but let it suffice to note here that the prevalence of the primacy-of-justice thesis in the psychological literature may yield another reason, in addition to the above-mentioned ones, why liberal thinkers (and indeed thinkers of many other persuasions) have become so wary of the notion of desert. Noticing that desert-based claims and emotions tend to figure prominently in people's actual conceptions of justice, while at the same time realizing that desert is very often not, and should not be, an overriding concern in moral decision-making, these theorists have felt a sense of unease. The temptation has then become strong, for those in the grip of the primacy-of-justice thesis, to reject or downplay the role of desert in justice rather than to dismiss the thesis which is responsible for this unease in the first place.

Fortunately, with the dust of Rawls's first-virtue account of justice having settled some time ago, consensus has gradually grown among philosophers that justice concerns do not exhaust moral concerns, not even political ones. As Sadurski correctly notes, it seems to be consistent with our general moral intuitions that 'there are certain actions which are evil without being unjust, in the same way as there are morally commendable actions to which the adjective "just" is not relevant', and that the 'identification of a just society with a good society *tout court* is troublesome' (1985, pp. 12–13). Adapting Ross's useful terminology, Galston claims, in the same vein, that 'the demands of justice, considered in isolation, are *prima facie* rather than absolute' (1980, p. 108), and Cupit points out that we can reasonably endorse some distributive precepts 'without implying that they are our principles of justice' (1996, p. 81). This line of thought is most clearly and emphatically brought out in Campbell's book on justice in which he, alert as he is to the perils of the primacy-of-justice thesis, refers to his specification of the virtue as a non-prioritizing one and claims that endorsing it does not commit one to any particular moral or political priorities. For instance, a person who admits that justice yields an important *prima facie* value could still, without self-contradiction, routinely favour other claims – say, those of humanity, charity or social equality – over it (2001, pp. 14–15). The relevance of this insight for social-science research is that even if the scientist finds his respondents claiming, say, that people ought to get what they need or that managing directors should only earn five times as much as assembly-line workers, it is wrong to conclude that these views necessarily reflect the respondents' views of justice (see Swift, 1999, p. 343): that is, *unless* the scientist has taken care to make his research design determinate enough to yield exclusively judgements about justice, in particular, rather than the morally right, in general.

By accepting that justice is a virtue – an admission that most theorists would be willing to make which will not be impugned here – one has accepted the fact that a proper description of a state of affairs as just gives one a moral reason to promote it, provided, that is – as a moral externalist would plausibly add – that one has a desire to be moral in the first place. The course of our discussion so far has, none the less, revealed an unsettling discordance of opinion in regard to not only the scope but also the relevance of justice: as to what kind of a virtue justice is (primarily a personal or primarily a social one) and how compelling are the reasons it yields for reaction and action (*prima facie* or absolute). While my exploration of those issues has been rather broad-brush, enough has been said, I hope, to indicate why, given the methodological perspective adopted in Section 1.2, we have good logical, psychological and moral reasons for considering justice as being fundamentally a personal virtue and a non-prioritizing one. To progress further, a commonly taken step in the exploration of a moral virtue is, so to speak, to 'consult the oracle': go back to Aristotle and see what he said about it. A considerable part of the contemporary literature on the virtues is, after all, little more than a series of footnotes to Aristotle's discussion, and I say that without a tinge of irony or any intention to discredit the literature. If I did, I would be hoist with my own petard, since my treatment of the desert-based emotions in the following chapter, for instance, draws heavily on Aristotle's original exploration.

In this case, however, simply turning to Aristotle proves not to be good enough. There are, of course, many salutary lessons to be learnt from Aristotle's extensive discussion of justice in the *Nicomachean Ethics*. The famous dictum of justice consisting in treating equals equally and unequals unequally, is stimulating, if somewhat lacking in substantive bite; Aristotle's insistence on justice as a character trait, and only derivatively as a social value, tallies with the line of thought already suggested in the present section; and various observations that he makes in his treatment of what he calls 'particular justice' foreshadow important distinctions, later made clearer by other theorists, between procedural and distributive (as well as rectificatory) justice (1985, esp. pp. 116–25 [1129a–1131b]). Aristotle becomes, however, uncharacteristically obscure in his specifications of what he calls 'general justice', which – while open to conflicting interpretations (cf., for example, Curzer, 1995, versus Irwin, 1988) – seems to incorporate actions of all the other virtues, calling to mind the inflated justice concept that we have previously seen to follow from the primacy-of-justice thesis. Moreover, since Aristotle's account of justice in the *Nicomachean Ethics* fits badly with his ordinary architectonic of moral virtue, and both kinds of justice posited by him, the 'general' and the 'particular', seem to relate merely to cases where one is the distributor or recipient of goods rather than a bystander uninvolved in the distribution process, his account seems seriously incomplete. Curzer may well be right that we need Aristotle's treatment of the desert-based emotions in the *Rhetoric* to complete his general account of justice (Curzer, 1995, pp. 233ff.), as distinct from his account of 'general justice'. I will have more to say about that in Sections 3.2–3.3.

The time has now come to take the plunge and return to the crucial question already posed in this section: to *which* states of affairs does the just person aspire? In other words, what is the virtue of justice *about*? Let me first make it clear that it is not my intention in this book to articulate and defend yet another Theory of Justice (at any rate not with capital letters); nor do I plan to give a critical overview of previous theories. I will assume that the reader has at least a working knowledge of the most famous attempts at such theory construction of late, for instance those of Rawls and Nozick, and will not add to the already abundant attention they have received. This book is about desert, and most particularly desert-based emotions; what I have to say in it will be relevant to a general view of justice only in so far as desert-related concerns reasonably enter into the formation of such a general view. Nevertheless, if only for the sake of exposition, I will state presently what I take *distributive* justice to be (I leave *retributive* justice out of consideration here). I have chosen a characterization that I deem to be as uncontroversial as such a characterization can possibly be. Readers may still find elements of my characterization variously weighty; they may even choose to reject some of them and hold others in abeyance. To anticipate such responses, let me simply say that arguments for any possibly controversial parts of the characterization will gradually emerge in the course of my discussion in following chapters.

First a somewhat platitudinous point: I agree with Feather and many others that 'fairness' is a general term applicable to all areas of justice (1999, p. 24). More specifically, I take Rawls's dictum of 'justice as fairness' to express an analytic rather than a substantive truth. There may be certain uses of 'fairness' abroad where the term has taken over the whole sense of 'morally right' or 'justified' (cf. Hooker, 2000, p. 46), but those uses merely invite confusion. Some philosophically informed respondents participating in a social-science research might understand 'fairness' to refer specifically to Rawls's conception of justice; however, the sense of the term would then need to be made clear to them in advance. For all relevant purposes, justice simply means fairness. Obviously it can be controversial to explicate what fairness is, but that is because the characterization of justice itself is in part contestable (although I will, in what follows, try to overlook, as far as possible, putative contestability related to far-fetched dilemmas and borderline cases). Given this point, saying that justice is fairness is not meant to provide an explanation, merely a synonym.

Justice as Entitlements and Deserts

A more substantive point that I want to make is this: justice involves a combination of *entitlement* claims and *desert* claims, where the focus is sometimes on the former, sometimes on the latter (see Feinberg, 1970). A just person is, roughly speaking, a person concerned with bringing about states of affairs where those two kinds of claims are given sufficient consideration. A just society is, again roughly speaking, a society where the majority of persons are just in the above sense and where the claims in question are in fact given sufficient consideration in private and public affairs and institutions. While these are the basic ingredients in my theory of justice (with small letters) – that is, in the minimal theory designed to do the work required for my purposes in the following – some elaboration is in order.

Entitlements involve moral rights and procedural claims grounded in public practices: in legal, or quasi-legal, rules, real or hypothetical. To qualify as just, it is necessary that these entitlements be impartial with regard to the set of people to which the claims or rights apply. Being impartial means that they must be applied in a non-arbitrary, unbiased and consistent manner to everyone in the relevant category. Gert's definition of 'impartial' is salutary here: 'A is impartial in respect R with regard to group G if and only if A's actions in respect R are not influenced by which members of G benefit or are harmed by these actions' (1998, p. 132; cf. Hooker, 2000, pp. 23ff.) This condition rules out favouritism. In a public exam, the answers of all students shall be marked according to the same criteria, whether or not they happen to be among the teacher's pets; the specific qualities of a student only enter into consideration in so far as they determine beforehand whether he or she is entitled to take the exam in the first place.

Deserts involve claims about people getting their due, grounded in values that are 'natural' in Feinberg's sense, that is, prior to any system of public bestowals: institutions, practices and rules (1970, pp. 56, 86). A full analysis of the grounding values, the basis or bases of desert, is a tall task, the execution of which must await the following subsection. Let it suffice here to say provisionally, following Miller, that desert is 'a matter of fitting forms of treatment to specific qualities and actions of individuals which are generally held in high regard' (1976, p. 85). Contrary to entitlement claims, desert claims are thus by their very nature both partial (allowing us to take into consideration other qualities of the people involved than those simply concerned with group membership) and personal.

Let me add a few clarificatory observations. First, entitlements can, as such, never be a basis for desert, not even *prima facie*: we deserve many things to which we are not entitled and we are entitled to many things which we do not deserve – and even if it should be the case that we also deserve the things in addition to being entitled to them, the corollary desert claim will be independently grounded. Second, this does not mean that a desert claim must be independent of all public institutions and their rules; desert claims are often logically dependent on the *point* of such institutions and rules; for instance, we cannot conclude that a student deserves to get the highest grade in an exam without, at least tacitly, appealing to the point of exams (see Cummiskey, 1987, p. 18). However, this does not change the fact that such a desert claim will be grounded independently of the claim, for instance, that the student is entitled to the highest grade in the relevant exam simply because he or she answered more questions correctly than did any other student.

Third, entitlements can *protect* desert claims: we can have a rule prescribing that deservingness shall prevail in a certain domain, but once again the rationale of the desert claim(s) in question will be logically independent of the entitlement; protecting is not the same as grounding.

Since justice requires two different strands, entitlements and deserts, to braid into a single skein, conflicts are likely to ensue and so they do. In the 2002 Winter Olympics, the men's 1,000 metre short-track speedskating produced a bizarre finish with four of the five competitors falling on the final bend, leaving as the winner the Australian Steven Bradbury, who under normal circumstances would have been an also-ran. Bradbury was justly awarded the gold medal, in the sense of being entitled to it, given the rules of the competition, but it would, other things being equal, seem odd to say that he won his gold justly in the sense of having deserved it. Some philosophers have tried to push such possible conflicts aside by claiming that *only* deserts or *only* entitlements matter for justice. Hospers's often-quoted remark that justice 'is getting what one deserves; what could be simpler?' (1961, p. 433) is a good example of the former kind of manoeuvre, as is Nozick's (1971) entitlement (procedural/historical) theory of justice a good example of the latter. Such manoeuvres, however, look hopelessly counter-intuitive when applied to examples such as the above, where both an entitlement claim and a desert claim seem to make sense as claims of justice or injustice. Neither does it help matters to take refuge in ordinary language, in which entitlement claims are often couched in terms of desert. There are admittedly various contexts in daily conversation in which '*A* deserved to get *x*' is used as shorthand for '*A* was entitled, by the rules of the relevant "game", to get *x*', but such usage is correctly dismissed by most justice theorists as fuzzy and confusing. Miller aptly refers to such judgements as 'sham' desert judgements which have really to do with entitlements or, alternatively, with desert in a metaphorical sense, for instance where the deserving subject is not a person (1999, pp. 137–8). Olsaretti (2003b, pp. 196–7) adds a helpful observation about frequently made statements in ordinary discourse which employ the term 'desert' but which are parasitic on an independently formulated conception of justice, for instance the statement 'he deserves to get a heart transplant as soon as possible', where the apparent desert claim is grounded in the prior belief that justice requires providing for people's basic needs. Such claims, she correctly points out, are vacuous 'rubber-stamp claims', irrelevant to an understanding of desert as an independent value relevant to justice.

Feinberg's discussion in *Doing and Deserving* is the classic source for genuine conflicts between entitlement and desert claims in the domain of justice, and it has inspired a plethora of conflict stories: about candidates winning a mastership at a college (or winning a presidential race) to which they are entitled but which they do not deserve, about the lazy stick-in-the-mud legitimately, but undeservedly, inheriting the family fortune and so forth. For those who have ever taught at a school or a university, the idea of a student ending up, through serendipity, with the highest grade, which others might have deserved more, should come as no novelty. To repeat and underline an earlier observation, there are numerous cases where someone is entitled to something without deserving it, as well as cases where someone deserves something without being entitled to it. Of course, there are also many cases where the desert and entitlement claims go hand in hand; we could talk about an outcome which is, jointly, in accordance with both claims as being 'absolutely just' – although not necessarily, given my earlier rejection of the primacy-of-justice thesis, 'morally right, all things considered'. Another possible way to describe such an ideal state of affairs, from the perspective of justice, would be to call it 'merited', but I will deliberately avoid the term 'merit' in my exploration here for two reasons. The first is that while some writers use 'merit' synonymously with 'overall justice', others view it as synonymous with 'desert'. Yet others (and this is perhaps the most frequent use) consider merit a subset of justice, but broader than desert, that is, as a genus term referring to any esteemed quality of a person – say, the person's beauty, irrespective of his or her responsibility for it – while desert constitutes a species of the genus – requiring some kind of personal responsibility, say for the beauty – so that every case of desert is a case of merit but not vice versa (see, for example, McLeod, 1999, p. 67; Pojman, 2001, p. 92; Wilson, 2003, p. 278). I dare not add more to, nor try to sort out, this conceptual disarray. The second reason for avoiding the term 'merit' is the opprobrium which has become attached to it in some quarters via the term 'meritocracy', coined by Michael Young (1961) as a negative label for a dominating class of harsh and overprivileged high-achievers.

To return to the conflict cases, Feinberg points out in his classic study that desert claims have a *ceteris paribus* or *pro tanto* force in moral debate, but he thinks that such claims can rather easily be overridden and that they represent only a part ('and not necessarily the most important part') of the domain of justice. More specifically, Feinberg considers claims about desert, on the one hand, and entitlements or rights, on the other, to originate from 'altogether different parts of our ethical vocabularies' (1970, esp. pp. 56, 60, 80, 86). Coming at the issue from the other side, one might say that entitlement is not the only criterion of justice either, nor even, necessarily, the most important one (see, for example, Sadurski, 1985, pp. 120ff.). What we end up with, then, is in a certain sense a pluralistic view of justice, both with regard to the elements of justice (desert versus entitlement) and to the role of justice as one value among many making up the morally right. Nuyen has challenged Feinberg's strict distinction, pointing out that desert and entitlement 'do belong to the same ethical vocabulary'. There is, however, not much to be gained from his argument to that effect over and above the obvious truth that both entail claims 'of justice' (1997, esp. pp. 225–6, 228). In that sense, they are, of course, not 'altogether different', but the fact remains, to which Feinberg meant to direct our attention, that desert and entitlement often give rise to claims that have different rationales and are radically at odds with one another.

Unfortunately, many social scientists seem to be unaware of the subtle distinctions at work here, a fact which, understandably, does not help in either the gathering or the interpretation of empirical data about ordinary people's conceptions of justice. We will see examples of that later (Sections 4.1 and 4.2). Either the terms 'entitlement' and 'desert' (or 'deservingness', as social scientists prefer to call it) are used interchangeably, or 'entitlement' is presented, unhelpfully and without argument (even by such a leading authority as Melvin Lerner), as an umbrella term, covering all claims associated with justice. The psychologist Norman Feather constitutes a welcome exception with his nuanced understanding of different justice claims, and he has even conducted some interesting research based on the entitlement–desert distinction, examining conflicts between conceptions of what certain groups of people deserve on the one hand, and are entitled to on the other (2002).

How can we strike a balance between the claims of entitlement, on the one hand, and desert, on the other, when the two part company? What is, in such circumstances, the just state of affairs? To recapitulate, what I have suggested, in line with Feinberg and those who have joined the discursive field laid out by him, is that desert claims are typically weighed in the balance when deliberating on the just state of affairs, and the same applies to entitlement claims when those can be identified in the case in question, but that neither kind of claim is, normally, sufficient by itself for an 'on balance' or 'all things considered' judgement of justice. To go further than that, to specify what relative weight to give to each consideration in each instance, would require a whole moral theory – something that will not be provided here.

I do not claim any originality for the general characterization of justice that I have presented so far in this section. I deliberately chose as uncontroversial a conception of justice as possible, one harking back to Feinberg and one which also bears a resemblance to the 'non-prioritizing equalitarian–meritorian' analysis of justice which Campbell provides in an accessible introductory text (2001, esp. pp. 12–15) – at any rate in so far as 'equalitarian' for Campbell refers to the equality and impartiality of entitlement rules, but not to equality of outcomes. Rather than making do with an *argumentum ad verecundiam*, however, let me give three reasons why I think this characterization is a good one in light of the conditions for a fruitful conceptual study already broached in Section 1.2.

First, it respects common usage, both of laypeople and of experts. An important element of the usage of laypeople, an element which went missing for some time in philosophical analyses, is that desert forms an important criterion of justice (see, for example, an overview of the empirical evidence in Miller, 1999, ch. 4). As to the usage of the 'experts', various theorists have in recent years tried to reinstate desert as such a criterion (although not the *only* criterion), elevating it from its Rawlsian role as a pariah in justice accounts; I happily jump on that bandwagon. As someone once said, it is as silly to try to work out a theory of justice without any recourse to desert as it is to work out a theory of chastity without mentioning sex (cited in Flew, 1984, p. 155). Sadurski (1985) is one of those who want to reinstate desert; another is Geoffrey Cupit in a skilfully crafted book on 'justice as fittingness', 'fittingness' being for him simply 'an alternative idiom' in which to describe desert (1996, p. 46); and yet another, in a more limited way, is Miller (1999). According to the terminology adopted at the beginning of the present book, most recent accounts of justice, while not desert-*monistic*, are either desert-*sensitive* or desert-*prioritizing*, as opposed to the desert-*ignoring* justice theories of a quarter of a century ago. Miller (ibid.) terms his desert-sensitive account of justice a 'pluralist view' and contrasts it with both a 'negative view' (corresponding to what I have called 'desert-ignoring') and a 'positive view' (an amalgam of what I have called 'desert-monistic' and 'desert-prioritizing').

I would like to say, in passing, about Cupit's work mentioned above that while it is full of incisive insights, I find his general view of the relationship between justice and desert/fittingness somewhat mysterious. For Cupit, to act unjustly is to act unfittingly, but to act unfittingly is not necessarily to act unjustly (1996, p. 2). That is, there is desert outside justice but no justice outside desert. The arguments for both these points strike me as weak. In support of the first, Cupit adduces the claims that animals and the natural environment 'may deserve to be treated with respect even if it is not unjust to fail to so treat them', and that persons showing contempt for judges in courts of law, for instance by refusing to stand up, may be said to be treating them unfittingly, although not unjustly (ibid., pp. 3, 47). There may be reason for saying that the higher animals deserve certain treatment, provided we can, or in so far as we can, ascribe personhood to them – in which case they are simply to be understood as persons – but as it stands (including the natural environment as a bearer of deserts), Cupit's claim seems highly counter-intuitive. The case of the irreverent behaviour towards a judge does not fare much better; is not the offensive person being (at least potentially) unjust in this regard by failing to exhibit respectful behaviour to which the judge is entitled? In support of his second point, that there is no justice outside desert, Cupit tenders a complex argument meant to show that the injustice of ignoring an entitlement can be explained as a failure to treat someone in accordance with desert – it being true, for example, that when a person receives through legitimate entitlement a place at a university which another applicant would have deserved more, the former 'does not deserve the place'; it being false, however, 'that he deserves not to have it'. Cupit's central point here is that (conversely to the first example) 'when we are deliberately denied what we have qualified for under established rules – in circumstances where the relevant rule has not been disestablished – we are [undeservedly] treated as someone to whom that which has been qualified for should be denied' (ibid., pp. 123, 130–35). My response to that is to say that while there is a way in which the injustice in question *may* intelligibly be described in such exclusively desert-encompassing terms, there is very little reason to do so, since we have a much more intuitively plausible way of describing it: namely, simply as a violation of an entitlement. After all, Cupit does distinguish between entitlements and deserts, and his reformulation forces us to invoke *two distinct kinds* of desert violations, of not deserving *x* and of deserving not to have *x*, where Ockham's razor and common usage only demand one. All in all, I do not think Cupit has given us sufficient reason for departing from ordinary usage here, which is a pity since his is an otherwise impressive attempt to reforge the link between desert and justice.

The second reason for recommending my suggested specification of justice is that it is arguably coherent, both internally and with respect to related concepts, honouring morally valid distinctions (such as that between desert and entitlement, and between justice and the morally right). The third and final reason is that it yields a serviceable account, which can accommodate a variety of substantive views and commend itself to writers of otherwise diverse moral persuasions. My characterization thus allows for continued contestedness, both non-essential *conceptual* contestedness (since a successful characterization of the kind I propose will, *ex hypothesi*, not be essentially contestable; see Kristjánsson, 1996, ch. 7) and essential *substantive* contestedness on various issues involving and surrounding justice, for example, on (a) the nature of the threshold an entitlement has to pass to count as even potentially just, (b) the nature of the threshold an entitlement passes when it starts to infringe upon deserts, (c) how much value we should ascribe to desert, (d) the weight of justice in judgements of moral rightness, and so forth. Possible disagreements on some of these substantive issues will not, I hope, debar the reader from finding my exploration of desert and desert-related emotions worthwhile in itself. What the reader needs to accept for continued interest is simply that: (1) while justice is a virtue, it is not tantamount to moral rightness, (2) desert forms an important element in justice, if not the only one or even, necessarily, a prioritizing one, and (3) sometimes desert trumps entitlements but sometimes it is eclipsed by entitlements.

Basis or Bases of Desert?

As I have already noted more than once, desert has in recent years been regaining ground in philosophical discussions of justice after reaching its lowest point during the period when the theories of Rawls and Nozick set the agenda for justice talk. Perhaps MacIntyre was right, after all, in his insistence on the philosophical deficiencies of both of those theories: in particular, that they exclude a rich and embedded-enough conception of a moral community for the notion of desert to make the sense that it does in real life (1984, pp. 248–51).

But what exactly, then, is desert all about? So far I have done little more than to point out, in line with the post-Feinbergian orthodoxy, that desert is a 'natural' notion, prior to public institutions and entitlements. 'Prior' can be understood here both historically – at the societal, as well as the individual (psychological), level – and logically, in the sense that desert claims can sometimes be used to criticize as internally unjust the rules that underlie institutions and entitlements. Those rules cannot, however, be used to criticize desert claims in the same way, that is, *qua* desert claims – although they can be used to criticize them *qua* justice claims and even morally outweigh them sometimes as claims of that sort, which is an altogether different matter (cf. Sadurski, 1985, pp. 18ff.). I also cited Miller's sketchy formal characterization of desert as 'a matter of fitting forms of treatment to specific qualities and actions of individuals which are generally held in high regard' (1976, p. 85). What we need to know now, however, is precisely what those 'qualities and actions' are and why they are so highly regarded.

A helpful starting point is the work that has been done recently on the formal structure of desert claims and the wide consensus which has been formed on what that structure is. According to this, desert is a triadic relation between (i) a person *P*, (ii), a negative or a positive outcome or state of affairs *S* (that is, harm/loss or benefit/gain) deserved by *P*, and (iii) a basis, *B*, in virtue of which *P* deserves *S*, where *B* relates to some fact(s) about what *P* is or does (based on Feinberg, 1970, p. 61). I explain later why I prefer to talk about a negative or positive 'state of affairs' rather than a 'mode of treatment' as Feinberg does (see also Miller's reference above to 'fitting treatment'). Among the ways in which a desert claim can go wrong, according to Feinberg, are (a) by relating to some facts which are not relevant or appropriate in the context of ascribing desert or (b) by relating to facts which, while potentially relevant, are simply not, as it happens, facts about *P* (ibid., p. 59). Understanding the logic of a concept is always the first step towards grasping its substantive point, but the essential questions remaining here are, first, what counts as a relevant fact about *P*, that is, what constitutes a legitimate desert basis, and, second (a question essentially implicit in the first), whether there is only one such basis or many.

Before tackling those questions, let us briefly consider whether deserving and not deserving are contradictories or merely contraries. Is it possible that *P* neither deserves *S* nor does not deserve *S* in virtue of *B* – that is, is there a concept *of non-deserving* (or, as some would call it, 'negative desert') as opposed to *deserving* or *not deserving* ('positive desert')? I will answer that question in the negative. The most obvious reasons are conceptual clarity and economy, but I take it that common usage agrees as well. Were *P*, for example, to gain some windfall unrelated to any putative desert basis – no fact about what *P* is or does being relevant to whether *P* deserves the windfall or not, or where such facts about *P* as could be deemed relevant happened to weigh equally for and against *P*'s deserving it – ordinary language would simply describe that as a case where *P* does not deserve the windfall. I will follow suit in what follows. Hence I deem Olsaretti's argument against a compensatory notion of desert misguided in so far as it is based on rejecting the claim that the statement 'P does not deserve to be subject to harmful untoward intervention that she is not responsible for' entails 'P deserves not to be subject to the untoward intervention' (2003b, p. 198). I believe there is an indisputable conversational entailment at stake here, if not a strictly logical one. This does not undermine Feinberg's helpful distinction between 'polar' and 'non-polar' desert (1970, p. 62). In some cases ('polar'), we would be interested in whether *P* either deserves a gain or deserves a loss; but in others ('non-polar'), whether *P* deserves or does not deserve a gain, or deserves or does not deserve a loss. That, however, does not change the fact that there are two possibilities in each case: of deserving or not deserving a gain (or a loss), although in some of them not deserving a gain implies deserving a loss (and vice versa), while in others it does not. This has to do with the nature of the baselines in question to which I will turn later in this section.

Let us now revert to the nature and number of the desert basis/bases. Following Feinberg, the received wisdom has become that the nature of *B* can be varied and that there is actually not only one basis but many. Olsaretti refers to views that uphold this wisdom as 'ecumenical', as opposed to 'selective' (2003a, pp. 5–6). Feinberg thinks that the bases differ with regard to the nature of *S*, and he lists five 'major classes' of *S* – awards of prizes; assignments of grades; rewards and punishments; praise, blame and other informal responses; reparation, liability and other modes of compensation – each with its own distinctive, if sometimes overlapping, desert basis (1970, pp. 62ff.). This 'different goods, different desert bases' account is echoed in much of the post-Feinbergian literature, as well as in popular sources. For instance, Miller maintains that 'This [what kind of desert] will clearly vary from one good to the next' (1976, p. 118) and Ben Rogers, in a newspaper column, states without argument that 'there are many sorts of deserts' (2002, p. 21).

The most important follow-up to Feinberg's original idea is George Sher's detailed analysis in his book *Desert*. While taking his cue from Feinberg, Sher's approach is different in that he engages directly with the different desert bases without connecting them to different classes of *S*. This implies that the same *S* could at times be assessed differently with respect to different desert bases. It is not only that *P* might exclusively deserve S_1 in virtue of B_1, S_2 in virtue of B_2 and so on, but that *P* might deserve S_1 in virtue of both B_1 and B_2 but not deserve it in virtue of B_3 and B_4; deserve S_2 in virtue of B_1 and B_3 but not in virtue of B_2 and B_4, and so on.

Sher's plan is an ambitious one, namely to 'provide the sort of comprehensive treatment of desert that has so far been lacking'. While accepting that it would 'be most satisfying if all major desert claims turned out to have a single compelling normative base', he does not think that this is the case at all, but rather that they 'owe their justification to irreducibly different principles and values'. People deserve (a) the predictable consequences of their free acts, (b) the objects of their sustained efforts over time, (c) punishment commensurate with the wrongness of their acts, (d) prizes for their competitive performance and (e) (for various reasons) happiness/

rewards as a result of their virtuous character and good deeds – but these desert bases turn out, according to Sher's analysis, not to be grounded in any single value but in a number of more fragmented ones (1987, esp. pp. x, xii, 20, 151). Sher thinks that the above bases will cover all the most significant types of cases about which desert claims are made, and it is salutary at this point to list the sorts of assertions that he has in mind (ibid., pp. 6–7):

1 Jones deserves his success; he's worked hard for it.
2 Smith deserved more success than he had; he gave it his all.
3 Walters deserved the job; he's the best-qualified applicant.
4 Wilson deserved to be disqualified; he knew the deadline for applications was March 1.
5 Jackson deserves more than minimum wage; his job is important and he does it well.
6 Baker deserves to win; he's played superbly.
7 Miss Vermont deserves to win; she's the prettiest entrant.
8 Anderson deserves his twenty-year sentence; he planned the murder.
9 Brown may have known he wouldn't be caught, but he still deserves to be punished.
10 Winters deserves some compensation; he's suffered constant pain since the shooting.
11 Lee deserves a reward; he risked his life.
12 Benson deserves some good luck; he's a fine person.
13 Gordon deserves some good luck; he's had only bad.
14 McArthur deserves a hearing; he's an expert on the subject.
15 Cleveland deserves better publicity; it's an interesting city.

I think these examples are of varying relevance. Some of them I would simply dismiss as what Miller calls 'sham' desert judgements, as explained above: judgements really having to do with entitlements, or judgements where the deserving subject is not a person. Case 15 is a typical example of the latter, and I would consider cases 3, 4 and 7 to refer to entitlements: to assessments according to institutional rule-based criteria. Since Sher is well aware of the distinction between deserts and entitlements and surely knows of the many instances in which ordinary language mixes up the two, one wonders why he chose those three assertions as potential candidates for explanation along the lines of the suggested desert bases in the first place.

We need not, for present purposes, go deeply into the nature of each desert basis that Sher proposes, but a few clarifications are in order. As to (a), the expected-consequences basis, Sher takes it to be 'possible to infer from the premise that it is good that persons act autonomously the conclusion that it is good that they have certain things that flow from their autonomous acts' (ibid., p. 38). Aware of the obvious objection that *P* can hardly be said to deserve the predictable gain of his autonomous choice if that choice is an evil one, Sher argues that the desert in question is then simply offset by the negative value of the way the person exercised his freedom. The same applies also, *mutatis mutandis*, in the case of (b), the sustained-effort basis. Already, here, one senses something going amiss. Is the gain of Hannibal Lecter's desire for human flesh *prima facie* deserved in virtue of its resulting from the expected consequences of Hannibal's autonomous and sustained efforts, but then simply overridden in the end because of the negative moral value of its causal antecedents? Would it not be more appropriate to say that Hannibal does not deserve his ghoulish reward from the start? I will return to this case later. Notice also that Sher does not think that (e), the rewards-of-virtue basis, is a unitary one, grounded in a single principle, but rather that it is to be traced to a 'number of more local sources' (ibid., p. 110). So there is not only heterogeneity among bases but also within them.

Feinberg and Sher's analyses of desert bases add a second dimension to the claim that justice is a pluralistic notion. It is then, so it seems, not only the case that other considerations are relevant to judgements of justice apart from desert claims; it is also the case that the bases of the desert claims themselves are heterogeneous and have no single justification (see, for example, ibid., p. 230). Now, pluralism of this sort does not necessarily imply relativism; in default of a single justification or a single denominator, it might still somehow be possible to rank conflicting desert bases in order of salience. Sher's example of the way in which a given desert basis resulting from expected consequences or sustained effort can be overruled by certain moral considerations seems to indicate that his is not a radically relativized notion of plurality. After all, in everyday life people are prone to say that *P* deserves or does not deserve *S*, full stop; one does not often hear claims to the effect that *P* deserves *S* in virtue of one desert basis but not of another – or even that *P* deserves *S* in one respect but not another. The simplest explanation of that would, of course, be that people are working with a single desert basis rather than a fluid multiplicity of overlapping bases; but then again, simple explanations are not always the best. They must have something else to recommend them, and in this case, in fact, I think they do.

I will say more about that shortly, but first a nod is in order to an article that seems to bring the very idea of distinct desert bases to its most natural conclusion. The reason for saying that is that its author, Julian Lamont, frames the idea of a common-core concept (here: desert) around which different conceptions (here: different bases) revolve – like planets around a single star – in language well known from debates about moral and political concepts, thus giving it an aura of familiarity and logical respectability. Lamont argues against the presumption, underlying much of the relevant literature, that the disputes about what constitutes desert can be resolved by a closer and closer analysis of the concept itself. This presumption is false, Lamont claims, because desert is not 'internally determined': it 'gives no unique set of conceptual and moral requirements'; rather, it requires external values and goals to make it determinate. That is, when people make desert claims, they are not merely telling us what desert itself requires; they also, unwittingly, introduce external values and make their judgements in the light of those values. However, since these add-on values are diverse and conflicting, the desert claims themselves become diverse and conflicting. For example, no scrutiny of the concept of desert will answer the question whether an advertised fellowship for the applicant 'with the greatest mastery of computer science' should, on grounds of desert, go to the brightest applicant or to the one who has worked hardest. The answer will depend on whether you value more natural brightness or hard work (1994, esp. pp. 45, 49, 54, 58).

This analysis is strikingly redolent of the 'essential contestability thesis', originally formulated by W. B. Gallie (1955–56), which became fashionable in moral, and especially political, conceptual studies a while ago. The point of Gallie's thesis was specifically to explain how a concept could have a non-relative core and be amenable to a clear formal definition (like Feinberg's 'desert') while at the same time being essentially contestable in the sense that there can never be any warrant for the belief that one interpretation of it is better than another, since these interpretations bring to the concept conflicting conceptions. To rephrase Lamont's point about desert in those terms, he might say that while it is definitely one and the same concept of desert which forms the bone of contention, different external values attached in people's minds to at least one of the variables (namely *B*) can support radically different interpretations about what desert really is, even within the fixed terms of the original specification (cf. Connolly's analysis of *freedom* as an essentially contested concept, 1983, esp. pp. 166–7).

The main problem with the picture painted here is a familiar one: is the allegedly common core of the concept of desert also essentially contestable or not? If it is, then the essential contestability thesis collapses into implausible and uninteresting conceptual relativism: there is simply no specific concept of desert abroad, and when people think they are arguing about desert, they are merely talking at cross-purposes. If it is not itself essentially contestable, however, then there seems no special reason to think that good arguments cannot be given for one conception being closer to this non-contestable core than another (see further in Kristjánsson, 1996, s. 7.1). Perhaps it is true that people bring their conflicting values to the concept of desert, but it may equally well be true that some of these values are more reasonable than others, given the role this concept plays in moral discourse. Why dismiss out of hand the claim of the conceptual naturalist that moral and political concepts have particular points and purposes in human relations, given the common nature of human beings and the natural environment they inhabit, and that these points can be critically argued for (see my earlier discussion in Section 1.2; for a further elaboration, see Kristjánsson, 1996, ss. 7.2–7.3)?

These are, of course, merely rhetorical questions. Rather than engaging here with the general issue of conceptual contestability or relativity in the moral domain, let me in what follows propose a number of specific arguments for the highly 'selective' view that desert admits of a single basis, *moral virtue*, and that the other commonly suggested bases are either reducible to that basis, in so far as they form reasonable grounds for desert claims, or simply uphold other distinct values which have nothing to do with desert. A quick look at the most prominent literature on desert will show a profusion of claims in opposition to this proposal. Miller blatantly claims that 'the kind of desert which is relevant to social justice is rarely *moral* desert' (1976, p. 87); Galston explains that desert-related facts 'need not be moral characteristics' (1980, p. 170) and so forth. I will, however, not let the received wisdom deter me here, but would like to suggest rather that Rawls may, after all, have hit the mark with one of his premises for the dismissal of desert as a ground for distributive justice, namely that the most plausible understanding of desert does imply a thick, substantive conception of the human good (although he arguably drew the wrong conclusion from the premise). The thick, substantive conception in question is that desert requires gains and losses to be distributed according to people's moral virtues.

Before arguing for this understanding of desert, let me first spell it out in more detail. The idea of a tight connection between virtue and desert is, of course, not novel. In what Hurka calls a 'golden age for moral theory', the heyday of objective consequentialism from Sidgwick to Ross, virtue and desert were two commonly recognized intrinsic goods, and desert was typically understood to mean 'the proportionment of happiness to virtue' (Hurka, 2001, pp. 6–7, 16; cf. Ross, 1930, p. 27). I do not intend to elaborate here on Hurka's (2001) own interesting comparison concerning the common formal (mathematical) structure of desert and virtue, nor do I intend to follow in the footsteps of the 'golden-age' objectivists since their theories of intrinsic goods contain a lot of baggage that I would not want to carry. My intent, rather, is to claim that given the post-Feinbergian view about the logical structure of desert and its salience as a consideration of justice, desert is best understood as having a single basis: moral virtue. This claim might seem to let in through the back door the plurality of desert bases that I want to avoid since modern-day virtue ethics tends to posit a number of irreconcilable virtues. Does the invocation of moral virtue as a desert basis not mean that *P* might typically deserve *S* on the grounds of one virtue that *P* possesses, but not deserve it on the grounds of another virtue that *P* does not possess, with no way of choosing between the two? One way to counter that suggestion would be to rely on the somewhat antediluvian theory of the unity of the virtues, according to which each virtue implies all the others; one cannot have one without having all. Rather than doing that, however, I prefer to rely here on an Aristotelian account which implies the possibility of ranking people in order of comprehensive moral worth according to their possession of important virtues. For those wary of the pluralist tendency in the currently popular virtue ethics, an alternative formulation of my original claim might, then, be that people deserve *S* or do not deserve *S* solely on the grounds of their *moral worth*. If someone is put off by the idea of the unequal moral worth of persons, it does well to remember that believing that different persons, such as Nelson Mandela and Saddam Hussein, might have unequal *moral worth as persons*, depending on their demonstrated level of moral attainment, is not tantamount to considering them of unequal *worth as moral persons* (see Hare, 1996, pp. 239–40). The idea of unequal moral worth still leaves sound moral reasons for respecting every moral agent's civil liberties and human rights, as well as sound moral reasons against moral separatism and political elitism (see further in Kristjánsson, 2002, s. 4.4). Rather than letting the vagaries of modern virtue ethics force me to use the language of moral worth, however, which could be misunderstood and misinterpreted, I will in what follows stick to my original formulation of desert as based on 'moral virtue'.

The idea on which I want to build is a deep-seated pre-theoretical (or perhaps I should say, pre-academic) one: namely, that in an ideal world everyone would, other things being equal, reap as he has sown. The good should, ideally, prosper, while those who swim in sin should sink in sorrow. This pre-reflective, primordial notion of desert seems to be grounded in every known culture and religion (see Pojman, 2001, p. 98–9). Far be it from me to recommend this as an overarching principle of *morality* since I am sympathetic neither to an unmitigated primacy-of-desert thesis (with respect to justice) nor to a primacy-of-justice thesis (with respect to morality). I do, however, think that this is how people do, and should reasonably, think about *desert*. How exactly we calculate the deserts in each given instance is another story. It is obvious that a villain does not deserve to become president and that a saint does not deserve to be tortured, but, needless to say, there are various marginal cases where one might reasonably ask, for instance, whether a person of moderate virtue deserves to win 100,000 pounds in the lottery or simply deserves praise for his good efforts. As with many other moral quandaries, in so far as such quandaries can be properly resolved, the answers will require considerable moral wisdom and experience. In any case, there would usually be a host of other moral considerations to take into account in such a situation apart from the desert-based ones, should the situation actually require some action (interference) on our part as opposed to simple reaction. And even when it only calls for a reaction (emotion) on our part, there are, typically, other emotions relevant to the case at hand which adjust the desert-based ones up or down. I will return to this question of calculations in Section 4.3. What we can reasonably say, at this point, is that a morally perfect person in a world of limited resources, such as ours, deserves as much in the way of those resources as is commensurate with not interfering with other people's chances of getting what they deserve. Notably, however, in a perfect world a morally perfect person would not only get all he or she deserves but more, since desert is not the only moral value (cf. Pojman, 2001, p. 106).

The notion of desert that I have now sketched is *global* in the sense that moral virtue is its only and all-encompassing desert basis. It is, by contrast, *not global* in two other possible senses of the word. It does not imply, as I have repeatedly stressed, that desert is the overriding moral concern, nor does it imply that a morally virtuous person never deserves any misfortune. In our world as it is, most overall virtuous persons will still fall short of perfect moral virtue (perhaps even, in an imperfect world, no one can be morally perfect); hence they may deserve misfortune proportionate to their (minor) faults. Similarly, an overall non-virtuous person may deserve a reward when deviating in a positive way from his general tendency. Returning, however, to the sense in which this notion of desert is global, allow me to reiterate and stress that the idea is not of moral virtue as an overriding desert basis but as an exhaustive one. Consider again the case of Hannibal Lecter, or of a gang member who likes to torture others for amusement, and let us exclude here, for the sake of argument, the uninteresting possibility that both are insane, hence unable to exercise their personhood and not desert-evaluable. My claim is, then, that Sher's proposed 'expected-consequences' and 'sustained-effort' bases provide *no reason* whatsoever, not even a *prima facie* and easily overridden one, for counting the outcomes desired and aimed at by the two persons (of flesh-eating and torture) deserved. Someone might object by saying that these outcomes are still the objects of reasonable choice and for any such object of *P*'s choice, there is a *prima facie* reason why *P* should be allowed to get it. I do not deny that flesh-eating and torture can be objects of reasonable choice, at least not in the Anscombean sense in which almost anything can count as an object of reasonable choice under some description, even drinking a 'saucer of mud' (Anscombe, 1976, p. 71, discussed in Kristjánsson, 2002, pp. 48–9). However, it is one thing to say that something is an object of *P*'s reasonable choice and that there is a *prima facie* reason why *P* should be allowed to get it – any attempt to curb *P*'s getting it thus being a constraint upon *P*'s freedom which stands in need of justification. It is quite another thing to say that for any object of *P*'s reasonable choice, there is a *prima facie* reason for considering it deserved that *P* gets it. There are strong intuitions in support of the first claim (see, for example, Connolly, 1983, pp. 151–2), fewer, if any, for the second, but it seems to me as if Sher systematically conflates the two. By excluding Hannibal's efforts as a putative desert basis, I am not saying that effort-making only gives rise to desert when it is conscientious effort aimed at doing good. The effort involved in activities that are neither good nor evil may also constitute a desert basis. But that does not necessarily mean, as Sher seems to think, that effort has a specific value as a desert basis independent of moral virtue. More plausibly, it can be taken to mean that a moral virtue may sometimes be trained and kept going even when not directly aimed at the good: relief workers not only feed the poor; they also work out in the gym, read newspapers and so forth.

In addition to being global, the account I am suggesting of desert is *cosmic*, in the sense Miller has given to the notion of 'cosmic desert'. While it is *prima facie* good that people get what they deserve, to say that a state of affairs (*S*) is undeserved is not *necessarily* to say that someone is morally responsible for *S*, or that anyone (except God, perhaps, on the day of reckoning) has, as things stand, a duty to *do* anything about it. The idea of cosmic justice may be held independently of the idea of desert based on moral virtue. However, I do not present it here as a logically independent thesis. Rather, I consider it to follow from (a) the Feinbergian notion of desert as simply one ingredient (and not necessarily the most important ingredient) in justice and justice as simply one ingredient in moral rightness, coupled with (b) the fact that there are obviously many cases where a human being cannot do anything about an undeserved state of affairs apart from reacting to it emotionally in the proper way.

Miller claims that a cosmic conception of desert carries no implications for human action and that it is, consequently, morally and politically irrelevant (1976, pp. 114–15). That contention, however, is only supportable on the basis of two questionable assumptions: (1) that mere hypothetical possibilities are not morally/politically relevant and (2) that only actions, not emotions, matter for morality. These assumptions are not only questionable but also, in my estimation, simply wrong, because (1) much of moral development and moral reflection takes place in the God's-eyes-view realm of the hypothetical: 'It is undeserved that this innocent child is dying of an incurable disease, and if we could, we should be doing something about it.' Understanding the thrust of such an assertion is an indispensable milestone on the way to moral maturity. Furthermore, (2) emotions (including desert-based emotions focusing on the actualization, or lack thereof, of cosmic desert in particular cases; see later in Chapter 3) are morally salient in recording, conveying and establishing our moral values – feeling the right things at the right times is a necessary part of the good life (see Section 1.2) – regardless of how particular emotions are allowed at particular times to translate into action. The idea of moral virtue as the single basis for desert, as I have explicated it, does indeed imply that desert claims are very often emotion claims, grounded in a desire for 'poetic justice', rather than direct incitements to action. But they are no less morally or politically significant for that reason. This is why Miller is only half right when he says that if Smith deserves to win a race but Brown actually wins it, then this is '*no* reason' to give Smith the prize, or to regard it as just that he gets it, except in some sense of justice 'which carries no implications for human action' (1976, pp. 114–15). There may be no reason to *give* Smith the prize (since Brown is entitled to it, and it would have pernicious consequences to try to abolish the rules of competitive sport), but Smith's deserving to get the prize arguably gives us a pretty good reason for *regarding* it as potentially just – if overridably so – that he gets it. And that is a morally relevant fact, in the sense in which moral hypotheticals and moral emotions are relevant as cornerstones of moral maturity.

Olsaretti refers to cosmic accounts of desert, such as the one I am presenting here, as upholding a 'telic' desert principle, one that is relevant for assessing outcomes or states of affairs, as opposed to a 'deontic' desert principle which is used primarily to assess or guide actions (2003a, p. 8). The reader should thus understand why I have chosen to talk about 'outcomes' or 'states of affairs' rather than 'treatment' as one of the term variables (*S*) of desert. Instead of Miller's characterization of desert as 'a matter of fitting forms of treatment to specific qualities and actions of individuals which are generally held in high regard' (1976, p. 85), I would suggest 'a matter of a fit between states of affairs and specific moral qualities and actions of individuals which are generally held in high regard because they are moral'. Desert claims seek a tailored fit between *P*'s moral virtue as a desert basis (*B*) and the states of affairs (*S*) in which *P* lands, not merely between *B* and other people's treatment of *P*.

The Comparative Nature of Desert

It is commonly claimed that distributive justice is a *holistic* notion in that the justice of any assignment to an individual depends on the larger distribution of benefits in society. In contrast, desert claims are – so we are told – *individualistic*; their legitimacy can be established without looking at what others are receiving. This claim, which has been most carefully worked out by Scheffler in his important article 'Justice and Desert in Liberal Theory' (reprinted in Scheffler, 2001), draws on an earlier distinction made by Feinberg (1980) between distributive justice as an example of *comparative* justice, and desert as a principle of *non-comparative* justice. In the case of the latter, Feinberg claimed that each person's due is determined in isolation from considerations about others, thus suiting it admirably for the context of retributive justice, whereas such considerations about others inevitably enter into assessments of overall distributive justice (for an analysis and discussion, see Olsaretti, 2003a, pp. 17ff.). Recently, serious criticisms have been raised to this distinction, criticisms where it is argued that desert has a comparative as well as a non-comparative element. On such a view, we cannot assess the justice of an assignment of benefits or burdens to a particular person without knowing whether that assignment is part of an overall distribution that satisfies people's comparative deserts – and that implies a view of justice that, although desert-based, is also holistic (see Scheffler, 2003b). These criticisms have led Scheffler to modify somewhat his position. He now concedes that desert can be given a 'variable' as well as a 'fixed' interpretation in justice and that the former is not incompatible with distributive holism. He still, however, holds to the view that most desert claims about allocations rely on a fixed principle, especially those concerned with *economic* desert. Thus, in Scheffler's view, as responsible agents, we are not precluded from rejecting distribution in accordance with 'economic desert', although we may admit that desert has an essential role to play in our practice of treating others as responsible agents (as presupposed by our 'reactive attitudes') and that desert does have distributive implications, as well as retributive ones, in certain practices involving praise and blame, the allocation of prizes and so forth (Scheffler, 2003a; 2003b).

I would go much further than Scheffler and, indeed, some of his critics by insisting that *all* desert claims are comparative, and hence that all such claims (*qua* justice claims) are holistic, for the simple logical reason that comparisons unavoidably matter for determining what is a person's due in the first place. All desert claims involve, in my view, at least an implicit reference to a *baseline of expectations*. Such claims are about people getting their due with respect to benefits or burdens. If these claims did not involve an implicit reference to a baseline of expectations, there would be no way to determine what should count as a benefit or a burden in the first place, let alone a deserved or undeserved one. For example, I cannot be indignant over someone else's undeserved good fortune unless I deem that person to have enjoyed some fortune which people of a similar kind, in a similar position, would not have expected to enjoy, compared to what they deserve. In most cases, the baseline of expectations will be a *statistical* one: that is, referring to what people of a similar kind could have statistically expected under similar circumstances. In some cases, however, we might want to employ a *moral* baseline: for instance if someone ventures by accident into an area where most travellers are kidnapped by guerrillas and that person happens to be so kidnapped, we might want to say that the baseline of expectations is one in which a person is not kidnapped, since that would be the morally (as opposed to the statistically) expected outcome. We would rightly consider it a (relative) loss for a dope peddler if he sold much less of his illegal commodities than could be statistically expected, even though the morally ideal situation would be one in which no illegal substances were sold on the streets. If there is a conflict between a statistical and a moral baseline, the one that we should rightly employ is the one that would be preferred by the person whose deserts we are determining (cf., in a different context, Nozick, 1972, pp. 112–16). To take a couple of more examples, a child who died of hunger in a poverty-stricken area could be considered as having suffered a loss, although most children in that area died of hunger, as long as such deaths could reasonably be prevented through human intervention; in other words, a moral baseline would rightly apply. By contrast, if the world were constituted such that everyone were doomed to die of hunger before the age of thirty, and nothing could be done to avert it, then a person who died of hunger before that age could not be considered to have suffered a loss, since that fate would be in harmony both with a statistical and moral baseline of expectations.

Determining the relevant baseline of expectations is only the first step in a three-step process of establishing a desert claim. In the second place, we must compare the outcome of the person in question (*P*) to the baseline of expectations in order to decide whether *P* has experienced a gain, a loss or a neutral outcome. Notice here that in some cases there is no chance of a neutral outcome. Let us say that there is, statistically, a 50 per cent chance of an acceptance, a 50 per cent chance of a refusal when a man proposes to a woman There is no in-between possible: you are either faced either with the bliss of an acceptance or the humiliation of a rejection. Those would be cases of what Feinberg calls 'polar desert' (see earlier): you are doomed either to lose or to gain. In other cases, of 'non-polar' desert, the neutral outcome is the most common one: we are then interested in whether *P* deserved to win or not to win (say, in a lottery draw), where not winning is the neutral outcome, or deserved to lose or not to lose (say, a wallet when walking through a dangerous park at night), where not losing is the neutral outcome. In the third place, we must finally compare *P*'s comparatively established outcome (gain, loss or neutral) to *P*'s deserved outcome: to what we think was *P*'s due according to basis of desert that we deem relevant in the specific context (that is, according to my earlier specification of a unitary desert basis, to *P*'s level of moral virtue). If there is a discrepancy in either direction, *P*'s state of affairs is not deserved: *P* has either been, comparatively speaking, undeservedly fortunate or undeservedly unfortunate. If there is no discrepancy, that state of affairs is deserved. As we have seen, this process of forming a desert claim is essentially comparative, implying, *qua* justice claim, 'holistic' comparisons with the general distribution of the relevant benefits across society, compared to what people deserve. So, in this sense, at least, it is true that all desert claims are socially comparative (cf. Sadurski, 1985, pp. 14ff.), although it does not mean that they must all involve a comparison to the speaker's own lot (see further in Sections 3.2–3.3).

What is the root of the claim about the non-comparative nature of desert that I have now rejected? I think its root, and simultaneously its fault, lies in a mistaken consideration of 'sham' desert judgements, many of which, as we have seen, are judgements where ordinary language simplistically and misleadingly couches entitlement claims in the language of desert. It would be quite normal to say in everyday life, for instance, that *P* 'deserved' to get an 'A' in the maths exam having answered all the questions correctly, and this claim would hold good irrespective of what others happened to get in the exam. Such statements give 'desert' the impression of being non-comparative, of being a purely 'individualistic' notion. Yet this claim is, as it stands, not really a desert claim, but rather an entitlement claim in disguise. The reason for this is not that a desert claim must be independent of all public institutions and their rules; desert claims are, as noted earlier, often logically dependent on the *point* of such institutions and rules. The reason is rather that what this particular claim means is simply that *P* was *entitled* to get an 'A' according to certain institutional rule-based criteria regarding exams (that if you answer all questions correctly, you will get an 'A'); it does not constitute a desert claim until the basis of the desert is provided: some relevant desert-conferring fact(s) about *P*, such as *P* deserved to get an 'A', say, because of superior efforts during the term or well-honed intelligence. Alternatively, perhaps, *P* did *not* deserve an 'A', although entitled to it, because it was only through serendipity that all the questions were answered correctly, while the industrious and bright P_1, who should have deserved an 'A', undeservedly failed to get it because of illness during the exam. When we enter the field of such real, as opposed to 'sham', desert claims, the illusion of the non-comparative nature of desert quickly dissolves.

As noted earlier, I am not the first person to entertain doubts about the notion of non-comparative desert. But I would like here to distinguish my argument above from some other criticisms recently directed at this notion, some of which are less radical than mine, but at least one of which is more radical (and, I submit, unreasonably so). Shelly Kagan (2003) argues that an adequate theory of desert will need to include both non-comparative and comparative principles. He considers cases where such principles seem to clash, such as one in which persons *A* and *B* are equally deserving and *A* is getting what is deserved, but *B* is getting more. Should *A*'s lot then ideally be improved or not? Or think of a case where *A* is more deserving than *B* but *B* has more than *A*. Even if *A* is already getting what he deserves, should his lot not be ideally improved even more so that he gets more than *B* (ibid., p. 97)? From my point of view, these cases seem to have an air of artificiality about them, for they assume that the relevant comparison class comprises only two persons. In most real situations, we are concerned with what people sufficiently similar to the person in question normally (statistically or morally) can be expected to get. If *A* and *B* are simply two out of millions of similar persons in a similar situation, the fact that *B* gets more than deserved would not suffice to raise the baseline of expectations for *A* to any substantial degree. Let us suppose, however, that *A* and *B* are in a unique situation, where *A*'s lot can only be compared to *B*'s and vice versa. Then, on my account, there would be no question of the rightness of *A*'s receiving more in both of Kagan's examples; of course *A* should. The only reason why these examples raise a problem for Kagan in the first place is his insistence that there is, for each person, a particular level of well-being that is 'absolutely' (non-comparatively) deserved (ibid., p. 94), but that is a claim I would strongly deny.

Thomas Hurka also thinks that we need to supplement a theory of comparative desert with a notion of non-comparative desert in order to fill certain 'gaps' in the former. These gaps are that (a) if all we know is that a person with a certain degree of virtue is enjoying a certain amount of pleasure, the comparative notion of desert has nothing to say about the degree of desert value this situation contains, and (b) if persons *A* and *B* are equally virtuous, the comparative notion assigns the same value to the situation where they both enjoy one unit of pleasure and the situation where they both enjoy a thousand units. Hurka finds these gaps 'unacceptable' (2003, p. 50), but I find them perfectly logically acceptable, if practically implausible. What is 'unacceptable' about them, from a practical perspective, is the assumed level of ignorance of the relevant situations: that is, the underdetermination of the given scenarios. Underdeterminate research scenarios give us, as we will see many examples of in this book, underdeterminate moral conclusions. If it is really so that we know absolutely nothing about some given persons except their level of virtue and their level of pleasure (or well-being) – in other words, that we know nothing else about the nature of the situations in which they find themselves or what other people can statistically and/or morally expect in such situations – then we simply have no idea of whether they are experiencing a gain, a loss or a neutral outcome, let alone whether their outcome is deserved or not. This indicates, as I see it, not a weakness in the comparative notion of desert, but rather one of its strengths as a social, holistic moral principle.

Owen McLeod agrees with me that we can do without the distinction between comparative and non-comparative desert and thereby avoid the nettlesome questions of how to reconcile putative conflicts between them (2003, p. 125). McLeod, however, throws the baby out with the bathwater by upholding a desert-monistic theory of justice, which rejects not only non-comparative desert but also any notion of non-comparative justice (since justice is equated with desert). This lands him in serious trouble when attempting to explain cases such as one in which a student *P* receives an 'A' in an exam by answering all the questions correctly, but where some other students whose answers were inferior also receive an 'A' (ibid., p. 129). McLeod is forced to conclude that *P*'s receipt of 'A' is here *tout court* an injustice to *P*, and to concoct a complicated theory of the 'economics of receipt' to explain why. McLeod inadvisably deprives himself of the possibility of saying that in one sense of justice, that is, justice as entitlement, *P*'s grade is just, whereas in another, justice as desert, it is not. While my account of the non-comparative nature of desert is, thus, more radical than that of Kagan and Hurka, it does not extend as far as McLeod's account, namely to justice in all of its senses.

2.2 For a Single-basis View of Desert: the Intuitive Appeal and the Question of Needs

Why do I take my account of moral virtue, spelled out earlier in this chapter, as the single desert basis to best capture that elusive term, variable *B*? Put compendiously, I think that it is, for four distinct reasons, the most philosophically illuminating and serviceable account available: (1) it has strong *intuitive appeal*; (2) it helps to account for the sense in which *need* is, and also the sense in which need is not, relevant for justice (and, indeed, the same goes for *equality*, as we will see in Section 2.3); (3) it sheds light on the controversial issue of if and to what extent *responsibility* is required for desert attribution; and (4) it best accords with *social-science research* on what people actually think desert is. Let me postpone an elaboration of reasons (3) and (4) until Section 2.3, but start here with numbers (1) and (2).

The examples typically given to elicit people's intuitions concerning justice and desert tend to be seriously underdescribed. Archetypically so is Kohlberg's staple story of Heinz's sick wife whose only chance of survival was the expensive drug Heinz could not afford to buy from that penurious chemist. Should he steal it or not? Or to put it differently, should the entitlements of private property or the needs of a sick dependant carry more moral weight? It is no wonder that people, especially young people, most often failed to come to any rationally argued-for conclusion when confronted with this story (which involves a typical justice dilemma rather than a general moral dilemma) – a fact which eventually led to Kohlberg's serious underestimation of people's moral acumen. The core of the problem here is that we do not know enough of the dying wife's deserts in the first place in order to be able to weigh them against the relevant entitlements. Had the example included a clear clue about her moral virtue – 'She was a paragon of virtue' or 'She was a vicious gang member' – we could have passed a judgement about her deserving the medication or not (which would then have helped us sort out whether her need had any grounding in desert). This example shows the strong intuitive appeal of virtue as a desert basis. It is not only the case that the wife's other possible desert bases would have been overridden in the event that she were a vicious gang member; all other desert-based considerations would simply have ceased to matter (as opposed, perhaps, to humanitarian concerns). This is also, to cite a personal anecdotal example, why all the seven-year-old pupils in my son's class ceased supporting Michael Schumacher, the successful Formula 1 driver, after they read in the media that his grandmother was living in dire straits and, without any good reasons from Schumacher, never received any visits from her grandson. A multi-millionaire who showed such lack of concern for his grandmother simply did not deserve to win any Grand Prix races – so my son and his classmates concluded – irrespective of his other accomplishments!

If we look again at Sher's list of fifteen paradigm assertions about deserts, passing over those I have already excluded as 'sham' desert judgements (3, 4, 7 and 15), we notice that all the remaining ones include a moral element. While seriously underdescribed as far as helping us to pass judgements of desert on grounds of all-round moral virtue, the intuitive appeal of those assertions lies, I think, precisely in their reference to particular moral virtues and vices (cf. Moore, 2000, pp. 323–4, 435). In default of any knowledge about the rest of *P*'s virtues and vices, we must rely on the information we have. We know that, if nothing else, Jones is diligent (in 1), Smith hard-working (in 2), Jackson conscientious (in 5), Baker ambitious and well prepared (in 6), Anderson and Brown criminally minded (in 8 and 9), Winters a brave sufferer (in 10), Lee courageous and altruistic (in 11), Benson generally virtuous (in 12), Gordon under-rewarded (in 13) and McArthur a person of wisdom (in 14). These are all moral virtues and vices (while there is a thin line here between moral, intellectual and other virtues, recall that Aristotle includes wit in his list of moral virtues, and wisdom, as distinct from mere knowledge, has traditionally been thought to include a moral element) and they explain not only the intuitive appeal of those assertions *qua* desert claims but, more generally, the appeal of all of Sher's other proposed desert bases, not merely (e), happiness/rewards as a result of virtuous character and good deeds. The potential allure of considering people deserving of (a) the predictable consequences of their free acts, (b) the objects of their sustained efforts over time and also, to an extent (on top of simple entitlement considerations), (d) prizes for their competitive performance, lies in the fact that we think of people as deserving, other things being equal, the fruit of their hard work and effort. Diligence and perseverance in morally acceptable (praiseworthy or at least non-blameworthy) projects are, as such, moral virtues (see, for example, Pojman, 2001, p. 94). If, however, the hard work and effort are aimed at immoral outcomes, people do not merely become less deserving of the goods gained, but rather, as I have already explained, not deserving at all or even negatively deserving. Sher's category (c), punishment commensurate with the wrongness of their acts, obviously falls in line here, too. So it seems as if we may, after all, have managed to locate the 'single compelling normative base' which Sher sought (1987, p. xii) but which he did not find.

Notice that new information about *P*'s virtues may drastically change our intuitions about *P*'s deserts, as in the case of Steven Bradbury's serendipitous speedskating victory at the Olympics (see Section 2.1). Most people were ready to write it off as undeserved (although overall just, because of entitlement) but later changed their minds after it was revealed in the media that he had bravely suffered and come back from a life-threatening crash, as well as serious training injuries, some time ago. This also indicates that people's original reactions to Bradbury's victory as being undeserved did not rest so much on the non-moral concern that he had less skill as a skater than the other competitors but, rather, on the moral concern that he had not exhibited the same level of virtue (diligence, perseverance and so forth) as them in reaching the finals. After the revelations about Bradbury's courage, the considerations which pulled people in different directions were, thus, not a non-moral consideration about his not having been the 'best competitor' *per se*, and a moral one about his having been a paragon of courage, but rather two moral concerns about different moral virtues. To be sure, if skating were considered an immoral activity, or if Bradbury's competitors had used immoral means to acquire their superior skills (for instance, illegal drugs), we would not have been concerned about the undeservingness of Bradbury's winning the gold medal at their expense. The account of a single moral desert basis thus helps us make sense of competing intuitions about the relative weight of *effort* and *achievement* in desert claims, including those relating to deserved salaries. Simply being hard-working is not a desert basis if the hard work has a negative moral value; working hard on morally worthwhile and prospectively successful projects, on the other hand, belongs to the desert basis of moral virtue. Achievement through pure luck and morally unsound achievements do not constitute grounds for desert; morally sound achievements achieved through effort do. So effort and achievement turn out not to be as conflicting as they are often made out to be; both count in desert claims in so far, and only in so far, as they are instantiations of moral virtue. To be sure, however, the *practical* problem remains of how to reward a person for morally sound and potentially successful efforts that fail, through bad luck, to result in achievement.

Turning now to the second of my four arguments for the superiority of my single-basis account of desert, many writers have wanted to place *need* as a core ingredient in justice, beside entitlement and desert (see, for example, Miller, 1976; 1999). Others have argued vehemently against such an inclusion (for example, Sadurski, 1985). It is not difficult to make out a case for the satisfaction of *basic needs* being required by my single-basis account of desert. Everyone satisfying a minimal standard of moral virtue would deserve to have their basic needs satisfied, on that account, simply because that is the only way for them to remain desert-evaluable as moral agents; that is, having their capacity to deserve preserved (see further in Section 2.3), given the fact that lack of basic necessities undermines the possibility of autonomous choices. The more troublesome cases concern non-basic needs. Consider Miller's example of an elderly woman developing arthritis and needing a hip replacement. There is no connection between her condition and any service she has rendered or any injury she has suffered at the hands of others, and she has, so far in life, received her fair share of benefits. Miller concludes that in her case a justice-based claim for hip replacement would be purely one of need and not of desert (1999, p. 227).

Now, what would we normally want to say about the claim for medical treatment in such a case: that it is a claim of (a) justice *qua* desert? (b) justice *qua* entitlement but not desert? (c) justice *qua* need (as Miller thinks)? (d) not justice, but of another moral value (altruism, sympathy, care, love)? In this case, at least in our part of the world, (b) would seem to be the most normal formulation. Given that the woman resides in Europe, one would ask whether she were not entitled to hip replacement, and if so, why the national health service does not provide it. In the USA, the language of entitlement would also seem to be the most natural medium in which to discuss the case. If the woman has adequate medical insurance, she is presumably entitled to the operation, and if she does not, then one might want to argue that everyone should, ideally, be entitled to such insurance. In the third world, (d) would, as things unfortunately stand, be a more realistic formulation, unless the speaker wanted to bring to the fore questions of international injustice (first world versus third world). I think that people would not be as tempted as Miller seems to think they erroneously are to consider the claim based on the woman's health need as being one of desert at all. The word 'deserved' might often be used, but as Miller himself notes, sham uses of that word, where it actually refers for instance to entitlements, abound. Of course there may still be situations in which we would want to say that the woman really does deserve the operation in light of her moral virtue – but then her getting the operation would be considered just not because it is needed (although it is needed) but because it is deserved.

So my conclusion is that there is some truth both in the claim that need is relevant to justice and that it is not: it sometimes is and it sometimes is not. When it is relevant to justice, it is because it relates to claims about entitlements (most commonly), or deserts (less commonly), not because it is an independent ingredient of justice. When it is not, it relates to other values which may be as morally important as justice, but which are not reducible to justice.

Before turning to the other two reasons for the evident superiority of my account of the desert variable *B*, it is salutary to say a few words in passing about how my account of moral virtue as a single desert basis compares with another rare (in recent times) attempt at the same, by Eric Moore (2000). Moore first suggests a simple view of the connection between desert and virtue, namely that a 'person deserves good things for possessing a virtue or acting virtuously, bad things for possessing a vice or acting viciously, and that these two categories exhaust the desert bases' (ibid., pp. 421–2), but he is later led to qualify that view in various ways in light of further considerations. Let me first say that I am happier with his original view than with his qualified view. One of his qualifications I deem important, however, and would like to incorporate into my account, namely that children can reasonably be said to deserve *S* on the grounds of their budding virtues, or their potential for virtue growth (see my discussion of desert evaluability in the following section), rather than on the grounds of their already existing virtues. So *B* would, in addition to actual moral virtue, have to include, at least in the case of the young, prospective (other things being equal) moral virtue, or at least an acceptance of childish innocence as a budding moral virtue.

Moore's other major qualification involves total past receipts. He produces a number of stories which are meant to show that what matters for desert claims is not only *P*'s present moral virtue, but also whether or not *P* has received a fair share of good for virtuous actions, and fair share of bad for vicious actions, in the past. The idea seems to be this, to take one example: '*P* was such a scoundrel in the past, and although he has now turned into a paragon of moral virtue, he does not deserve any rewards for that yet since he has not atoned sufficiently for his past misdeeds.' While it is true that our estimate of *P*'s total past receipts may enter into our measurement of *P*'s comparative gain or loss, which is then to be desert-evaluated, I would agree with Miller, who points out that desert claims can be justified on the basis of both past and *present* facts about persons (1976, p. 93). I do not concur with those, such as Flew (1984, pp. 152–3) and Sadurski (1985, p. 118), who hold desert to be exclusively, or even essentially, a backward-looking notion, unless we regard the present as the limit of the past. Old sins do cast long shadows, and we might well want to qualify our judgement of *P*'s present-virtue-based deserts in light of his past vices. But equally, we might want to increase our positive estimation of *P*'s present-virtue-based deserts in light of *P*'s admirable efforts in turning away from past moral error – the formidable effort required for changing from a sinner to a saint. The same could also apply, *mutatis mutandis*, in the case of a 'good old dog' who later learnt bad tricks (I return to this point in Section 4.3). Since considerations of past receipts versus moral progress/regress would, I think, more or less cancel each other out in our desert evaluations, I do not find Moore's past-receipts amendment of his original 'simple view' either necessary or helpful.

2.3 Desert, Responsibility and the Empirical Evidence

In this section, I present two more reasons for accepting the single-basis account of desert: namely, that (3) it sheds light on the controversial issue of if, and if so in what sense and to what extent, responsibility is required for desert attribution, and (4) it best accords with social-science research on what people actually think desert is. To start with (3), recall first the common assumption that moral evaluation can only be properly directed at that for which a person can be held responsible. Various attempts at undermining this general assumption have failed (see Kristjánsson, 2002, s. 1.4). This general assumption, then, typically engenders a corollary assumption in accounts of desert: the 'desert-responsibility thesis', as Cupit calls it, entailing that lack of responsibility undermines a claim to deserve (1996, p. 39). Notice that the desert-responsibility thesis obviously does not imply that *P* deserves everything for which *P* is responsible (a shady businessman does not deserve the wealth amassed through his dishonest practices; see, for example, Feather's example, 2002, p. 339); rather, it means that responsibility is a necessary condition of desert attribution: of any rational claims about *P*'s deserving or not deserving *S*.

The desert-responsibility thesis is often considered a source of embarrassment for those accounts of justice which are exclusively, or even partly, based on desert. Given, on the one hand, the plausibility of this thesis and, on the other, the observation that people are not responsible 'all the way down' (beneath the surface of nature and nurture) for the talents and abilities that underlie their actions, it seems – to many contemporary liberals at least – that nobody may ever deserve anything at all, in the Feinbergian 'natural' sense. This is, as I noted in Section 2.1, one of reasons why the notion of desert fell, more or less, by the wayside in post-Rawlsian liberal thinking about justice. Other writers have tried to salvage the notion of desert by severing its link to moral evaluation and arguing that desert attribution is (commonly or even always) non-dependent upon responsibility.

There are, it seems to me, at least two arguments abroad here which need to be kept separate. The first is this:

1 There is no individual pre-institutional responsibility for action or character.
2 Desert requires such responsibility. Thus,
3 There is no such thing as desert.

And the second:

1 People are often correctly thought to deserve outcomes for the creation of which they are not responsible.
2 Moral evaluation of people necessarily requires responsibility. Thus,
3 Desert claims are not claims of moral evaluation.

While the second argument potentially rescues desert claims from complete oblivion (as claims of some sort of non-moral evaluation), it offers no reprieve for an account such as mine which considers all desert claims to be claims of moral evaluation, namely claims about *P*'s moral virtues and how well or badly *P* is rewarded for them.

Briefly stated, I think the second argument is invalid as the responsibility referred to in premise (1) need not be the same responsibility that is at issue in premise (2). Moral evaluation *does* require responsibility, and desert claims *are* claims of moral evaluation, but this does not mean that the responsibility required for desert claims is causal or moral responsibility *for the specific outcomes* about which desert claims are made. Such a direct-connection requirement is, as Hurka has noted in a different context, not essential to an account of desert: 'If a saintly person enjoys happiness not caused by his saintliness, that is still appropriate and good; if a vicious person suffers pain unrelated to his vice, that is what common sense calls poetic justice' (Hurka, 2001, p. 12, footnote 10). What kind of responsibility is then required for desert claims to be rational? In my opinion, only the Aristotelian kind of responsibility for our character traits: for allowing ourselves to become the sort of persons we are. On the Aristotelian account – as I explain in more detail in Section 5.2 – a period of early, more or less non-critical, habituation, where character traits are inculcated in us as children, is followed by the gradual growth of our own practical reason where we, so to speak, *choose* our own character by reassessing and adding to those traits with which we were originally inculcated. I am thus, for instance, responsible for a vicious trait in my character if I could *at some time* have avoided having it through making the right choices, even if its original filaments have *by now* solidified into unbreakable cables. It is precisely this kind of responsibility, I submit, which makes people *desert-evaluable*, namely the capacity for forming one's own character via right or wrong choices. We can call this a qualified desert-responsibility thesis (about moral character), as opposed to the traditional unqualified desert-responsibility thesis (about specific outcomes). Invoking the former thesis does not mean that I am implicitly replacing my original account of moral virtue as the basis of desert with an alternative account of desert based on one's past choices to promote one's virtue. On the Aristotelian understanding, there is no either–or here. A disposition to act or feel must have come about in a certain way – namely, the way described above – in a grown-up person for it to count as moral virtue in the first place.

In light of this qualified desert-responsibility thesis, I believe that the first argument above, while valid, leads to a false conclusion as its first premise is false: individual responsibility for character traits is, as Aristotle argues, possible. Sadurski is thus right that if hard determinism were correct, there would be no grounds for responsibility and, hence, desert (1985, p. 131). It does not follow, however, that 'it makes no sense to attribute desert, positive or negative, to persons for actions or facts over which they have no control' (ibid., p. 117). First of all, desert is not attributed for actions but for outcomes, and second, these need not be under *P*'s control for desert attribution to make sense – witness the intelligibility of a claim about a villain having deservedly been crushed to death in a landslide – as long as *P* is responsible for the moral characteristic which serves as the basis of the desert claim. This is why it does not make sense to attribute desert to animals, as noted before, unless we see them as possessing some kind of personhood (as involving a capacity for choice and character formation), and also why it is not appropriate to rest a desert claim on the fact of a person's beauty alone, unless the person has done something to preserve or enhance that beauty. Beauty may, however, regardless of responsibility, serve as grounds for an entitlement claim – as opposed to a desert claim – of justice, for instance in a beauty competition.

A possible objector might complain at this point that rather than explaining the link between desert and responsibility, my single-basis account of virtue and its concomitant qualified desert-responsibility thesis obscure it by failing to account for the many cases in which we are interested in *P*'s deserving a *particular* outcome – an outcome that *P* has brought about and is directly responsible for – rather than in the poetic justice of *P*'s deserving simply *any* outcome which corresponds to his or her level of moral attainment. Although I do not agree with Hurka's suggestion that there is somehow 'more desert-value' at stake when such a direct-responsibility connection is present (Hurka, 2001, p. 12, footnote 10), my 'cosmic' account of desert can fully accommodate our interest in the particular-outcome cases. That interest admits, I suggest, of two distinct explanations. First, and less interestingly perhaps, our knowledge of *P*'s overall moral standing is often limited; sometimes we do not know anything about *P* except the fact that *P* brought about a positive or a negative outcome and was or was not rewarded for it, in which case we must use those sole facts as our desert basis: '*P* spent a lot of time and money on charity work and was later rewarded for it with a presidential award.' Deserved or not? Lacking any further information about *P*'s motives and general moral standing, we are bound to answer in the affirmative. If we later find out more about *P*, such as 'he took advantage of his position as a charity worker to abuse children in his care', or even 'his commendable contribution to relief work was outweighed morally, if less directly, by the fact of being a wife-beater at home', we would quickly revise our judgement of *P*'s having deserved the award. Because of the already-noted underdetermination of the scenarios that psychologists tend to use to elicit people's intuitions of desert, this first explanation is highly relevant – as we will soon see – for the interpretation of the available empirical data.

Now, my objector might retort that there do exist prototypical cases of desert attribution where we would preferably want to *block* all information about the person other than the one directly relevant for a given desert claim about a specific, isolated outcome, rather than viewing our interest in that isolated outcome as some kind of second-best in the absence of all other information. I accept that such circumstances exist. In most cases, those could be explained as relating to our often-mentioned 'sham' desert judgements: judgements that are really about entitlement, such as a candidate 'deservedly' winning an election for having received the most votes, or a pupil 'deservedly' getting a higher grade than any other in his class in a maths exam for having answered the most questions correctly. In such cases, we would of course want to block any (other) desert-related information because the judgements are not really about deserts.

Second, and more importantly, however – and this I unabashedly acknowledge – there are specific modes of treatment which can, for *conceptual* reasons, only count as deserved if they come about as reactions to particular acts or omissions for which *P* is directly responsible. Certain rewards and punishments are cases in point: *P* only deserves to receive the reward promised for the capture of a particular criminal if, in fact, *P* has apprehended that criminal. However morally admirable *P* is in other respects is irrelevant here; *P* may deserve *a* reward for it, but *P* does not deserve *this* reward. In other words, the fact of *P*'s having apprehended the criminal is a necessary, if not a sufficient, reason for *P*'s deserving the reward in question (bear in mind that if *P* is a villain, *P* may not deserve a reward for anything whatsoever!). Similarly, if *P* is punished for robbing a certain bank at a certain date, *P* only deserves the punishment *for that* if *P* actually robbed the bank at that date, although *P* may, for some other reasons, deserve *punishment*. In some cases of this sort, we may have to add the fourth variable to the desert relation: namely, its source: P_1 deserves *S* in virtue of *B* only if *S* is brought about by a certain person or a set of persons P_2 falling under a certain description ('the judge in charge of this case' and so on). Notice that the particular desert claims here must not be confused with entitlements (although entitlements and deserts may often go hand in hand). The claim that *P* may be *entitled* to a promised reward for capturing the criminal is a separate one from the claim that *P deserves* the reward, and it is only the latter claim that need concern us here.

After this concession is made, however, about the existence of non-substitutable desert outcomes, the possible objector might want to press the original point further and ask whether those are not the typical cases of desert claims – which would then undermine both my view of desert claims as (a) being 'global' in the already-explained sense and (b) merely presupposing responsibility for one's own character traits rather than that for specific actions: 'Do desert claims not typically concern specific outcomes, not allowing the substitution of other outcomes in which, say, *P* receives the same level of utility?' I do not think that this is typically the case at all. The non-substitutable outcomes concern specific modes of treatment where certain kinds of Strawsonian 'reactive attitudes' are being expressed: in rewarding, punishing, forgiving and showing gratitude or resentment (cf. Cupit, 1996, pp. 168ff.). There is no reason to suppose that those take up more than a small part of desert claims. Most desert claims express appraising reactive attitudes that are more general, not just those specific ones; we are interested in *P* experiencing *some* gain or loss on the grounds of his or her good or bad moral character. It should be noted that even in cases of non-substitutable desert rewards, we would find it better that *P* received some other unrelated reward than none. If *P* did not receive the deserved reward for apprehending the criminal, we would take some heart in knowing that *P* later had a stroke of luck. The difference between non-substitutable and substitutable outcomes in this respect, however, is that in the case of the former, even after *P* has received the 'appropriate' level of benefits or burdens, we still find it undeserved that *P* did not receive the specific reward; in the case of the latter, by contrast, we feel desert has been fully done once the appropriate level has been reached.

The point about a conceptual connection between *some* actions and deserved outcomes related to those actions is cleverly and industriously exploited in Cupit's discussion of desert and responsibility (ibid., ch. 7). I would, however, take serious exception to his claim that this is the *only* conceptual connection between desert and responsibility. Cupit seems to think that any desert-responsibility thesis which goes beyond this simple conceptual point – be it the traditional one of direct responsibility being required for any deserved outcome (which I have denied) or one of responsibility being required for the general moral characteristics which underlie desert claims (as I have argued) – implies a denial of moral luck. (More counter-intuitively, Cupit also thinks of it as incompatible with the fact that non-persons, such as animals and the environment, can be said to deserve; I have responded briefly to that point in Section 2.1.) But moral luck matters for desert, Cupit claims, as it does for morality in general: the most beautiful girl deserves to win the beauty competition simply by virtue of her beauty. Her lack of responsibility for her beauty – as lying in her genes – is irrelevant (ibid., p. 170).

There are at least two ways to counter Cupit's claim here. The less elaborate one is simply to invoke a different set of intuitions. There is a long tradition of thought, harking back to Aristotle, which considers beauty and ugliness (and other physical endowments, for that matter) morally irrelevant unless they have something to do with 'training or attention' (Aristotle, 1985, p. 68 [1114a]). Are these intuitions not, perhaps, more considered and reflective than Cupit's? The more elaborate response would be to argue that moral luck is not an all-or-nothing affair, nor is there only one kind of 'luck' involved. *Circumstantial luck* does not undercut desert claims or other moral claims; it is very often a matter of luck in what circumstances we find ourselves, what kind of cards we have been dealt. What matters, however, for moral assessment is what we do with the cards that we have. A desert-responsibility thesis, of whatever sort, does not imply the denial of such luck. Other kinds of moral luck may, however, nullify deserts. The athlete whose performance is affected by what Miller calls *integral luck*, such as being tripped by another competitor, may still deserve to win the race more than the actual winner (1999, pp. 143ff.; cf. Nagel, 1979, ch. 3 and Kristjánsson, 2002,

s. 4.2). On Cupit's account, the truth of hard determinism would be irrelevant for the appropriateness of desert claims; this, however, is an implication that I and many other writers on this issue find unacceptable. By contrast, my account makes do with a minimal responsibility requirement that qualifies the contested desert-responsibility thesis without demolishing it, as I think Cupit's account does.

In Cupit's defence it could, however, correctly be pointed out that not all is gained by the admission that circumstantial luck does not nullify *P*'s deserts. I have already noted that moral luck is not an all-or-nothing affair, and although *single* desert claims may legitimately be made against the background of circumstantial luck, one could argue that the same does not hold for the distribution of *differential* deserts. If people's differential deserts depend on their differential circumstantial luck, then is the distribution of those deserts really just (see Olsaretti, 2002)? Again, there are two ways for me to respond. First, my version of the desert-responsibility thesis (*qua* desert evaluability) makes do with a minimal amount of circumstantial luck. On the Aristotelian understanding of moral education, on which I would rely here, any person who is not brought up as a child in singularly bad habits eventually becomes able to choose a life of virtue or vice. There is thus, according to my account of the responsibility required for desert attribution, much less difference across individuals with regard to the relevant circumstantial luck than on the traditional accounts. Second, for those few unlucky ones, brought up to become Hitler-*Jugend* officers or whatever, one could claim, on the grounds of various examples of young devils turning into old saints, that Aristotle was too quick in excluding the possibility of a viciously brought-up person seeing anything attractive about virtue later in life. Alternatively, one could argue that there is, in fact, nothing unjust about considering a person who has had the opportunity of choosing virtue and actually chosen it to be more deserving than a person who has not chosen virtue because he or she did not have the opportunity of doing so. The reason would simply have to do with Aristotle's well-taken observation about people's difficulties in bearing 'the results of good fortune suitably', and his reminder of the great many who do have the circumstantial luck to become virtuous but fall prey to arrogance, disdain of the less fortunate and even 'wanton aggression' (1985, pp. 100–101 [1124a–b]; cf. Kristjánsson, 2002, s. 4.2). A person surely deserves credit (that is praise and, hence, a higher level of well-being in so far as being praised raises one's level of well-being) for resisting such temptations, while other persons who did not have the chance to resist them do not deserve the same credit, although they obviously do not deserve any blame either for not doing what they could not do.

Responsibility, Equality and Justice

Before leaving the topic of responsibility, a few words should be said, in passing, about the sort of liberal accounts of justice that make most heavy weather of responsibility: so-called luck-neutralizing egalitarian theories of justice (for an overview, see Hurley, 2003). Luck-neutralizing justice egalitarians hold that distributive justice should neutralize those differences between people that are a matter of luck while respecting those for which people are responsible. The claim that luck-induced inequalities demand moral redistribution is, of course, nothing more than a particular application of the Kantian requirement of immunizing morality against luck. Those theories typically understand 'luck' simply as the inverse correlate of responsibility: what is a matter of luck for someone is what he or she is not responsible for.

Hurley (ibid.) holds those theories up for scrutiny, and her lengthy, eye-opening and exciting exploration builds up to a staggeringly unambiguous conclusion: there is no inherent connection between responsibility/luck and equality. While giving people only what they are responsible for would neutralize luck, giving them something else, for which they are not responsible, would not, even if the latter were equality-conferring. Responsibility may have a 'currency role' in determining *what* justice requires to be (re)distributed, but from this we cannot derive a 'patterning role': about *how* to distribute. Traditional luck-neutralizing egalitarians, who think that attempts to neutralize luck have some inherent tendency to achieve relatively more equal patterns of distribution and that this provides an independent justification for favouring such patterns, fall into, in Hurley's view, one or both of two logical errors: the egalitarian fallacy and the luck-neutralizer's dilemma. The *egalitarian fallacy* involves the inference from its being a matter of luck that two persons are unequal to its not being a matter of luck if they were to be equal. The *luck-neutralizer's dilemma* rests on the fact that luck can be understood either interpersonally or counterfactually. But on the first understanding, aiming to neutralize interpersonal bad luck specifies only trivially an egalitarian pattern of distribution, since interpersonal inequality is used to define bad luck; while on the second understanding, aiming to neutralize counterfactual bad luck does not, in any way, specify or justify an egalitarian pattern of distribution since eliminating the results of my luck would not necessarily have the same effect on me as doing the same for you would have on you. Perhaps the import of Hurley's argumentation here can best be summarized by saying that responsibility judgements are, for better or for worse, not primarily about relations or comparisons between persons.

The upshot of Hurley's exploration is not that responsibility has no role to play in justice theories, nor that the egalitarian implications are fully refuted or undermined, but rather that the role of responsibility must be relocated and reconfigured, and that the ideal of equality be furthered via side-channels that are both more subtle and more circuitous than those identified in prevailing luck-neutralizing accounts. Hurley sometimes speaks here as if more hinges on her exploration than the merits of the particular theories she criticizes: namely, that the very ideals of equality and proper distribution of goods are somehow at stake. I wonder whether they are. Is it really so philosophically/politically crucial to be able to reclaim egalitarian results from those theories? If an egalitarian concern is simply to favour 'relatively more equal patterns of distribution of *X* over relatively less equal patterns of *X*, other things equal' (ibid., p. 147), then one wonders why so much freight need be heaped on the notion of responsibility. Why cannot such equal favouring simply be grounded in reasons of expediency, compassion, generosity or social stability? Hurley's deliberately chosen narrow perspective does not rule out other angles on equality, but it is still noticeable that when she gives hypothetical examples of alternative perspectives, they are all justice-based: if not based on responsibility, directly or indirectly (through knowledge), then at least on fairness or desert (ibid., p. 201), even though she rejects desert as a principle of justice. Our old doubts about the primacy-of-justice thesis come once again to mind. Are we bound to assume that all questions of (re)distribution must be questions of justice? Could not a distributive pattern be justifiable morally although it is not just?

This is not to deny flat out the relevance of equality for justice. First, recall the impartiality condition about *entitlements*, mentioned in Section 2.1: to qualify as just, it is necessary that entitlements be impartial with regard to the set of people to which the relevant claims or rights apply. Impartiality here implies, in a certain sense, equality – namely, equality in the same sense as when we talk of 'equality before the law'. Second, equality is related to *desert* in two ways. More generally, the scale for weighing the deserts of different people is *equal* (in other words *the same*), as I have argued, that is, moral virtue, although the outcomes, as a matter of fact, may well be *unequal* (cf. Kristjánsson, 2002, p. 134, on the kind of formal egalitarianism inherent in Aristotle's non-arbitrary criteria for moral worth). More specifically, desert – naturally enough – calls for the rectification of undeserved inequalities: that is, because of their undeservingness, not because of their inequality as such (cf. Olsaretti, 2003a, pp. 14–17). I think, however, that these three notions of equality – related to entitlements and deserts, respectively – exhaust the role of equality in justice. There are many other good moral reasons for favouring equality of outcomes in this or that sphere of human life, but it obscures rather than illuminates to consider those reasons as intimately related to, or even as an independent part of, the ideal of justice.

The Empirical Evidence

Let us turn, then, finally, to the empirical evidence. Considerable information has been gathered by social scientists about people's conceptions of justice, in general, and desert (or 'deservingness'), in particular. Hareli (1999) complains that much of this material is biased because of the researchers' primacy-of-desert assumption: the assumption that judgements of desert and justice are interchangeable. True as that may be, it seems rather unfair of Hareli to cite Norman Feather as one of the theorists who are bound to this assumption. Feather is well aware of the distinction between desert and entitlement, as we saw in Section 2.1, and he does not equate people's judgements of desert with their judgements about justice in general, although he holds that the former provide a 'key variable' of the latter (1999, esp. pp. 1, 7, 15). Indeed, Feather's extensive research project on the 'psychology of deservingness' – while not entirely free from avoidable bias as we will soon see – seems to me to constitute the best theoretically grounded and methodologically convincing project of that kind available at present.

Taking his cue from Heider's (1958) pioneering work on balanced and unbalanced structures, Feather's theoretical model is based on the assumption that three main factors influence our judgements of whether *P* deserves an outcome that follows *P*'s action: (a) the perceived value of the action, (b) the perceived value of the outcome and (c) the perceived control (responsibility) *P* has over the action and its outcome. Balanced conjunctions between (a) and (b), that is, a positively valued outcome following a positively valued action (+ +) or a negatively valued outcome following a negatively valued action (– –), are generally perceived as deserved, while unbalanced ones (+ – or – +) are generally perceived as undeserved. No less important, in Feather's estimation, is factor (c): *P* is not seen to deserve an outcome for which *P* is not responsible, and *P* is seen to deserve a balanced action–outcome conjunction only when *P* has had control over (and was, hence, responsible for) those actions (1999, ch. 1).

We see that Feather's first and second factors involve the rather platitudinous assumption that desert is about good acts leading to good outcomes and bad acts leading to bad outcomes, while the third factor brings in the traditional, if less platitudinous, desert-responsibility thesis explored above. While the empirical evidence gathered by Feather seems to confirm the hypotheses derived from his model, critics have correctly pointed out that his findings provide scant information about the relative impact of the three factors: for instance, about whether the value of an action or its controllability matters more because these factors were 'covaried when manipulated' (Lupfer and Gingrich, 1999, pp. 168–9). To complicate things, Feather has suggested, in view of research carried out by himself and by others, that more factors may also be relevant here, such as 'liking or disliking, social identity, and moral character' (1999, p. 23), although these are factors that have not yet been sufficiently tested and compared. Feather does not explore the possibility that these extra factors might be interrelated, for example that liking or disliking *P* might influence our judgement of 'deservingness' in so far as these constitute reactions to *P*'s positive or negative moral character, or that we may be more willing to pass such judgements about people who belong to our in-group than about outsiders, simply because we know and understand the former better and feel better qualified to assess their moral standing.

A lot of empirical work obviously still needs to be done in this area but, aware as he is of the theoretical landscape, Feather seems at least to be on the right track. As I see it, the main problem with his empirical research is the typical methodological one of the underdetermination of study scenarios. His most often-cited support for the original action–control–outcome triad comes from subjects' responses to scenarios where (1) two high-school students achieve academic success, the former because of hard work despite low ability and the latter because of high ability despite little effort, and (2) where two other such students fail, the former because of illness and the latter because of lack of effort. Somewhat unsurprisingly, the research subjects deemed the former student more deserving of success in the first scenario, and the latter student more deserving of failure in the second (Feather, 1992). I agree with the already-mentioned complaint about the inseparability of factors here (value of action versus controllability of action). A more theoretically serious misgiving would, however, be this: is the reason for the strongly felt, foregone-conclusion nature of these findings perhaps a result of underdetermination? What if we had known something more about the moral character of these students, for example that the hard-working high achiever in (1) and the sick one in (2) were both moral blackguards, while their counterparts were paragons of moral virtue – might that not have influenced our overall verdict of their 'deservingness'? Are we concentrating on the students' responsibility for their respective outcomes in those scenarios only because we are completely ignorant of their moral character, and the extent to which they are responsible for it, rather than because we find the traditional desert-responsibility thesis about the connection between a deserved outcome and the responsibility for *that* outcome inherently attractive?

Fortunately, these do not need to remain merely rhetorical questions, for interesting research has recently been conducted in which Feather's original factors were not only manipulated independently but a new one added, namely his suggested but scantly tested 'character appraisal', operationalized via a list of typical virtues and vices of good and bad people, derived from a pilot study. The more complicated vignettes used in this research involved various combinations of moral character, outcome and responsibility (good character, positive outcome, low control; bad character, negative outcome, high control; and so forth). The results were striking. While Feather's original findings were corroborated to a certain extent, the dominant influencing factor turned out to be *moral character*, or, more precisely, the 'value of character'–'value of outcome' interaction. The traditional desert-responsibility thesis, on which Feather relied, was undermined in that, even when *P* was seen as having little responsibility for the action leading to the good or bad outcome, the outcome was typically deemed deserved or undeserved on the grounds of the value attached to *P*'s general character traits (Lupfer and Gingrich, 1999). The perceived poetic justice – or should I say the 'poetic desert' – of the villain-crushed-in-a-landslide cases was clearly there to see, as evidenced by the subjects' responses.

Despite the resurgence of a naturalist approach to morals in general, many philosophers still continue to ignore the empirical evidence concerning people's moral and political intuitions. I think they do so at their peril, as I argued in Section 1.2. In the present case, I have indicated how carefully obtained empirical evidence on people's intuitions concerning deserts clearly supports the single-basis account of desert and the qualified desert-responsibility thesis that I have presented and argued for in this chapter.

Chapter 3

Desert-Based Emotions

3.1 Our Reactive Attitudes: Emotionalizing Justice

As a complex virtue, justice seems to encompass, among other things, certain *desert-based emotions* that are at least developmentally – and arguably also, morally – important for an understanding of justice. It would be premature to assume at this point that these emotions can be morally justified and that the virtue of justice necessarily requires them. The purpose of this chapter is a more preliminary one: to explore the philosophical reasons for the rising interest in desert-based emotions and to offer a conceptual overview of some prototypical emotions of this sort. More specifically, in the present section, I examine the writings of three philosophers, Robert Solomon, Samuel Scheffler and Peter Strawson, that, from different perspectives, shed light – directly or indirectly – on the nature and moral/political salience of desert-based emotions. This section thus explains the considerations which have, *in fact*, motivated the recently growing interest in desert-based emotions as germane to justice; one might, of course be independently interested in such emotions without recourse to the role that they play (or do not play) in justice. Subsequently, in Sections 3.2 and 3.3, which form the more substantial part of this chapter, I identify and analyse two important classes of desert-based emotions having to do with the deserved and undeserved fortunes of *others* and of *oneself*, respectively. The reader will not reap from my exploration a definitive answer to the question whether those emotions are, generally speaking, virtuous – that awaits Section 4.3 – but should, I hope, at the end of this chapter have an enriched understanding of what *kind* of virtues they would have to represent, in order to really be virtuous.

Why are emotions relevant for justice? Robert C. Solomon, in one book and a couple of articles (1994; 1995; 2001), presents us with various answers to that question. While the reasons given in those answers are all interrelated and mutually supportive, I will divide them up loosely into conceptual, psychological and moral reasons.

The *conceptual* reasons must be understood against the backdrop of Solomon's general stance on morality and the emotions, a stance that he has defended in various earlier works. Solomon is, after all, one of the earliest and most outspoken frontrunners of the cognitive theory of emotions, according to which beliefs or judgements – which are, in principle, amenable to reason, cultivation and regulation – form an essential part of emotions, or *are* even (as Solomon used to emphasize at the beginning of his crusade) the emotions themselves (see my earlier discussion in Section 1.3). Theorists have through the ages (*pro* Plato but *contra* Aristotle) misdescribed the emotions as gatecrashers in the realm of reason, and emotionally inspired beliefs as disruptions of rational thought, but in doing so they wrongly tore the subject matter of morality in two. We must now revise this all-too-common conceptual account and return to a moral-sentiment theory of morality which considers the basis of morality to be found in our natural dispositions to have certain emotions. In the field of justice, for example, we need to acknowledge that this virtue does not have its origins in lofty Socratic insights but arises rather from the 'promptings of some basic emotions': some sympathetic, such as compassion, others antipathetic, such as envy; emotions which make justice 'both necessary and possible' (Solomon, 1995, pp. 31, 200).

These conceptual and general insights pave the way for Solomon's *psychological* reasons which have to do with both the origin and the nature of justice concerns in human beings. It is, in his view, simply a matter of developmental fact that the idea of justice consists originally of a constellation of feelings, which alone provide the psychological ground in which grand philosophical theories of justice can take root (ibid., p. 30). Any sound psychological account of the emergence of justice concerns in children will thus show us that the first appearance of a sense of justice is expressed in terms of a small class of emotional responses to the perception of certain resource-distribution situations and that, rather than disappearing or decreasing in importance, this earliest nucleus of feelings sustains justice concerns into adulthood, remaining essentially the same as when it first appeared in early infancy (for a concise overview of the relevant psychological literature, see, for example, Charlesworth, 1992). To think of pure rationality, divested of any emotional input, as a requirement for a correct understanding of justice, one must have become disengaged from those very facts about human existence which distinguish us, for instance, from the goddess of justice who is not only permanently blindfolded but, more importantly, above nature.

Solomon's radical naturalistic view of justice leaves various questions unanswered about the genealogy of justice *qua* psychological disposition(s). The standard options which come to mind when exploring his view would be: (a) an economic rational-choice model of justice internalization – mirroring social-contract theory in political philosophy – according to which children learn to believe in justice in order to attain some other goals which are both prior and external to justice, (b) a more Freudian-inspired emergent-motive theory of justice as a primordial drive or (c) an evolutionary account of justice as an adaptive mechanism, which might be suggested in conjunction with (a) or even (b) but could also be held separately from those. Solomon's psychological reasons for emotionalizing justice seem to be more or less neutral with regard to these options – into which I will delve more thoroughly in Section 4.1 – or at least not to exclude any of them.

Solomon's *moral* reasons for injecting emotions (back) into discussions of justice fit in with his Aristotelian emphasis on justice as primarily a personal virtue and only derivatively a social one. Justice is and must be, first and foremost, 'in us' as individual persons, in our attitudes towards each other, rather than in any particular social set-up with which the world presents us (1994, p. 300; 2001, p. 169). While such personalization of justice does, in a certain conceptual sense, imply its depoliticization, it does not do so in the introverted way criticized by certain political leftists, who have condemned the inculcation of personal virtues in moral education as an integral element of a right-wing agenda: recall, for instance, the criticisms commonly, if wrong-headedly, directed at the influential character-education movement in the USA, criticisms that I will explore in Section 5.2. The idea is not that social arrangements and institutions are irrelevant for justice, but rather that the overemphasis on 'systems' silences the individual voice crying out for justice and symbolizes an archaic (and some would say male-dominated) conceptualization of what counts as 'political': namely, the pure governance of reason alone (see, for example, Boler, 1999). Seen in that light, Solomon's emotionalization of justice could just as well be supported by radical feminists – recall their slogan 'the personal is political' – as by moral conservatives. It does not, in other words, depend upon political orientation in the practical sense.

The link forged by Solomon between justice and emotions should not come as a surprise to those philosophers who have paid any attention to the empirical findings reported in the psychological literature. People typically describe negative events in their lives as more immoral, more obstructive to plans, goals and personal relationships, and – most saliently here – as eliciting emotions that are more distressful and long-lasting, when those events are experienced as *unjust* (see Mikula et al., 1998, for one of many examples of such findings). The question remains, of course, whether these emotions are necessarily *desert-based* and relevant to my concerns in the present chapter. I will return to that question in the following section, but let it suffice to note here that since justice-elicited emotions are considered to have their roots in early childhood, they must focus primarily on justice in its pre-institutional sense (assuming that children at that age have not reached an understanding of institutional entitlements). In light of the Feinbergian dichotomy between pre-institutional desert-based and institutional rights-based justice, it would seem reasonable to suppose that the justice-grounding emotions in which Solomon is chiefly interested are, indeed, desert-based ones.

Solomon criticizes Rawlsians for ignoring the emotional elements in our 'sense of justice', although this criticism is not spelt out in detail (2001, pp. 172–3). Importantly, Rawlsians could disagree with Solomon's account on two distinct grounds. The first would apply if the emotions in question were considered predominantly or even exclusively desert-based; recall my review in Section 2.1 of how (Rawlsian) liberals rule out desert as a potential ingredient in justice for implying not only a fuller sense of individual responsibility than is required – or considered reasonable – by a liberal theory of justice, but also a 'thick', substantive notion of the human good that fails not only to remain neutral with regard to the plurality of the good but also to accommodate the equal moral worth of persons. The second and more general ground for Rawlsian scepticism may lie in the very idea of emotionalizing justice, as expressed by Solomon. That scepticism might, at first glance, seem difficult to square with Rawls's own (early) sympathetic nod to Rousseau's claim that the sense of justice is 'no mere moral conception formed by the understanding alone', but rather 'the natural outcome of our primitive affections', and his subsequent elaboration of how such an emotional capacity for a sense of justice is 'the fundamental aspect of moral personality in the theory of justice' (Rawls, 1963, pp. 281–2; Rawls cites Rousseau, 1911, pp. 196, 215). It seems true, however, that by the time Rawls wrote his *Theory of Justice*, this alleged 'capacity' had degenerated into a retrospective appreciation of, and attraction to, the abstract and emotion-free principles derived behind the Veil of Ignorance. In other words, Rawlsians only accept the emotionalization of justice after justice has been constructed *qua* principle – with the elicited emotions then being regimented by the principle – whereas for Solomon, emotionalizing justice means that emotions form and sustain the principle or idea of justice from the beginning. And that, of course, is an essential difference of opinion.

Samuel Scheffler reaches a similar conclusion about the relevance of (desert-based) emotions for justice, but he arrives at it, so to speak, the other way round from Solomon. Scheffler does not argue that because the prevailing liberal theories of justice fail to take account of emotions, there must be something amiss in them; rather, he infers from the non-persuasiveness of such theories that they might be better off by giving desert-based emotions their due.

To talk of the non-persuasiveness of liberal justice might strike the reader as somewhat odd; liberalism has, after all, been the dominant paradigm in Western political philosophy for decades, and no theory of justice stands comparison with Rawls's in terms of academic acclaim. The problem to which Scheffler points in his provocative paper (1992), however, is that this enthusiasm has never trickled down to the general public. He could have mentioned repeated empirical studies, both in the USA and in Europe (recorded by Frolich and Oppenheimer, 1992) that have failed to record public support for Rawls's famous 'difference principle' of justice, but Scheffler's worry is, in fact, a more general one: that the philosophical defences of liberalism appear to underestimate the importance of those human attitudes and emotions that find expression through our everyday practices with respect to desert.

Now, if disengagement from desert concerns is, as maintained here, an Achilles' heel of liberalism, liberals might be well advised to reconsider their typical misgivings about deserts noted earlier. They might, for example, want to incorporate some desert-based values into their value system by arguing that such values need not undermine the desired pluralism of the good, any more than does the value of autonomous choice which liberals have never been shy of promoting as a non-fallible, non-controversial value for all (see, for example, Sher, 1987, pp. 208–9). This is, however, not the tack taken by Scheffler. He is more concerned about the fact that liberals' rejection of desert – or their reliance on a watered-down institutional notion of desert – rests on a reduced conception of individual responsibility which is completely at odds with people's reactive attitudes of shame, guilt, indignation and so forth: attitudes that require a pre-institutional conception of desert and a strong sense in which individual persons are considered responsible for their own characters and destinies.

Such a claim obviously needs some expansion. First, it should be made clear that Scheffler does not assert that the reduced-responsibility assumption of liberalism is wrong; he simply explains why it has led, and may continue to lead, philosophical liberalism into political isolation. Although he does not say so directly, the general public in the West seems to be growing increasingly weary of the transformation of our societies into 'therapeutic wards' where each individual passes the buck of responsibility to societal structures. To express this in Scheffler's own, more sober, terms:

> if liberalism proposes to replace our ordinary notion of desert with the idea of legitimate institutional expectations, and if that proposal meets with political resistance, the possibility cannot be excluded that such resistance is responsive in part to an underlying tension between liberalism and the reactive attitudes, rather than stemming exclusively from contingent features of the prevailing political climate. (1992, p. 314)

The key notion here is that of 'reactive attitudes' and it is to that notion that we now turn.

Reactive Attitudes

Both Solomon (at least implicitly) and Scheffler (explicitly) draw on Peter Strawson's famous notion of *reactive attitudes*. In an influential paper, read to the British Academy in 1962, he gives an account of such attitudes that has since been considered vital to the perennial free will versus determinism controversy, providing insights that have often eluded participants in that debate. It may be, however, that greater philosophical illumination can be gained from Strawson's account by bringing it to bear on topics addressed in the present chapter.

Strawson famously draws a distinction between *reactive* attitudes, such as gratitude, resentment, forgiveness, love and guilt, and *objective* attitudes which exculpate an agent and/or his act from blame as having been influenced by an inner or outer incapacity of some sort (compulsion, accident, ignorance, insanity and so forth). The former attitudes form the basis of moral responsibility; to have such attitudes *is*, in Strawson's strict sense, to ascribe moral responsibility. When adopting the standpoint of reactive attitudes, we are engaging in normal human relationships; we are viewing others and ourselves as persons. When resorting to objective attitudes, we are, on the other hand, objectifying people; we think that, for some reason, what is specifically human about them or their acts is missing. The reactive attitudes can take a number of forms: they can be *other-reactive* – either personally reactive (such as my anger at person *B* for wronging me) or vicariously reactive (such as my anger that *B* wronged *C*) – or *self-reactive*, such as my guilt over my own moral improprieties.

Strawson then argues that the reactive attitudes are 'essentially natural human reactions': part and parcel of what it is to be a human person in a human society. Giving them up for a sustained objectivity of interpersonal attitudes, and the social isolation which that would entail, is, Strawson claims, not something of which human beings would be capable; even if it is not logically inconceivable, it is practically so (1962, esp. pp. 195–7). This is why we cannot take seriously the thought that a possible future validation of the truth of determinism could lead to a total decay of those reactive attitudes, with the ensuing consequence of all our practices of blaming and praising disappearing into thin air; for 'it is *useless* to ask whether it would not be rational for us to do what it is not in our nature to (be able to) do' (ibid., p. 204). In other words, the truth of determinism would be, in practice, irrelevant to attributions of moral responsibility and moral obligations: a conclusion seized upon, ever since Strawson's paper, by so-called compatibilists in the free will/determinism debate.

I am not the only one to find Strawson's ultimate suggestion rather unconvincing (Scheffler, for one, agrees: 1992, p. 312). Why should it be psychologically inconceivable for us to objectify all human acts if we really became convinced – however unlikely – that hard determinism is true? After all, we have in recent times seen more and more human characteristics, which used to be traced back to the locus of free will in the individual psyche, given genetic explanations. Furthermore, there is good reason to be suspicious of any view that replaces metaphysics with moral psychology. Much more persuasive about Strawson's account of reactive attitudes is, however, the implicit suggestion of how irreplaceable these attitudes are for the concept of desert and how they make intelligible the connection between a verdict of desert and its basis or bases ('*B* deserves this reward because of his praiseworthy act for which he was morally responsible', and so forth). Not only that: provided that we take these attitudes to be metaphysically warranted, and given their ubiquity in human relationships, we may easily be led to conclude, *à la* Solomon and Scheffler, that justice without those desert-based attitudes would be like *Hamlet* without the Prince.

The present chapter focuses on desert-based emotions and their role in justice. While Strawson's analysis of reactive attitudes is highly relevant for that topic, as Scheffler and others have noted and upon which I have, above, tried to elaborate, it would be an oversimplification merely to equate such attitudes with desert-based emotions. *First*, it is not clear that all of the Strawsonian reactive attitudes would even count as *emotions*. Judging from his description, some of them seem to have more in common with simple feelings, or even intentions, or beliefs, which are not necessarily emotionally imbued (about others' goodwill or lack of goodwill towards us), than with emotions in the traditional sense (1962, p. 192). Yet we have to admit, as I did in Section 1.3, that there is embarrassingly little agreement among emotion theorists – even within the reigning cognitive-theory camp – about the individuation of emotions and about the distinction between those beliefs and desires that in combination constitute particular emotions and those which do not. So for all we know, there might be a way to characterize all the reactive attitudes as emotions: either dispositional or episodic. *Second*, however, not all of those attitudes seem to have anything to do with justice: there is, for instance, nothing odd (logically or morally) about one's *gratitude* being directed at someone's supererogatory acts going far beyond the demands of justice, or about oneself being more grateful to a benefactor than would, strictly speaking, be deserved. *Third*, even within the majority of apparently justice-related reactive attitudes, not all are necessarily desert-based. For example, Krehbiel and Cropanzano (2000) have recently shown, in a psychological laboratory experiment, how pure procedural (institutional) justice, or lack thereof, works with outcome favourability to produce a variety of intense emotional states, such as guilt and anger. Furthermore, it could, for instance, be perfectly reasonable of me, given certain background conditions, to be angrily envious of my brother, *B* – with respect to some favour with which our father, *C*, had presented *B* but not me although I had the same procedural right to it as *B* – without my also being jealous of *B*, that is, without my believing that I deserved the favour as much or more than *B* (see Kristjánsson, 2002, ch. 5). In other words, justice-related emotions do not necessarily imply desert-based ones.

Despite these three important caveats, we have good reason to suppose that a significant number of reactive attitudes are, indeed, justice-related and – more importantly for our present purposes – that some of the most salient of the latter are specifically desert-based. I have already in this section suggested a *developmental* thesis about the psychological priority of desert-based emotions over other justice concerns; this is not only borne out in the psychological literature but also stands to reason if the reactive attitudes are really rooted in human nature rather than being 'artificial' in the Humean sense. Moreover, as I pointed out in Section 2.1, pre-institutional justice (*qua* desert) is *logically* prior to institutional justice in one important sense: desert claims can sometimes be used to criticize as internally unjust the rules that underlie institutions and entitlements, whereas those rules cannot be used to criticize desert claims in the same way – that is, *qua* desert claims – although they can be used to criticize them *qua* justice claims.

3.2 Other-reactive Desert-Based Emotions

Considerable literature exists on the relevance of desert-based emotions, such as vengefulness, for *retributive* justice (see, for example, Solomon, 1994; French, 2001). Less has been written about the role of such emotions in *distributive* justice. I propose, in what remains of this chapter, to single out for taxonomical classification an important class of distributive desert-based emotions having to do with reactions to others' and to one's own lot, respectively. I consider the former to fall under the rubric of 'other-reactive desert-based emotions' and the latter of 'self-reactive desert-based emotions'. Let me make it clear, at this juncture, that by a desert-based emotion I specifically mean an emotion that involves a belief about a state of affairs relevant for desert, coupled with a desire that 'desert be done'. By a desire for desert I simply mean – in line with my earlier exploration – a concern with matters of a proper fit between (a) states of affairs and (b) specific qualities and actions of individuals which are generally held in high regard; I deliberately leave open here the question of what constitutes the basis or bases of desert; that is, I will not assume that my single-basis view of moral virtue, expounded in Chapter 2, is correct, simply because that view is not needed for the work that lies ahead of me here.

I will confine myself to emotions that are, so to speak, positively desert-based: that is, they involve pain at undeserved fortune because it is undeserved or pleasure at deserved fortune because it is deserved. I do not exclude the possibility of negatively desert-based emotions: that is, pain at deserved fortune *because* it is deserved and pleasure at undeserved fortune *because* it is undeserved. I do, however, think that such emotions – which would count as particularly nasty – are rare. Much more common and important for our discussion are emotions such as pain at deserved fortune *irrespective of* its deservingness (that is, pain at deserved fortune *although* it is deserved but not *because* it is deserved) and pleasure at undeserved fortune *irrespective of* its undeservingness (that is, pleasure at undeserved fortune *although* it is undeserved but not *because* it is undeserved). While not desert-based themselves, I include those latter emotions in my taxonomical schemas as contrasts to the desert-based emotions.

One of the first things children learn – from bedtime stories, fairy-tales and TV-cartoons – is to cheer the 'good guys' and rejoice when they finally succeed, while booing the 'bad guys' and saluting their eventual downfall. If we hold in view the prevailing cognitive-theory model of emotions as made up of desires and beliefs (or judgements or construals; see Section 1.3) and consider here three parameters: (i) emotional pain and pleasure, or the perceived satisfaction or frustration of a desire/concern (see Roberts, 2003, p. 157), evoked by (ii) the belief that another person has enjoyed good fortune or suffered bad fortune, (iii) either deservedly or undeservedly so – then eight distinct emotions suggest themselves: (*A1*) pain at another's deserved good fortune, (*A2*) pain at another's deserved bad fortune, (*A3*) pain at another's undeserved good fortune, (*A4*) pain at another's undeserved bad fortune, (*B1*) pleasure at another's deserved good fortune, (*B2*) pleasure at another's deserved bad fortune, (*B3*) pleasure at another's undeserved good fortune and (*B4*) pleasure at another's undeserved bad fortune.

Despite the recent resurgence of emotion research among philosophers, this group of emotions, surely among the most pervasive and intense of all, has not garnered the attention that one might have expected, with the exception, perhaps, of (*A2*) and (*A4*) – as the different varieties of sympathy (pain at others' misfortunes) have figured prominently on philosophical agendas at least since the days of David Hume and Adam Smith. I explore the nature of all these emotions in the following, but to rectify somewhat the imbalance of recent discussions, I propose to focus specifically on pain at others' good fortune (*A1* and *A3*), on the one hand, and pleasure at others' bad fortune (*B2* and *B4*), on the other. Yet, in order to secure an understanding of these four emotions, we need to consider all of the eight emotions in question and the relations between them. Thus I cannot shirk saying something also about pain at others' misfortune, and even pleasure at others' good fortune, although the former has already been widely explored and the latter may, at first glance, seem rather uncontroversial and hence – at least morally, if not psychologically and logically – uninteresting ('like motherhood, we are all for it').

Aristotle's is probably the most comprehensive and ambitious account ever of fortunes-of-others emotions. If only for that reason, Aristotle's work constitutes a natural springboard for inquiries into the nature of those emotions. To begin with, Aristotle's account of *pity* is well known and has come under much renewed scrutiny of late. According to Nussbaum, pity in Aristotle's account – as an emotion directed at another person's misfortune or suffering – rests on three jointly sufficient beliefs: (i) that the suffering is serious rather than trivial, (ii) that the pitier's own possibilities are similar to those of the sufferer and (iii) that the suffering is not caused primarily by the sufferer's own culpable actions (Nussbaum, 1996, p. 31; see also Ben-Ze'ev, 2000, p. 329, on belief (ii)). Before going any further, however, let us follow Nussbaum and others in switching terms: what Aristotle is talking about here is clearly the emotion that we would refer to nowadays as 'compassion' rather than 'pity'. The term 'pity' has, from the Victorian era onwards, acquired an element of condescension and a stance of superiority that it did not have formerly (see, for example, Nussbaum, 1996, p. 29; Blum, 1987, p. 233), features which have even made some writers question the moral worth of the emotion which the term denotes (see Callan, 1988, for a harsh, if not quite a Nietzschean, debunking of the moral value of pity). In the following, I assume that Aristotle's *eleos* is 'compassion', while reserving the term 'pity' for another emotion in which Aristotle had less interest.

Let us, then, consider the three above-mentioned belief conditions of compassion delineated by Nussbaum. We can refer to them as the conditions of *size*, *empathy* and *responsibility*. The *size* condition is uncontroversial. The suffering for which we feel compassion must be weighty enough: we will not, normally, feel compassion for someone with a slightly pricked finger. The *empathy* condition also seems reasonable: compassion requires the imaginative processes needed for empathizing with another person, identifying with the other's plight, and that, in turn, requires a grasp of one's own vulnerabilities – and hence one's resulting liability to misfortune – as similar enough to those of the sufferer. However, empathy is not a sufficient condition for compassion: being able to identify with a sufferer is also a necessary condition for taking pleasure in (rather than bemoaning) the suffering; furthermore, empathy does not, as such, involve motivation towards alleviating the other's difficulties, as compassion normally does (see, for example, Clark, 1997, p. 45; Goldie, 2000, p. 215; I return to the notion of empathy in Section 4.1).

More problematic than the other two is the *responsibility* condition: the requirement that the sufferer must not be primarily responsible for his or her own plight. A distinction must first be made between *moral* and *causal* responsibility. A person can be morally responsible for an outcome, or for the correction of an outcome, without being part of the causal link leading up to it. Conversely, causal responsibility does not necessarily produce moral responsibility: although I am causally responsible for your not being able to drive faster on the highway, simply in virtue of my driving in front of you at a normal speed, I am not thereby morally responsible for your being late for work. Let us assume that moral responsibility is at issue here: that compassion will not (rationally) be felt if the sufferers are primarily morally responsible for their own plight. The problem with this reading is that it does not seem to correspond exactly to Aristotle's explication of compassion. He says that compassion is pain 'at an apparently destructive or painful evil happening *to one who does not deserve it*' (1991, p. 152 [1385b], my emphasis). Nussbaum acknowledges, with various textual references, that Aristotle sees the object of compassion as 'undeserving' of its suffering. She seems, however, to want to equate that point with the claim that grief is not primarily the result of the sufferer's own fault (1996, p. 33). Nussbaum is not the only one prone to such conflation; as we saw in Section 2.3, in an often-quoted psychological research project on the perceived importance of deservingness in success and failure situations, it is assumed that when participants attribute (moral?) responsibility for a negative outcome to a person, they are at the same time attributing deservingness (Feather, 1992).

There are two reasons for questioning this equation. First and more obviously, the sufferer's lack of responsibility for the suffering is not – along with the *size* and *empathy* conditions – sufficient to warrant compassion, witness the case of a much-hated villain crushed in a landslide. Second, the sufferer's responsibility is not sufficient to exclude compassion: we may well feel compassion for a smoker diagnosed with lung cancer although we know that the responsibility for the cancer, through choosing to smoke, is the smoker's own. Nussbaum explains such cases as ones of perceived 'discrepancy between fault and punishment': compassion resting on the belief that the latter has unduly exceeded the former (1996, p. 33). However, consider a man illegally crossing a railway track. He knows that it is highly unlikely that a train will be passing by in this particular place and takes the risk, knowing, however, that should a train arrive while he is crossing, he would certainly be killed by it. Now, the train arrives and kills him. It seems strange to say, should we feel compassion, that it is because the 'punishment is disproportionate to the fault': no other 'punishment' than death was possible should a train arrive, and the person was fully aware of the risk. Nussbaum might claim that we feel compassion because the punishment is disproportionate to the *risk*, rather than to the *fault*, but a much more straightforward and plausible reason for our feeling compassion in such a case is that we consider the person's death undeserved. Perhaps he was a kind person, this was his first notable violation of the law, and so forth. If the person were a notorious highwayman, we would be less likely to experience compassion, and yet the 'punishment' would presumably be equally disproportionate to the risk. This seems to indicate that what matters here is desert, pure and simple, rather than responsibility, or even rather than desert based on an intermediate condition of responsibility. Thus I think there is good reason to take Aristotle literally and consider compassion to be pain at another's *undeserved* bad fortune (*A4*). That helps, among other things, to account for the repeated findings in psychological research linking participants' reports of compassion with the perceived undeservingness of the misfortune in question (see, for example, Brigham et al., 1997), and with their emphatic anger at the person responsible for the misfortune as the attention turns from the victim to the culprit (see, for example, Hoffman, 2000, pp. 96ff.). Let me further suggest – in line with the spirit if not the letter of Aristotle's account – that 'pity', in the modern sense, is best understood as pain at another's *deserved* bad fortune (*A2*).

Pity requires a similar *size* condition as compassion – we do not pity a person for trivial inconveniences – and the *empathy* condition hardly suffices for distinguishing between compassion and pity either. For although the stance of superiority and even condescension in pity may seem to be alien to empathy (see, for example, Snow, 1991, p. 197), some emotional congruence or identification is required for a grasp of the other's bad fortune as bad fortune. That is, although the other person's suffering is caused by an error which 'I would not have committed', I can hardly understand it as human suffering at which I am pained without realizing that, *under different circumstances* (for instance, if I had been brought up in a different way), I might also have been capable of committing the error and suffer similar torments. Indeed, although pity is normally considered morally inferior to compassion, the redeeming moral feature of pity may lie precisely in its embodiment of the attitude of solicitude or care which is impossible without the capacity to put oneself in others' shoes and see things from their perspective. Some empirical research even suggests that there may be a limit to the extent that awareness of the victim's misfortune as deserved can temper the observers' emphatic distress, at least when they are directly involved in attending to the victim (Stotland, 1969).

It seems, then, reasonable to suppose that what distinguishes compassion from pity is the third condition, which we have now seen is best understood as a *desert* condition rather than as a *responsibility* condition (cf. Blum, 1987). This would, for example, help to explain the origin of two beliefs normally associated with pity: first the belief that the other's position is unalterably inferior (hence the pitier's commonly depreciating attitude) and second, the belief that we have less reason to offer help to those pitied than to those for whom we feel compassion (see Ben-Ze'ev, 2000, pp. 328–9). We tend, in general, to view those deserving a good as (morally) superior to those not deserving a good, and when resources are scarce, we may well feel inclined to allocate such resources to the former rather than the latter.

Aristotle hardly mentions pain at another's deserved bad fortune except to push it aside as morally unworthy, for 'one who is distressed at undeserved misfortune will take pleasure or be unmoved by misfortunes of the opposite sort [that is, deserved]; for example, no good person would be distressed when parricides and bloodthirsty murderers meet punishment' (1991, p. 156 [1386b]). Aristotle, who is unable to see anything in pity except misplaced compassion or 'morbid sentimentality' (those words are Nerney's, 1991, p. 84), may have been led astray by the rigidity of his own classification of the emotions under scrutiny here (see later in this section). It may, nevertheless, be true that 'morbid sentimentality' is an excess of sympathetic emotions in general; much has been written recently about burn-out symptoms in the 'caring professions', symptoms characterized by emphatic distress so painful and intolerable that it is transformed into an intense feeling of personal distress which, in the end, may move the person out of the sympathetic mode entirely (see, for example, Hoffman, 2000, p. 198).

In addition to 'compassion' and 'pity', the term 'sympathy' is very much part of our everyday vocabulary. Most writers agree that 'sympathy' is a wider notion than the other two. Not only does it encompass the extensions of both 'pity' and 'compassion', 'sympathy' also refers to pain at less serious misfortunes and is thus not subject to the *size* condition that both pity and compassion must satisfy (see, for example, Snow, 1991, p. 197; Ben-Ze'ev, 2000, p. 337). Unfortunately, 'sympathy', in this sense, is sometimes referred to as 'compassion', which invites confusion (witness Goldie's 2002 paper on 'compassion', which is evidently about sympathy).

If we now turn to emotions involving pleasure at others' good fortune, the first thing that stands out is the lack of proper terms in English. Tesser (1991) gives examples of terms in Yiddish, Spanish and Portuguese capturing emotions of this kind (p. 131). In my own native language, Icelandic, there exists a verb, *samgleðjast* (to feel pleasure at another person's fortune/happiness), but for some reason no respective noun. Notably, in German, there is no word similar to *Schadenfreude* to describe such an emotion, for example no '*Freudenfreude*'. Ben-Ze'ev suggests that the reason may lie in the less differentiated nature of positively evaluating emotions and the fact that pleasure at someone's fortune is 'quite similar to the general emotion of joy or happiness' (2000, p. 355). The eighteenth-century moral-sentiment philosophers might have wanted to talk about 'sympathetic enjoyment' here; Ben-Ze'ev opts for the rather cumbersome noun 'happy-for'. Since I think that there is good reason to follow Aristotle in distinguishing pleasure at deserved good fortune (*B1*) from pleasure at undeserved good fortune (*B3*), I will refer to the former as 'gratulation' but to the latter as 'happy-for'. I frankly admit, however, that this is an arbitrary decision, made for convenience of exposition and based on a linguistic fiat, not on any philosophical or linguistic rationale. In any case, what matters here is the underlying concepts, rather than the words used to describe them.

After introducing the emotion of what he calls 'happy-for', Ben-Ze'ev has uncharacteristically little to say about it. Perhaps he thinks, as I suggested earlier, that pleasure at others' good fortune is too simple and morally uncontroversial to merit much discussion. After all, we all know that happiness is made to be shared, and that to love other people is to love their joys. Aristotle suggests, however, that the matter may not be as simple as that, for although pleasure at deserved good fortune will be felt by any 'fair-minded person' (1991, p. 156 [1386b]), pleasure at undeserved good fortune indicates that the person is overly gratulatory. Aristotle claims that while the latter emotion 'has not so definite a name', it is reminiscent of 'gluttons' who 'accept all food' (1984, p. 1934 [1221b]). Our *liking* the other person may be more than just an intensity variable, promoting what I call 'happy-for' to the higher level of gratulation, as Ortony and his colleagues seem to think (1988, pp. 93–4), for we are more likely to like a person whom we deem good and, thus, worthy of good fortune. The account here of Ortony et al. is, however, marred by not accepting deservingness as a variable in the individuation, but only the intensity, of fortunes-of-others emotions.

In his out-and-out rejection of the emotion that I call 'happy-for', Aristotle seems to ignore rather obvious cases where pleasure at another person's undeserved good fortune does not constitute a moral fault; where it is at least morally neutral if not laudable. Suppose, for instance, that a normal person has some kind of windfall that is only conducive to that person's own well-being and does not harm or hurt anyone else. Even if we assume that the windfall cannot count as deserved – in respect of the person's efforts or history – rejoicing in such a case seems, from a moral perspective, rather non-moral than immoral and, if the person is our friend, even morally commendable. It will not do to respond here, on Aristotle's behalf, that this would be a case where the fortune is non-deserved rather than undeserved, for he clearly understands 'undeserved' as a contradictory, rather than a contrary, of 'deserved' – that is, he understands desert concerns as 'bipolar' rather than 'unipolar', to employ Roberts's useful terminology (2003, p. 144) – and I will follow suit, for reasons that I mentioned in

Chapter 2. Nerney suggests that Aristotle decries pleasure at another's undeserved good fortune because it betrays *ingratitude* to those responsible for the good fortune (given that it was not the sole responsibility of the person enjoying it), in particular ingratitude to divine powers (1991, p. 84). I believe, however, that Aristotle's rejection of happy-for is forced on him, much like his rejection of pity (in the modern sense), by his own rigid classificatory system which leads him to think that it is psychologically impossible for a 'fair-minded' person to experience pleasure at undeserved good fortune. I say more about that later.

Next on our agenda is righteous indignation (hereafter, for shortness' sake, only *indignation*). Indignation (*nemesis*) is defined by Aristotle as the emotion of 'being pained at undeserved *good* fortune'; more specifically, 'being distressed at the evidence of unworthy success' – wealth and power and such things – which others have recently received. It is in this sense that the term 'indignation' will be used in what follows, distinguishing it from other common, but wider, uses of the term, in which 'indignation' is understood as (a kind of) resentment over wrongs suffered by ourselves or others (for such a wider use, see, for example, Neblett, 1979). Indignation, says Aristotle further, 'arises from the same moral character' as compassion, and 'both emotions are characteristic of a good moral character' (1991, pp. 155–7 [1386b–1387a]). In Aristotle's schema, there is a clear distinction between indignation and anger (*orge*), where the latter is felt towards people who have slighted oneself or one's friends; there may, however, of course be cases where another person's undeservedly realizing good fortune involves, or results in, harm to oneself or one's friends, in which case anger may be experienced on top of indignation (on this distinction, see Coker, 1992, pp. 72–3).

Most commentators agree that something goes seriously amiss when Aristotle tries to fit indignation into his usual architectonic of a mean flanked by the faults of deficiency and excess. In the *Nicomachean Ethics*, where indignation gets only cursory treatment, Aristotle defines it as a mean between the excess of *phthonos* (envy) and the deficiency of *epichairekakia* (*Schadenfreude*): 'For the properly indignant person feels pain when someone else does well undeservedly; the envious person exceeds him by feeling pain when anyone does well, while the *Schadenfreude*-ful person is so deficient in feeling pain that he actually enjoys [other people's misfortunes]'(Aristotle, 1985, p. 49 [1108b]); Irwin translates *epichairekakia* as 'spite', but *Schadenfreude* is, I believe, more precise, as we will see later, and I amend his translation accordingly.

In the *Eudemian Ethics*, the deficiency of indignation is, by contrast, said to be happy-for (others' undeserved good fortune), but the excess remains the same, that is, envy (1984, p. 1934 [1221a]). Coker, for one, corrects Aristotle's account, in order to make it more consistent with the doctrine of the mean, by positing *defective indignation* ('pleasure or lack of pain at undeserved good fortune') as the deficiency (1992, p. 68). I agree that some rectification of that sort is needed, although I would have omitted the pleasure part; it seems enough to say that the deficiency of indignation is indifference to distributive injustices, characterized by lack of distress when someone has more than deserved. I think, however, that the excess part should also be corrected in order to make the account of indignation as a mean completely coherent. Being pained too much at good fortune, even deserved good fortune, is not the same as envy. Envy admittedly comes in many guises, but common to all types of envy is *A*'s resentment towards *B* because *A* believes *B* has got, or is about to get, a thing (an object or a state) which *A* wants, coupled with the desire for this something to be taken away from *B*, so that it can fall to *A*'s lot instead, or at least for *B*'s relative advantage over *A* as possessor of this thing to be eliminated. I exclude here the emotion that Aristotle named 'emulation' (*zelos*) (1991, pp. 160–62 [1388a–b]). Although this emotion is often referred to in ordinary language as 'envy' (more precisely, 'admiring envy' or 'emulative envy'), most writers agree that it should not be considered a type of envy at all (see Kristjánsson, 2002, s. 5.1). The focus in envy is on our own inferiority with respect to another person and on how this can be rectified. In contrast, a man who is excessively indignant need not be making any comparisons with himself or even his friends (as happens in cases of envy where a person is envious on a friend's behalf); he need not wish that the fortune in question fall to his (or his friend's) lot – he simply grudges the fortune of that person of whom he is indignant, and wants to take the fortune away from that person. For this reason, I suggest that the excess of indignation, which is emotion (*A1*) in our original schema (pain at others' deserved good fortune), be categorized as *begrudging spite* rather than envy.

The Issue of Schadenfreude

Finally, then, let us take a close look at (*B2*) and (*B4*): pleasure at others' deserved and undeserved bad fortune, respectively. A caveat must be added here to the claim at the beginning of my discussion of fortunes-of-others emotions that emotions from this group have not come under much recent scrutiny. Notably, during the last few years, *Schadenfreude* has suddenly been accorded pride of place in the popular media. For once, the results of a philosophical exploration have resounded with a blast in the public consciousness, as the recent rage for *Schadenfreude* seems directly inspired by John Portmann's book, *When Bad Things Happen to Other People* (2000). We read not so long ago in *Newsweek* that 'the German concept of rejoicing in the misfortunes of others is thriving in the ruins of the New Economy' and that seeing the 'dot-com set' getting a bracing taste of the downside is deeply satisfying for many (Breslau, 2000). *Mademoiselle* went even further by informing us that 'there's a virtual all-you-can-eat schadenfreude buffet going on' at the moment (Bried, 2001). Both magazines used examples of people chortling at anything that inhibits flagrant exhibitions of dot-com wealth. Portmann's message, that the notion of desert or deservedness lies 'at the heart of *Schadenfreude*', that *Schadenfreude* 'rides on the coat-tails of justice' and is thus 'morally acceptable' (2000, p. 4), seems to have touched a particular cord with those delighting in crashing stock prices and dot-com bankruptcies. More generally, '*Schadenfreude* is about wrongs being righted and is an emotion which is all right to feel' suddenly became the received wisdom of the day. Portmann may have to revise his observation that the term *Schadenfreude* 'has *not* caught on in America' (ibid., p. 182); in fact, both the magazine articles that I have quoted from here refer approvingly to his own analysis of it. In Ben-Ze'ev's extended study of various emotions, appearing at about the same time as Portmann's book, *Schadenfreude* is also said to incorporate the belief that 'others deserve their misfortune' (2000, p. 356), with the result that the emotion is then – at least partly – morally condoned. I will argue in what follows that this conception of *Schadenfreude* betrays an inadequate grasp of the relationship between pain at others' good fortune and pleasure at others' bad fortune and that it distorts, for various reasons, the real focus of (*B2*): pleasure at another person's deserved bad fortune as *satisfied indignation*.

First, let us revert once again to Aristotle's discussion. One who is distressed at undeserved misfortunes 'will take pleasure or be unmoved by misfortunes of the opposite sort [that is, deserved]', Aristotle says, 'for it is right to rejoice in such cases' (1991, p. 156 [1386b]). Although he later adds that it is 'evident' from his discussion of indignation 'at what sort of people in misfortune and evildoing and lack of success one should rejoice or [at least] not feel distressed' (ibid., p. 158 [1387b]), he decides, unfortunately, to leave this emotion unnamed. I propose to call it 'satisfied indignation', and the rationale for that term will reveal itself presently. Nerney names it 'Anger Fulfilled' (1991, p. 84), but it should be clear from the distinction drawn between anger and indignation in the previous subsection why I feel that is not a particularly apt term. We have already seen *epichairekakia* mentioned above by Aristotle in connection with indignation, and it is clear from his references to it in the *Rhetoric* that he understands it as pleasure at others' undeserved bad fortune. I will follow Cooper in translating *epichairekakia* as *Schadenfreude*, rather than simply 'spite' or 'malice', as the latter terms are broader and seem less transparent in this context (cf. Cooper, 1996, p. 242; Irwin uses 'spite', as already noted, in his translation of Aristotle, 1985, and Kennedy, in his translation of Aristotle, 1991, uses 'malice').

As noted above, *Schadenfreude* has become a buzzword in the popular media, inspired by some recent philosophical analyses. We need not, however, look long to realize that the *Schadenfreude* under discussion there is not Aristotle's *epichairekakia*. Ben-Ze'ev translates *Schadenfreude* as 'pleasure-in-others'-misfortune' and claims that among its typical characteristics are that '(1) the other person is perceived to deserve the misfortune, (2) the misfortune is relatively minor and (3) we are passive in generating the other's misfortune' (2000, p. 356). Explaining the second factor, Ben-Ze'ev says that in the event of a severe misfortune, the element of deservingness is missing and then, typically, pleasure-in-others'-misfortune turns into pity. He concedes that people often feel pleased when a vicious criminal suffers a serious misfortune, but claims that it is only because we have raised our standards of what constitutes a major misfortune by comparing it with the even more serious crime that the criminal committed (ibid., pp. 358, 362). As far as the moral value of pleasure-in-others'-misfortune is concerned, Ben-Ze'ev maintains that if we correctly distinguish this emotion – in view of its connection to deservingness – from cruelty or sadism, we realize that it is 'not strongly negative from a moral viewpoint' or, in any case, 'no worse than many other emotions' (ibid., pp. 374, 376).

Portmann claims, like Ben-Ze'ev, that the notion of desert lies at the heart of *Schadenfreude* and that through this emotion we approve of and even celebrate the suffering of others for reasons we take to be moral. In so far as they really *are* moral, that is, to the extent that *Schadenfreude* signifies love of justice or repugnance to injustice, 'this emotion is a virtue'. Portmann does not, in contrast to Ben-Ze'ev, place any size restriction on the comeuppance in which we rejoice, but explicitly allows significant injuries (2000, pp. 4, 35, 42, 55–6). I agree with Portmann that there is no typical size barrier to the misfortunes in which people take pleasure, and I agree in fact, substantially at least, with what both he and Ben-Ze'ev say about the moral value of pleasure at others' deserved bad fortune. However, I do not think that equating this emotion with *Schadenfreude* rings true. In fact, I think that their conceptual analysis of pleasure in others' misfortune or suffering relinquishes its connection to *Schadenfreude* in direct proportion to its achieving its connection to desert.

For one thing, this analysis pays the conceptual price of having no commonly used term left to refer to the non-morally inspired pleasure at others' *undeserved* bad fortune. Ben-Ze'ev seems to think that this emotion is too rare to merit much scrutiny or that, when it exists, it is simply the same as cruelty or sadism. Portmann, on the other hand, suggests that this unethical emotion be referred to as 'malicious glee' (2000, p. 200). He elsewhere admits that the account of *Schadenfreude* he develops 'may surprise native German speakers' but seems not too worried about that, as his intention is not to provide an 'etymological sketch but a moral evaluation of the emotion' (ibid., p. 5).

Although my misgivings about Ben-Ze'ev's and Portmann's terminologies are more than merely etymological, it does well to start here with a nod towards the German notion of *Schadenfreude*; this is after all a German word although it has relatively recently been imported into English. In 1930, Martha Moers wrote an enlightening piece about *Schadenfreude*, from the perspective of moral education, in a journal of pedagogy. There, she cleverly delineates the different forms that this emotion may assume, from the mildly morally negative joy of seeing another person in an embarrassing, comical situation, to the seriously morally negative joy aroused by the severe misfortune of a good person whom we have maliciously envied. She then considers the emotion, sometimes thought to fall within the rubric of

Schadenfreude, where one's joy is motivated by the satisfaction of justice having been restored when a bad person suffers misfortune. If the justice motive is really pure, Moers says, if it is unpolluted by any malicious elements, then this is 'hardly to be considered a reprehensible tendency' in a person. Indeed, in such a case, we should not speak of *Schadenfreude* at all: what the case presents, rather, is '*Pseudoschadenfreude*', as Moers calls it (1930, p. 131, my emphasis). For Moers, as in fact for most German speakers, there exists nothing that might be called 'morally proper *Schadenfreude*'; there does, however, exist an emotion characterized by a sense of justice when a haughty person stumbles into bad luck or when a villain is brought to book.

There is a long philosophical and pedagogical tradition, harking back to Aristotle, of understanding *Schadenfreude* in precisely the way Moers does. Schopenhauer's diatribe on *Schadenfreude*, where he describes it as the 'worst trait in human nature', is often quoted in the literature, and Kierkegaard, no more forgivingly, considered *Schadenfreude*, the 'even more hideous cousin' of envy, lurking in a 'dark corner' of the mind (cited in Schoeck, 1969, pp. 170, 172) – to mention but two historic examples. Schopenhauer relates *Schadenfreude* directly to cruelty, as we saw Ben-Ze'ev do above. I think that may overdo the negative moral assessment of *Schadenfreude* somewhat, for, arguably, we need to distinguish between (1) the joy of actively promoting and witnessing another's suffering, (2) the joy of seeing another suffer although the suffering was not caused by us, (3) the joy of witnessing another's misfortune though not enjoying the suffering as such and (4) the joy of witnessing another's deserved misfortune as a restoration of justice. While the joys in (1) and (2) smack of cruelty, or even sadism (surely the worst trait in human beings), these joys are not *necessary* elements in *Schadenfreude*; only (3) is.

If we add (4) as a necessary or, at least, a typical element in *Schadenfreude*, as Ben-Ze'ev and Portmann want to do, we not only dishonour the discursive tradition about this concept – by letting our characterization of *Schadenfreude* become disengaged from the accounts from which the traditional discussion has taken its material and impetus – we also end up obliterating the distinction between two emotions with radically different foci. The focus of the traditional notion of *Schadenfreude* (from Aristotle's *epichairekakia* to Moers's real *Schadenfreude*) is pleasure at misfortune, without any moral concern – although distinguishable from pleasure in the suffering *qua* suffering through sadistic emotional identification with the sufferer. Once the pleasure at misfortune *qua* deserved misfortune enters in, we are, by contrast, dealing with an emotion whose focus is the alleviation of our previous indignation: the restoration of justice. We *felt* indignation because of the very fact that another person was getting more than deserved; now the injustice has been remedied and we feel relieved. This is why I call this emotion, which Aristotle left unnamed, 'satisfied indignation' (cf. McNamee's similar characterization of it as 'satisfaction', 2003, p. 13). To be sure, we may decide to call the emotion by some other name. If, however, we choose to call it *Schadenfreude*, as Ben-Ze'ev and Portmann have done, we risk ending up in conceptual confusion – even if we find some other term to designate the traditional concept of *Schadenfreude*, we invite a no-ending conflation of the two – and also risk being responsible for rabble-rousing in society where demagogues will be more than ready to inform the public that actually '*Schadenfreude* is all right, as moral philosophers have now demonstrated.'

Before the recent excitement about *Schadenfreude*, at least, people did not seem to have shared Ben-Ze'ev's and Portmann's intuitions about the concept: witness a recent psychological study which showed that the manipulation of deservingness in different (videotaped) scenarios had 'no effect' on the participants' sense of *Schadenfreude* (Brigham et al., 1997, p. 366). It may well be, however – and this is only a hunch – that people are sometimes tempted to use the word *Schadenfreude* not only for real *Schadenfreude*, as pleasure at others' undeserved bad fortune, but also for pleasure at others' deserved bad fortune when that emotion is rational but not morally proper: that is, when it should be morally outweighed by other considerations. If this is true, it strengthens rather than weakens my point about the deficiency of a moral concern that is inherent in the concept of *Schadenfreude*.

To end my discussion of our pleasure at others' bad fortune, a few words are in order about the connection between (malicious) envy and *Schadenfreude* (in the traditional sense). This connection is well established not only in the philosophical literature and psychological research, but also, arguably, in the public consciousness. Aristotle says that the *Schadenfreude*-ful person 'is also envious' (1991, p. 156 [1386b]); recall Kierkegaard's words about *Schadenfreude* being the 'hideous cousin' of envy; Goldie points out that sometimes 'the frisson of *Schadenfreude* that we feel at another's downfall will reveal in us a previously existing malicious envy of which we were not aware' (2000, p. 27); McNamee reminds us of the Catholic doctrine of how envy leads first to sadness, then gossip, then *Schadenfreude* and finally hatred (2003, p. 10); and numerous examples of psychological research strongly support linking the experience of envy with the experience of *Schadenfreude* (see, for example, Smith et al., 1996; Brigham et al., 1997). The idea here is simple enough: when someone you have maliciously envied suffers bad luck, you get a malicious joy buzz. Where such linking has *not* been documented in psychological experiments (see, for example, Feather and Sherman, 2002), the reason seems to lie in the in the overly broad specification of *Schadenfreude* employed, as pleasure at another's misfortune *simpliciter*. Since many of these cases will be cases of 'satisfied indignation' rather than real *Schadenfreude*, it is no wonder that a strong connection cannot be identified between the experience of pleasure at another's misfortune, so broadly construed, and envy.

Does the fact of the connection between real *Schadenfreude* and envy, however, not subvert my earlier point about satisfied indignation as a remedial emotion having a different focus – does not *Schadenfreude* then also have a restorative focus? The answer to that question is twofold. First, *Schadenfreude* does not, whereas satisfied indignation does, require a sense of restoration. Although *Schadenfreude* commonly follows upon the heels of envy, it is also quite common in cases where envy has not previously been experienced, especially in cases of minor misfortunes (a passer-by slipping on a banana skin, and so on). Second, even when *Schadenfreude* serves as a remedial emotion, the sense of what has been restored is both conceptually and morally different from that which is involved in satisfied indignation. In such kinds of *Schadenfreude*, our (distorted) sense of equality with another person is restored; in satisfied indignation, our sense of justice is restored. Needless to say, the former will often self-deceptively camouflage as the latter, but the experience of 'pure *Schadenfreude*', without any misconceived self-righteous allusion to justice, is not an uncommon phenomenon either.

Justice as an Emotional Virtue

After the necessary revision and retooling of Aristotle's skeletal account of the fortunes-of-others emotions, they can, for clarity's sake, be represented as in Figure 3.1.

The emotions in bold are, obviously, according to my specification, those of the desert-based emotions in question. To choose these four fortunes-of-others emotions as prototypical examples of desert-based other-reactive emotions is, I think, reasonable, in view of the following two factors. First, these four emotions are *purely* other-reactive; the standing of the subject experiencing the relevant emotion, for instance the subject's perceived superiority or inferiority with respect to the object, has nothing to do *logically* with the conceptualization of the emotion (*contra* Ben-Ze'ev, 2003): I may, in principle, be equally indignant of *B*'s undeserved good fortune irrespective of my social standing with respect to *B*, although it is, no doubt, psychologically true that this standing influences how frequently and intensely such an emotion is felt – witness Ben-Ze'ev's reminder of the Aristotelian claim that worthless and unambitious persons are not inclined to

	A: PAIN	
	Good fortune	*Bad fortune*
Deserved	(*1*) Begrudging spite	(2) Pity
Undeserved	(*3*) **Indignation**	(*4*) **Compassion**

	B: PLEASURE	
	Good fortune	*Bad fortune*
Deserved	(*1*) **Gratulation**	(2) **Satisfied indignation**
Undeserved	(*3*) Happy-for	(*4*) *Schadenfreude*

Figure 3.1 Fortunes-of-others emotions

indignation (ibid.). And second, these four emotions are also purely desert-based in the sense that they are not sometimes desert-based and sometimes not, or invariably mixed with some other emotions. None of the other frequently chosen examples of desert-based emotions is as 'pure' in these two respects. *Anger* is, for instance, about someone having wronged *me* (or someone close to me), and anger can also be rights-based rather than desert-based (see Krehbiel and Cropanzano's research results, 2000, mentioned earlier) – although even in such cases anger may involve the belief that the culprit deserves to be punished (see Roberts, 2003, p. 204), which is another matter. *Envy* may be desert-based (when coupled with indignation, eliciting 'indignant envy'), but equally often it may be rights-based ('angry envy') or simply lacking any purported moral basis at all ('invidious envy'; see, for example, D'Arms and Jacobson, 2000, p. 82). Ben-Ze'ev, while agreeing that there is often no moral concern in envy, still thinks that all envy has a desert or justice component (2000, p. 287; 2003), but he fails to realize that if that were so, then all envy would involve a moral concern, for all desert claims belong to the moral domain even if they can often be overridden by other moral considerations (see further in Kristjánsson, 2002, pp. 153–4). To take one more example, *jealousy* is, as I have argued elsewhere, always desert-based, but jealousy is a very complicated emotion – technically speaking a 'compound emotion' – which includes in addition to indignation at *B*'s superior position with regard to me, anger at a third party, *C*, for providing *B* with a favour that I think I deserve as much or more than *B*, and envy towards *B*, namely a desire for *B*'s relative advantage over me to be eliminated, preferably by taking the favour away from *B* and giving it to me (cf. my earlier remarks in Section 1.3 on compound emotions; see further in Kristjánsson, 2002, ch. 5).

No philosopher has understood the emotional corollaries of justice better than Aristotle, and it is to him that it is now time to return. What stood out at the beginning of the present subsection (see the diagram above) was little more than Aristotle's account of the fortunes-of-others emotions, duly pruned and adjusted. If certain obvious anomalies concerning the fit of those emotions to Aristotle's architectonic of a golden mean are removed, and the scattered pieces from Aristotle's two books on ethics and his *Rhetoric* are put together, we seem to end up with a consistent and morally suggestive account of justice as an emotional virtue. What is more, this account may provide the missing link needed to make Aristotle's comprehensive account of justice in the *Nicomachean Ethics* coherent and complete (for such an interpretation, see Coker, 1992, and more particularly, Curzer, 1995). It is often complained, as I did in Section 2.1, that there are lacunae in Aristotle's description in the *Nicomachean Ethics* of 'general' and 'particular' justice – because, for instance, both kinds of justice are limited to actions where the agent is both a distributor and a recipient of goods. If, however, we consider Aristotle's account of emotional justice to complement his account of social justice, we end up with a combined theory of all-round justice.

There is good reason to believe that Aristotle meant to be doing more than independently justifying four different emotions regarding others' fortunes: indignation (*A3*), compassion (*A4*), gratulation (*B1*) and satisfied indignation (*B2*). Not only does he think that these emotions all 'come from the same moral character' (1991, p. 156 [1386b]); he specifically says in the *Eudemian Ethics* that there is a single inclination, namely *nemesis*, which is characterized by 'pain felt at either good or bad fortune if undeserved, or to joy felt at them if deserved' (1984, p. 1954 [1233b]). Here Aristotle uses the term *nemesis* not only for indignation (*A3*: pain at others' undeserved good fortune) but for the mean temperament of being equitable towards the fortunes of others. This may explain why Aristotle chooses the verbal noun *to nemesan* ('being indignant') rather than *nemesis* in his extensive account of indignation in the *Rhetoric*: he wants to leave *nemesis* for the broader sense of a complex mean–temperament involving a number of interrelated emotions. However, Aristotle does use *nemesis* for indignation in the *Nichomachean Ethics*. (Recall that *Nemesis* was originally the name of the Greek goddess responsible for good measure, embodying godly envy of too much happiness.) In other words, Aristotle's view seems to be that there exists a general disposition to be pleased or pained – on the right occasions, for the right time and in the right measure – at other people's good or bad, deserved or undeserved fortune, and that the four emotions above represent this general disposition *qua* golden mean on different occasions, while begrudging spite (*A1*), pity (*A2*), happy-for (*B3*) and *Schadenfreude* (*B4*) constitute different excesses of the mean (Coker, 1992, talks about '4-*nemesis*' in this context; Curzer, 1995, about 'poetic justice'). What Aristotle tries to capture here is the sense of justice as a personal, emotional virtue: a virtue that binds good, reasonable people together in a community of feeling and judgement and lays the ground for justice as a social institution. Notably, Aristotle might be inclined to call it a 'natural virtue' rather than a 'full virtue', since it can also be possessed by children lacking in practical wisdom (*phronesis*) (1985, pp. 169–70 [1144b]).

There are considerable strengths to be found in the general line of Aristotle's thought here. Nevertheless, we should be wary of taking on board all of his particular insights, for it seems that his search for symmetry and precision in the mean–temperament of emotional justice gets the better of him at times. This search for perfect symmetry may explain his rather quick and badly argued case for rejection of pain at deserved bad fortune and pleasure at undeserved good fortune that we witnessed earlier.

Aristotle's core claim in this context is that 'when someone is distressed at the acquisition or possession of something, necessarily he rejoices at its deprivation or destruction' (1991, p. 156 [1387a]). This will be obvious in the case of the four justified emotions, emotions that are bound – since they all 'come from the same moral character' – to accompany each other: a person who normally feels compassion in the appropriate circumstances will also normally experience satisfied indignation in the appropriate circumstances, and so forth. The idea, however, seems also to be that each excess of an emotion belonging to the mean-temperament in question psychologically excludes another justified emotion from forming part of the mean. This works rather well in the case of begrudging spite and *Schadenfreude*; it is easy to imagine begrudging spite as contrary to gratulation and *Schadenfreude* as contrary to compassion. It is, in other words, psychologically plausible to think of a person disposed to begrudging spite as not being (by way of psychological necessity) disposed to gratulation – and *mutatis mutandis* for *Schadenfreude* versus compassion. What Aristotle says, however, about the relationship between happy-for and indignation, on the one hand, and pity and satisfied indignation, on the other hand, does not seem as psychologically plausible. He who is pleased at undeserved good fortune will show excess, Aristotle says, 'in not grieving even at the prosperity of the undeserving' (1984, p. 1934 [1221b]). That is, being dispositionally pleased at even undeserved good fortune will (psychologically) *result in* being deficiently indignant. Furthermore, Aristotle's description of compassion and satisfied indignation implies that a disposition to feel pity (pain at deserved bad fortune) is psychologically contrary to a disposition to feel satisfied indignation: pleasure at deserved bad fortune (1991, p. 156 [1386b]). But why should not a person who is generally indignant when his peers experience undeserved luck sometimes be capable of being happy for, say, a friend whose stroke of luck is not strictly speaking deserved? And it is difficult to imagine why a person who often feels pity, that is to say pain at someone else's deserved suffering – for example, at the plight of the drug addict who has brought his misfortune upon himself – cannot, in other cases, rejoice when someone reaps the whirlwind. Aristotle has not tendered any psychological argument, as opposed to an argument from logical symmetry, to the effect that pity and happy-for will issue in morally deficient satisfied indignation and indignation, respectively, when the occasion calls for those emotions in their full measure. Here, the rigidity of Aristotle's system seems to get the better of him and make him violate his own famous injunction of not looking for greater precision in subject-matters than that of which they, by their nature, admit.

3.3 Self-reactive Desert-Based Emotions

Could a conceptual account be given of desert-based and non-desert-based *fortunes-of-self* emotions – *qua* prototypical self-reactive emotions – similar to the above reconstructed Aristotelian one of *fortunes-of-others* emotions: that is, relying on the same three parameters of pain/pleasure, good/bad fortune and deservingness/undeservingness? This question poses an interesting challenge, one that has been conspicuously underresearched by philosophers. Perhaps philosophers have been deterred by the lack of an Aristotelian precedent (Aristotle's work is, after all, the natural starting point of most philosophical emotion research); perhaps there is something about the fortunes-of-self emotions which makes them less amenable to systematic classification. I will return to this latter consideration in due course, but first it should be noted that psychologists have not been as shy of addressing this topic as philosophers. Before proceeding further, it would be germane to mention a few points here about work done by the former.

Much recent research in psychology on what I have here called other-reactive and self-reactive emotions has taken place within the so-called self-evaluation maintenance (SEM) model, according to which another's performance (relative to one's own) can be consequential for the maintenance of one's self-evaluation. In this model, a distinction is made between *reflection* and *comparison* processes, with the suggestion being that one's self-evaluation is commonly raised through pleasure in the reflected glory of another's outstanding performance, where the performance is in an area of low relevance to the subject, whereas one's self-evaluation is commonly lowered through pain at comparison with another's outstanding performance, where the performance is in an area of high relevance to the subject (see, for example, Tesser and Collins, 1988; R. H. Smith, 2000). A sceptical reader may immediately think of counter-examples where, for instance, one experiences self-enhancing satisfaction at someone else's good fortune, in an area of either high or low relevance to oneself, because the fortune is deserved. Such examples would, however, miss the mark, for the reflection/comparison distinction is not meant to capture logical variables, but rather frequency or intensity variables which have been brought out in psychological experiments.

The terms of this proposed distinction, 'reflection' as opposed to 'comparison', are somewhat misleading, however, when coming from psychologists, for the psychological consensus seems to be that *all* the emotional reactions in question involve 'some sort of comparison between the self and another person' (Smith, 2000, p. 175; cf. Ben-Ze'ev, 2003). Now, there is clearly an almost platitudinous sense in which all the emotions explored in the previous section and the present one are *comparison-based*: they all involve an implicit reference to a baseline of expectations. Otherwise, there would be no way to determine what should count as good or bad fortune in the first place. For example, I cannot experience indignation at someone else's undeserved good fortune unless I deem that person to have enjoyed some fortune which people in a similar position would not normally have expected to enjoy (see Section 2.1). Let us call such an object–object comparison (between the object at hand and the object of expectations) a *weakly comparative* one.

It seems to me that an important distinction here is typically overlooked in the psychological literature. As we saw in Section 3.2, people can evaluate the fortunes of others without any reference to their own situation. This is logically impossible in the case of fortunes-of-self emotions: one must always evaluate the fortunes of oneself with reference to an object, be it (a) another person or persons here and now; (b) the object of statistical expectations or (c), though perhaps rarely such as in some cases of shame, the object of a self-constructed ideal. If we call such subject–object comparisons *strongly comparative*, then we can claim as a distinguishing mark between fortunes-of-others emotions and fortunes-of-self emotions that whereas the former are not necessarily strongly comparative, the latter are.

The psychologist Richard H. Smith is the author of an ambitious article which aims at the classification of what he calls – somewhat misleadingly in light of the above discussion – 'social comparison-based emotions', but which I would call simply fortunes-of-others and fortunes-of-self emotions. Smith suggests that each emotion can be categorized in terms of whether it results from an upward or downward comparison, whether it produces a positive or negative experience for the self, and whether it produces a positive or negative experience for the other. He also suggests that each emotion involves a characteristic focus of attention (the self; the other; a dual focus), and that each emotion can be broadly characterized as having either an assimilative or a contrastive nature. Collectively, all these criteria yield a rather complex diagram of the emotions. What need concern us in the present section are the specifically self-reactive emotions, which in Smith's schema are four: optimism, pride, depression/shame and fear/worry (2000).

While initially helpful, Smith's classification stands in need of some modification. First, fortunes-of-self emotions are, I have argued, strongly comparative, and Smith goes even further than that by assuming that *all* the emotions in his classificatory schema are strongly comparative. Yet none of the self-reactive emotions yielded by his schema are strongly comparative in their everyday senses: there is, for instance, nothing odd about a Robinson Crusoe being either depressed or optimistic irrespective of any comparisons with other persons, either real or imaginary. We may, however, partly overlook this problem for two reasons. First, Smith sometimes speaks as if there exist special social comparison-based uses of the emotion terms in question, and that it is such uses that he is specifically invoking, for instance, social comparison-based depression as opposed to general depression (see, for example, his discussion of social comparison-based pity, ibid., p. 191; yet he is less than ringingly explicit on this point). Second, there may be something about self-reactive emotions in general, when referred to in ordinary usage, that makes them less easily differentiable than many other kinds of emotions. I take this into account in my diagrams below by referring to each kind of fortunes-of-self emotion as 'a kind' of a more general emotional attitude.

My second complaint about Smith's account is that he does not invoke *desert* as a logical variable; he makes, for example, no distinction between pain at deserved, and at undeserved, bad fortune (with respect to oneself or others). To avoid making this complaint sound question-begging, we need to address the question of whether this alleged emotion variable is perhaps arbitrary, or whether, for instance, in the case of pain at deserved bad fortune, we are simply dealing with two distinct emotions, such as sympathy *and* anger. Once again, we are hampered by the lack of a general theory about emotion individuation. What we can say, however, is that psychological research has brought out the powerful role played by injustice in the elicitation of a number of different emotions (see., for example, Mikula et al., 1998). Moreover, the *beliefs* underlying, say, begrudging spite (pain at another's deserved good fortune), on the one hand, and indignation (pain at another's undeserved good fortune), on the other, as well as their typical *behavioural patterns*, seem to be different enough for us to suppose that we are dealing with two different emotions. The *feeling* component may well be identical, but then, in fact, it often is even in radically different emotions. It becomes, admittedly, more difficult to distinguish between the relevant beliefs and behaviours when the self is incorporated into the perceived desert structures, but psychological research seems none the less to indicate that there, also, desert is an important variable (see Feather, 1999, esp. pp. 241–3, on the incorporation of the self in desert structures).

In light of this elaboration of my second modification of Smith's schema, let me now propose a classificatory schema of fortunes-of-self emotions (Figure 3.2), applying the same parameters as in Figure 3.1.

This classification is more nuanced and, arguably also, more sensitive to salient psychological and moral differences than is Smith's classification of self-reactive emotions. Since the terms I have chosen are more or less self-explanatory, I will only expand briefly on their meanings here. Persons who feel pain at their own deserved good fortune with respect to others can, plausibly, be said to suffer from some kind of self-hate, whereas those who feel pain at undeserved good fortune experience a kind of shame, which can appear as guilt when their enjoying the fortune implies a violation of moral obligations (the latter has been well researched in the psychology literature; see, for example, Montada and Schneider, 1989; Schroeder et al., 1995). Persons who feel pain at their own deserved bad fortune experience self-pity, in the same sense of pity (as distinguished from compassion) as invoked in the case of the relevant fortunes-of-others emotion. Ordinary language does not

	A: PAIN	
	Good fortune	*Bad fortune*
Deserved	(*1*) A kind of self-hate	(*2*) A kind of self-pity
Undeserved	(*3*) **A kind of shame**	(*4*) **A kind of self-depression**

	B: PLEASURE	
	Good fortune	*Bad fortune*
Deserved	(*1*) **A kind of victorious joy**	(*2*) **A kind of satisfied shame**
Undeserved	(*3*) A kind of serendipitous joy	(*4*) A kind of masochism

Figure 3.2 Fortunes-of-self emotions

offer a term such as 'self-compassion' for pain at undeserved bad fortune; let us refer to it here as a kind of self-depression, which of course will often co-occur with anger at the agent(s) responsible for the undeserved bad fortune. Persons who feel pleasure at their deserved good fortune experience a kind of joy, namely victorious joy, which can appear as, or issue in, pride if one attributes (some) responsibility for the fortune to oneself. Joy must, however, be seen as both logically and developmentally prior to pride (see, for example, Charlesworth, 1992, pp. 266–7). I have decided to call pleasure at one's undeserved good fortune 'a kind of serendipitous joy'; recall here that I assume that the pleasure is not caused by the fact that the fortune is undeserved but rather takes no account of that fact. Pleasure at one's deserved bad fortune is a kind of satisfied shame: namely, the satisfaction/elimination of the shame felt at undeserved good fortune. This emotion will frequently, I believe, disguise itself as a kind of self-irony. Finally, pleasure at one's undeserved bad fortune must be seen as a kind of masochism, which might, in some cases, enter the sphere of the pathological.

The terms in bold cover the desert-based emotions in question (*A3*, *A4*, *B1*, *B2*), just as in the diagrams classifying the fortunes-of-others emotions. If we take seriously Aristotle's suggestion that the four desert-based fortunes-of-others emotions form parts of a general emotional disposition, *nemesis*, as pain felt at either good or bad fortune if undeserved, or joy felt at them if deserved, then our four desert-based fortunes-of-self emotions should form parts of the same disposition. One could even argue that Aristotle's suggestion and my analysis of the desert-based fortunes-of-self emotions are mutually supportive in the sense that Aristotle's suggestion might be seen to indicate that such emotions also exist with respect to the self, as well as with respect to other persons, and that my analysis strengthens his original suggestion of an underlying unity at work in all desert-based emotions.

Before this section draws to a close, let me make three observations about evident differences between fortunes-of-others and fortunes-of-self emotions.

First, recall the places where Aristotle's 'perfect-symmetry hypothesis' seemed to break down in the case of fortunes-of-others emotions (Section 3.2). It did not seem psychologically plausible to suppose that a psychological tendency to being 'happy-for' (another's undeserved fortune) should necessarily exclude a tendency to indignation, nor a tendency to pity exclude a tendency to satisfied indignation. Somewhat surprisingly, perhaps, Aristotle's hypothesis appears more plausible with respect to the corollary fortunes-of-self emotions: that tendencies to serendipitous joy and self-pity generally exclude tendencies to shame and satisfied shame, respectively. This may indicate that we make higher moral demands of ourselves than of others – to whom we are more willing to give the benefit of the doubt – by assuming, for instance, that if I am a person prone to self-pity in cases of deserved bad fortune, I become too morally weak to be able to experience satisfied shame in such circumstances. By suggesting that a tendency to serendipitous joy might exclude a tendency to shame, I am not saying that someone could not rejoice at his good fortune when coming across a banknote on the pavement, but suffer shame if he receives a huge inheritance from someone he has never met; the first benefit is, after all, small and the second large. I am rather suggesting that in cases of benefits or burdens of roughly similar 'quantity', Aristotle's perfect-symmetry thesis seems more plausible in the case of fortunes-of-self than fortunes-of-others emotions. Now perhaps people do not worry about the consistency of their assessments of what other people deserve as much as about the consistency of their attitudes to their own deserts, or there are some other factors which make our emotional responses more fixed in our own cases. If my hunch here is valid, the construction of our emotional landscape does not seem to concur with the common assumption that people find it easier to produce excuses for their own faults than for those of others (unless such excuses are primarily explained as the results of self-deceptions). Rather, I think, people are prone to consider self-pity as morally inferior to pity and serendipitous joy as morally inferior to happy-for (someone else's undeserved good luck).

Second, fortunes-of-self emotions seem – as we saw in the discussion of Smith's account – to be less easily distinguishable from more general emotional attitudes than the fortunes-of-others emotions; hence they appear as 'kinds' of this or that in Figure 3.2. We seem, this time perhaps less surprisingly, to have a more complex understanding of ourselves than of others. Third, the desert variable may be less psychologically clear-cut in the experience of our own fortunes than in those of others. We can, for instance, experience joy both at our deserved and undeserved good fortune with the difference between the two being, arguably, a more nuanced one than in the case of the corollary fortunes-of-others emotions. Perhaps the reason for the greater complexity and subtlety of self-reactive emotions, in general, is similar to the one for why there are more emotions focused on negatively evaluated than positively evaluated states of affairs (Ben-Ze'ev, 2003): namely, that the former have more functional value in our lives. These three distinguishing points, at any rate, indicate that if emotions do have a narrative structure, as many philosophers argue (see Section 1.3), the stories we tell about ourselves may be rather different from the ones we tell about others.

Let us finally revert to the question of what kind of virtue the desert-based emotions might represent if they really are virtues. Recall here the earlier distinction between three kinds of virtuosity in emotions, as manifested in 'emotion virtues', 'emotion-regulating virtues' and 'emotion-combining virtues' (Section 1.3). To concentrate on the last of the three, an emotion-combining virtue involves an emotional disposition to experience a number of particular emotions at the appropriate times, although it may itself also appear as an independent emotion. If Aristotle's general *nemesis* is a virtue, it is evidently a virtue in precisely this last sense: triggering the appropriate emotions at the appropriate times – including the eight desert-based fortunes-of-others and fortunes-of-self emotions that I have analysed in this chapter – while also itself constituting an independent emotional virtue. These eight emotions would, then, in a sense, depend upon this overarching virtue for their virtuousness. Enough has been said to indicate the *possible* moral standing of desert-based emotions and their role in justice. Much more needs to be said, in the following chapter, about their *actual* developmental role and moral status. What stands out at the end of the present chapter, I hope, is that justice theorists can only ignore those emotions at their peril.

Chapter 4

From Development to Justification

4.1 Developmental Accounts

Let us start this chapter with some basic facts with which social-science research has provided us. Justice, in general, and desert, in particular, have been shown to be universal concerns across cultural groups. While these values manifest themselves in somewhat varying ways in different places, there remains – so social scientists aver – something that can be distilled from those differences and called a universal sense *of* (or *for*) justice: an orientation towards the just that can be associated with the human capacity for cognition and feeling. The latter is highly relevant here. Contemporary research in developmental and social psychology implicates emotions more and more in the experience and development of a sense of justice, with young children all over the world seeming to *feel* the sting of injustice from an early age. This is manifested in their capacity to experience emotions of compassion, indignation and so forth, and to demonstrate their feelings of fairness and unfairness in their relationships with others. Even the jungle boy studied by the eighteenth-century doctor Jean Itard is reported to have reacted with great rage when undeservedly treated, supporting the conclusion of psychologists that no cultural conventions, as expressed through particular socialization practices, are necessary for the emergence of the most primitive, desert-based, sense of justice. Thus Strawson's 'reactive attitudes', many of which are desert-based, have been confirmed to be, if not ineluctable, then at least as a matter of fact ubiquitous in human life: original passions in Hume's sense (see, for example, Simmons, 1981; Damon, 1988; Masters, 1992; Charlesworth, 1992; not to mention the abundant social-psychology research on the 'belief in a just world', surveyed in Section 4.2).

Now, tracing the origin of a conception is not the same as providing a moral justification for it. Nevertheless, there is good reason to think that an understanding of the development of justice concerns in children may shed some light on the origin, role, salience and, perhaps, ultimately the content of the full-blown notion of justice, thus helping us to evaluate it morally. This is why a hard look at developmental theories of justice is now in order.

In this section, I first sketch some traditional accounts of moral internalization, in general, and justice internalization, in particular, with a quick survey of the strengths and weaknesses of each account. I have already (in Section 1.2) registered my agreement with Simmons, who claims that the obvious starting point for the construction of philosophical perspectives on justice should lie precisely in the 'origin and development of social justice principles' (1981, p. 41). We must, however, be mindful here of Carr's well-taken point, of which I made use in my argumentation in Section 1.2, that the very notion of moral development is an inherently normative one. Picking up Carr's general thread, my subsequent concern in the present section is to spell out the way in which normative concerns unavoidably enter into the design and interpretation of empirical research on children's development of justice conceptions – with special emphasis on Damon's well-known stage theory of development. As I will argue, normative considerations steer the design and interpretation of empirical research into the development of justice conceptions by providing assumptions both about what counts as a conception of justice in the first place (and what does not), and about what counts as a better (or worse) conception of justice. Only through mutual adjustments between different levels of 'factual bruteness', rather than between different levels of the purely descriptive and the purely evaluative, can we reach out to the perplexities of this morally loaded issue and arrive at a research project that can contribute both to a psychological and to a philosophical understanding of justice.

Following my discussion of Damon, I turn to another eminent developmental psychologist, Hoffman. I explore his theory of natural empathy as the fount of children's morality. After outlining the theory and its empirical underpinnings, I offer a philosophical (conceptual and moral) critique of some of its aspects. While Hoffman's theory offers valuable insights into the ways in which justice, like all moral concerns, relies on and relates to the child's original capacity for empathy, it underestimates, I argue, the emotionality of justice itself as a pre-institutional concern and overestimates its status as an abstract principle. This discussion paves the way for the input on 'just-world beliefs' from social psychology that I examine in Section 4.2, and ultimately my moral defence of desert and desert-based emotions in Section 4.3.

Theories of Justice Internalization

There are, as we know, various competing general theories abroad of moral internalization, and these different theories are variously well equipped for dealing specifically with the development of justice concerns (a process hereafter, for brevity's sake, referred to simply as 'justice internalization'). In order to understand better the thrust of the more specific theories of Damon and Hoffman, a brief mapping out of the general theoretical landscape is in order.

Social-learning theories (for example, Bandura, 1977) claim that children's moral cognitions and inclinations derive from social learning – that is, from children's experiences with other social agents – and are gradually moulded through reinforcement and modelling/observation. Although these theories tend to be a bit more complex than the old saying that rewarding good behaviour makes children good, they share with this saying an optimistic, positive vision of the possibilities of moral education. On the negative side, social-learning theories have been criticized for insufficient attention to the formation of that very self which is then subsequently moulded and conditioned. Serious doubts have also been raised about the idea of morality as a set of standards that adults foist upon an unknowing child. In the case of justice, this idea contradicts the common observations that first, children tend to experience intense justice-based emotions of their own accord from an early age, and second, the development of justice concerns seems to be a dominant, universal theme in child development and not merely the contingent processing of one pro-social conception among many transmitted to children via certain learning situations.

Economic theories of moral internalization take their cue from the ideal of *homo economicus*, who is motivated for the most part by self-interest when interacting with others, but who – by dint of a formalist rationality – gradually codifies a moral (social-exchange) system for mutual benefit (see, for example, Walster et al., 1978). These theories tend to appeal to moral formalists of all sorts, be they guided by social-contract theories of morality or a 'morally purer' Kantian formalism. Via the Kantian link, some followers of the influential cognitive-developmental school of child development have been sympathetic to such economic theories, which they have then combined with a developmental thesis about how justice concerns gradually develop through increased cognitive skills and higher levels of intellectual development. This model of justice internalization has, however, come under heavy fire of late, especially from adherents of the recently popular 'belief-in-a-just-world' theory. Just-world theorists claim – for a number of reasons which will be spelled out in Section 4.2 – that economic theories are ill suited for making sense of justice internalization. Moreover, economic theories, with their heavy emphasis on formal, rational processes, tend to be rather vague about the role of emotions in justice internalization.

Psychological theories of moral internalization form a diverse category. Pure psychoanalytic theories of justice as a 'cultural superego' – theories hampered, as is the psychoanalytic method in general, by the paucity of controlled experiments – are no longer as prominent as before, but among others that have recently come into vogue is the above-mentioned just-world theory in social psychology (influenced by Freudian psychoanalysis, Gestalt psychology and Mead's symbolic interactionism) that I examine in detail in Section 4.2. According to this theory, people possess a basic, primordial 'justice motive': a motive rooted in the emotionally driven childhood realization that immediate gratification of desires can and should be delayed in favour of long-term gain (Lerner, 1981). While strong on the relation between justice and the emotions, the just-world theory has, as we will see in due course, a hard time explaining differences, both individual and societal, in the strength of the 'justice motive'. Moreover, the theory's educational implications are particularly unclear since it is open to question both how morally commendable this alleged motive is and, once formed through psychological processes, how amenable it will be to cultivation and coaching.

Biological theories explain justice internalization, like all moral internalization, in terms of its adaptive value: 'The only scientific explanation' of moral behaviour is 'evolution by natural selection. There is no serious alternative except divine creation, but that is not science' (Walsh, 2000, p. 845; cf. Mackie, 1985, pp. 215ff.). These theories, which see justice motivations as 'hardwired', have less trouble than some of the previously mentioned theories in explaining the universality of people's sense of justice (which they consider traceable to non-human primates) and its inherent emotionality (as simply one ineluctable facet of its evolutionary function). However, many philosophers and psychologists have serious reservations about the 'evolutionary' perspective on morality in general, believing that it involves unfounded determinism, a 'genetic fallacy' and some highly controversial factual claims about what makes human beings function. Those reservations typically carry over into their assessment of the explanation of justice internalization that is offered by biological theories. Moreover, even many of those essentially sympathetic to the idea of a natural (inborn sentimental) basis of justice motivations and practices want to reject the 'hardwired explanations' of (socio)biological theories as *irrelevant*: 'We do not need a further intellectualization by way of sociobiological theory of the facts of life of which we are all aware ... This is how we are, what it is to be human' (French, 2001, p. 99).

It is, in fact, open to debate whether to count biological theories as a special category of justice-internalization theories here, since the former are normally held in conjunction with (or as a further supplement to) either economic or psychological theories of justice internalization. Indeed, various other combinations of the above theories are possible, for example accounts that hold justice-based emotions to be partly natural and partly socially constructed (cf. de Sousa, 2001; see also Hoffman's view described later).

Damon's Stage Theory

All of the above-mentioned theories share the goal of answering the *why* question of moral (or, more specifically, justice) internalization: *why* does it occur? They are generally less precise on the *how* question: the nitty-gritty details of what exactly takes place and at what time. A notable attempt at addressing this latter question, in the case of justice, is William Damon's stage theory of justice conceptualization (1981), to which I now turn.

Let me first make it clear that my aim here is not to explore, let alone detract from the merits of, Damon's general stance on the moral development and moral education of children. Damon is, after all, one of the world's leading child psychologists and his book, *The Moral Child*, one of the pivotal texts behind the rising post-Kohlbergian optimism about the possibility of making children both 'smart and good' through concerted efforts at school and in the home. I am in full sympathy with this optimism, as I am with Damon's claims that adults have long 'been blind to the full moral potential of the child' (1988, p. 4), and that from an early age 'children are acutely aware of moral concerns' (ibid., p. 1). I would not take exception either to Damon's contention that the sense of outrage felt by a four-year-old when pleading 'This is not fair' can be every bit as intense as that of an adult (ibid., p. 1). The question remains, however, what 'This is not fair' means to the child and how it is related to justice. It is, particularly, Damon's structural-developmental theory of justice conceptions that evokes my concern here.

In order to explore Damon's theory, his efforts in constructing it must be understood against the backdrop of Kohlberg's more historically (in)famous theory of moral development (I am referring here to the 'Kohlberg' of textbook fame rather than the more nuanced, but lesser known, thinker who emerged in the 1970s). The gradually developing consensus among commentators seems to be that while Kohlberg's untempered Kantian rationalism – his lack of interest in children's moral emotions and actual behaviour as opposed to their grasp and employment of abstract moral principles – seriously undermines his theory as one of general moral development, his findings have still bequeathed to us a wealth of information about one important facet of such development: his subjects' understanding (or lack thereof) of *justice* (for a quick overview of the literature, see Kristjánsson, 2002, s. 6.2). One way of interpreting Kohlberg's classic story of Heinz's sick wife, whose only chance of survival was the expensive drug Heinz could not afford to buy from that parsimonious chemist, is to understand it as embodying the potentially conflicting claims of entitlements (here, the rights of private property) versus deserved needs (here, of a sick dependant) as discordant ingredients in justice (see my discussion in Section 2.2). The story would then fall neatly into line with similar dilemma stories in which justice literature abounds: for instance, about a presidential candidate winning elections justly in the sense of having got the most votes, but unjustly in the sense of having won it undeservedly by duping the voters. What, in such a case, was the overall just outcome? Stories of this kind are notoriously difficult to decipher and resolve; hence Kohlberg's rather pessimistic conclusions about 'moral maturity' – which were then, in truth, merely conclusions about the understandably ambivalent sense of justice people often have.

Damon avoids the trap into which Kohlberg fell by starting off with what seems to be a less loaded story relative to the object of his inquiry. This was, in Damon's case, to track down the level of children's conceptions of justice, not their level of general moral development. He began simply by asking children, ranging in age from four to twelve, to imagine a situation in which they were required to split up the proceeds from the sale to parents at a school fair of pictures that they themselves had made earlier in class. He then probed their conceptions of 'positive justice' with some intriguing questions aimed at ascertaining what mattered most for the children: effort, achievement, need, equality, moral standing or something else. Should the best-behaved kids get the most, or the poor kids, or the kids who made the most pictures, or those who made the best pictures, or should, perhaps, everyone get an equal share? Based upon repeated studies of this kind, conducted in different countries, Damon advanced his stage theory, the briefest outline of which is as follows.

Four-year-old children think of 'positive justice' as reflecting their own self-centred wishes ('I should get it because I want to have it'); four- to five-year-old children's choices still reflect personal desires, but they posit criteria which adults would find morally irrelevant ('We should get most because we are girls'); five- to seven-year-old children think of justice in terms of strict equality ('Everyone should get the same'); six- to nine-year-old children have shed the equality conviction and, instead, think of justice as desert ('He should get more because he is better'); seven- to ten-year-old children's choices reflect the need to balance competing claims, including those of the low-contributing poor ('Poor kids should get the money'); finally, eight- to twelve-year-old children try to coordinate the claims of reciprocity (desert) and equality through more sophisticated ways of justification which often cannot be expressed in a single sentence (Damon, 1980, 1981; notice that the age levels overlap here because the proposed reasoning levels overlap). We could say that the oldest children have found their sea legs and begun to think of the intricacies of justice more as philosophers do: as something being *prima facie* just as distinct from being overall just, the latter to be adjudicated through *phronesis* in each particular case.

Eminent as Damon's theory is, it is not without its critics. Some claim that his original choice of a reward-for-work scenario biases children's answers in favour of a productivity-based justice and against a need-based one (Sigelman and Waitzman, 1991). Others, such as Huntsman, have failed to replicate Damon's findings in their own experiments and claim that the 'behaviour of the children seems to be dictated more by the characteristics of the situation than by age' (1984, p. 35). Huntsman may have hit the mark with his observation that there are inherent difficulties in 'matching adult expectations to children's perceptions of just behaviour' and that although Damon insists that his 'higher levels' simply mean 'older levels', the notion of qualitative differences cannot be avoided. Huntsman goes so far as to suggest that cognitive-developmental explanations may, all in all, be less apt than 'normative explanations' in capturing the justice concerns at stake in Damon's research (ibid., pp. 38–9).

Huntsman comes close to anticipating Carr's point about the inherent normativity of the notion of moral development. That notion seems to presuppose the idea of a more or less finely tuned 'moral radar': a tool with a particular role that can be performed well or badly. What concerns me more about Damon's theory, however, is the 'unavoidability of the normative' in a more specific sense, namely, the sense in which a conceptual moral theory enters into the interpretation of his data.

What we notice at once is the primacy-of-justice thesis: all conceptions of resource allocation must be justice conceptions; all distributive principles must be justice principles (or as Damon would put it, principles of 'positive justice'). But why presume that other moral concerns, such as pity, benevolence or utility, cannot play a role here also, or even non-moral ones, such as pure self-interest (cf. Miller, 1999, p. 44)? Notice that the children were not asked what was *the just way* to distribute the money earned, as distinct from *the morally correct way*; and even if they had been asked that question, it is doubtful whether children (at least at the younger age levels) would have any clear conception of what the 'just' way, as distinct from the overall 'correct' way, would mean. One way to interpret Damon's data – let us call it interpretation II as opposed to his own, which is interpretation I – would be to claim that the children interviewed did not have any specific conception of justice; that they, rather, worked with a gradually developing set of intuitions about moral principles of distribution. On interpretation II, somewhat ironically, Damon, who set out to measure children's sense of justice, would then have ended up measuring their general moral development, in contradistinction to Kohlberg, who set out to measure the latter but ended up (at best) measuring the former.

Another interpretation of the data, call it interpretation III, could be that some of the conceptions embodied in the children's answers were concerns of justice, perhaps those having to do with equality, desert and need, whereas others reflected non-justice-related concerns. There are, additionally, those justice theorists who strongly oppose the inclusion of equality and need as components in justice (however morally salient such values are from a non-justice-related perspective; see my discussion in Chapter 2), and they might want to propose interpretation IV: justice conceptions come to the fore *qua* desert considerations in the six- to nine-year-old group and continue to exist, albeit with other mixed non-justice-related elements, in the older groups, while the pro-need and pro-equality concerns detected would be due to humanitarian and egalitarian values which have nothing intrinsically to do with justice. There are, of course, other possible interpretations in light of other well-known theories of justice. Rather than conscientiously reeling off all of them, let me simply underline the telling point, which is this: there is no way to adjudicate between the competing claims of Damon's own interpretation of his data as having exclusively to do with children's conceptions of justice, and the alternative interpretations II–IV suggested above, except through the invocation of a normative conceptual theory. There is no non-evaluative royal road to understanding what justice means, be it for children or for adults.

This claim is not meant to constitute a rebuttal of Damon's stage theory for resting on a normative premise (although I happen to consider the premise that he employed, namely the primacy-of-justice thesis, seriously suspect; see Section 2.1). No developmental theory of the kind he proposes, nor, indeed, any empirical theory of justice, can avoid resting on a normative premise (see further in Miller, 1999, ch. 3). What is at fault in Damon's theory is rather that there are no arguments proffered for the premise that he happens to choose; it is smuggled in at the interpretative stage under the guise of a self-evident truth about all distributive choices being justice choices. Social scientists such as Damon need to accept, and accommodate, the unavoidability of normative conceptual bases for their studies, just as philosophers need to accept, and accommodate, the unavoidability of empirical evidence for justifying normative theories. As I suggested in Section 1.2, only a two-way exchange can here deliver the rich understanding of moral concepts that we are after.

Why are social scientists often so eager to fight shy of normative considerations, to create an (illusory) appearance of standing above the normative fray? Probably for fear of importing 'impure' elements into their studies. In this case the 'impurity' would consist in allowing essentially relative evaluative elements to defile the brute facts of their research matter. This fear, however, rests on the belief that normativity necessarily implies relativity. But that is simply not true. Recall Anscombe's clever discussion of the 'bruteness' of facts (1981a). Saying that my grocer *carts* potatoes to my house and *leaves* them there is more 'brute' than a description of the grocer as having *supplied* me with a quarter of potatoes. The second description is, again, more brute than saying that I *owe* the grocer such-and-such a sum of money, but that description could, in turn, be brute relative to yet another description, say, of my having a *prima facie moral obligation* to pay the grocer. Each description is implied, conversationally if not logically, by the preceding one. So facts are not brute *per se*; they are only brute relative to descriptions and contexts. Notice in particular that the climb up and down the ladder of bruteness traverses any significant distinction between facts and values. There is no particular step in this ladder of bruteness where we can say that the factual has ended and the evaluative taken over. The social-science textbook staple about 'normative conclusions only following from normative premises' is refuted by Anscombe's example if this is supposed to mean that evaluative descriptions can only follow from other evaluative descriptions (although it remains true that there is an important distinction between *facts* and *prescriptions*, which is quite another matter). There are descriptions of the non-evaluative and descriptions of the evaluative, but none is inherently less brute, or more brute, than the other (see further in Kristjánsson, 2002, s. 1.3).

What we need in both kinds of descriptions are *arguments* as to why those descriptions are more appropriate, in the given context, than some alternative. In Chapter 2, I tried, *inter alia*, to advance such arguments against the primacy-of-justice thesis, on the one hand, and for an account of justice as primarily a personal virtue, on the other. I also referred to the evolving consensus in the current literature that justice claims are not uniform, but rely, rather, on both entitlement claims and desert claims. Against this background, let me suggest that Damon and most of his critics may have been looking in the wrong places for facts that are 'brute relative to justice' (to use Anscombe's terminology): for facts that shed light on the development of children's conceptions of justice. They should not be looking at reasoned choices children make in socially institutionalized settings, such as that of reward for school work, but rather at their more natural (pre-institutional) reactions: the first inklings of justice concerns *qua* desert-based emotions. The outraged reaction of a two-year-old to being denied a turn on the swing, which Damon himself takes to be an early expression of a sense of injustice (1981, p. 57), is surely best understood as an emotional reaction rather than a purely intellectual one. As early as Rousseau – to recall a point from Chapter 3 – writers on children's moral development realized that justice is 'no mere moral conception formed by the understanding alone, but a true sentiment of the heart enlightened by reason' and, essentially, 'the natural outcome of our primitive affections' (1911, pp. 196, 215).

As with the other parameters of justice, steps in the direction of a more nuanced, subtle command of desert should, arguably, count as moral progress. That is why I would suggest the following research questions as fundamental to the exploration of the development of children's conceptions of justice: (1) When does the early emphatic distress children feel at others' suffering begin to transform itself qualitatively into compassion for undeserved suffering and pity for deserved suffering? (2) How, in general, do the desert-based emotions of anger, indignation, guilt, compassion, gratulation (pleasure over someone's deserved fortune) and so forth manifest themselves in children at different age levels? (3) When do children come to understand that the basis for an appropriate desert-based emotion must be some personal characteristic for whose creation the agent can be held responsible, rather than simply any characteristic with which he or she might be blessed through chance (such as beauty)? (4) When do children learn that other justice considerations may outweigh those of the desert-based emotions, for example, legal or quasi-legal entitlements? I believe that greater psychological and philosophical illumination would be gained by a research programme based on questions such as these than on the reward-for-work stories. While unabashedly normative, such a programme might, indeed, eventually yield a more tenable and productive developmental theory of justice than Damon's.

But do all these above qualms matter? Why should the social scientist be specifically interested in people's conceptions of justice *stricto sensu*, as distinct from the less precise judgements people – including children – make about proper distribution? If the philosopher refuses to grant these the status of justice judgements, is that not simply his problem? The standard philosophical answer to that would be to insist that justice judgements are often action-explaining and action-guiding in a way that more general allocation judgements are not. Experiencing an allocation situation as unjust on top of being, more generally speaking, morally wrong may motivate people to take action to alter it: action that they would have refrained from taking merely on the grounds of overall moral wrongness. However, a possible response by the social scientist – anticipated by Swift (1999, pp. 346–8) – would be to say that once you abandon the primacy-of-justice thesis and insist on the separation of the just from the morally right, the predictive value of justice judgements for action diminishes, since this opens up the possibility that judging a state of affairs as unjust will motivate you to no action whatsoever, providing that the situation in question can be justified through some other overriding concern (for instance, as being too costly to remove, perhaps). In other words, justice would not necessarily have motivational force any more and would thus be uninteresting from the predictivist-oriented standpoint of social-science.

This is, incidentally, the kind of response which tends to make philosophers wonder whether predictivism is not seriously defective as a model of social-scientific inquiry. However, even if we refuse to go that far, it does not seem to follow that because justice judgements are not always decisive for action, they are thereby social-scientifically unimportant, even from a predictivist-oriented standpoint. Quite the contrary: the observation that a person's interpreting a state of affairs as involving injustice may or may not lead that person to rise up in protest appears to make it even more important to chart people's allocation decisions from an early age and trace them back to their respective motives. For example, it would be highly interesting to know – in addition to the more specific research questions proposed above – from what age children generally start to distinguish between the criteria of moral rightness and justice: when are they capable of characterizing states of affairs as (a) unjust and morally wrong, (b) unjust but still morally right overall, (c) just but still morally wrong overall and (d) both just and morally right? Only by attending carefully to these distinctions can we begin to understand the role and weight of justice concerns in people's sense of proper or improper distribution and to predict with reasonable accuracy how likely agents are to react in some particular way or another to distribution issues in future scenarios.

If there is any lesson to be drawn from my critique of Damon's stage theory, it would be to remind us of the perils of looking at any single facet of children's moral views, including their alleged views on justice, *in vacuo*, without setting them against the background of their whole cognitive-motivational set. The fundamental virtue of the theory that I go on to consider in the following subsection is, precisely, that it takes the whole set into account.

Hoffman on the Development of Empathy and Justice

'To me, empathy is the spark of human concern for others, the glue that makes social life possible' (Hoffman, 2000, p. 3). The person who wrote those words, Martin L. Hoffman, has studied children's social and emotional development for the last three decades, especially in regard to empathy and its interaction with moral principles such as justice, and has gradually, in a number of journal articles, developed and expounded a theory of moral development which recently culminated in his book, *Empathy and Moral Development: Implications for Caring and Justice* (2000).

The past decades have seen expanded and intensified investigations into the nature and manifestations of children's pro-social reactions. Before delving into Hoffman's own theory, however, a brief overview of the presently received wisdom on such reactions is in order; for rather than producing a series of new empirical findings, Hoffman's contribution lies primarily in extrapolating from already-existing ones and systematizing them into a theoretical whole.

Any current textbook on moral development will tell us that the first rudimentary signs of empathy can be seen in children under one year and, indeed, even in babies as young as two to three days old when they respond to the cry of another nearby infant through mimicry. As the months pass, crying decreases and is replaced by worried attention. By the end of first year of life, there is, however, still no sign of children's deliberately trying to alter the emotions of others: they simply react to them. During the course of the second year of life this changes. Children now start to comfort their distressed peers or siblings: touching, patting or bringing cherished objects to them, in order to alleviate their distress. These expressions of concern seem to coincide in time with children's ability to recognize themselves in a mirror and to begin to refer to themselves as distinct persons. The years of two to four see the advent of a primarily self-centred type of reciprocity, of scratching the back of those who have already scratched yours: returning favours, for example, to 'deserving' persons. It is, however, generally not until after the age of six that we see examples of fully non-egocentric generosity/sharing, based on the recognition of others' needs, and so forth. By that time, psychologists start to speak of the 'altruistic' child: the child that performs pro-social acts motivated by a concern for others without expectations of being repaid (for a fuller account and references to primary sources, see, for example, Shaffer, 2000, ch. 10; Cole and Cole, 1996, ch. 10; Harris, 1989, ch. 2).

What are we to make of these developmental facts? How do they fit into a coherent theoretical picture of empathic moral development? Hoffman delineates five distinct 'stages' in the development of what he calls 'empathic distress', where each stage combines the gains of the previous stage(s). The first two stages encompass (1) the *reactive newborn cry* and (2) *egocentric empathic distress* (late in the first year), where children respond to distress as though they themselves are in distress, but where (2) is distinguishable from (1) in so far as it is more than an automatic response to an unpleasant sound; it is, rather, triggered and later alleviated by the appearance and disappearance of another's distress and can thus be called a precursor of pro-social motivation. Children's first helpful advances to others, during the course of the second year, mark the beginning of Hoffman's stage (3): *quasi-egocentric empathic distress*, in which children realize that someone else is in agony but confuse the other's inner states with their own and only know how to comfort the other through means that would alleviate their own distress. By stage (4), *veridical emphatic distress*, major developments have occurred, as children – late in their second year – learn to distinguish the other's inner states from their own, come closer to feeling what the other is feeling and start to adjust the chosen means of comfort to the other's preferences. Once the children reach stage (5), some time between the ages of five and eight, they start to feel *empathy for another's experience beyond the immediate situati*on, in the context of a larger pattern of life experience, owing for example to the other's chronic illness, economic hardship and so forth. The children now realize that others have lives that may be generally sad or happy and also learn to empathize with an entire group, as opposed to a specific individual (Hoffman, 2000, pp. 6, 69–84).

Importantly for our present purposes (a point to be exploited in the following subsection), Hoffman hypothesizes that beginning with stage (3), children's empathic distress is transformed in part into a feeling of 'sympathetic distress or compassion' for the victim and from then on, we can speak of a fully pro-social motivation (ibid., pp. 87–8). Somewhat confusedly, however, Hoffman chooses to let the single term 'empathic distress' refer to this empathic/sympathetic distress combination (ibid., p. 6), rather than invoking a new term from stage (3) onwards.

After introducing his five stages, Hoffman argues that while empathy's congruence with 'caring' is obvious, empathy is also substantially – if less obviously – congruent with 'justice principles'. Owing to this latter congruence, people will empathize with victims of justice violations and when they do this, they may be aware of both their empathic feelings for the victim and the activated justice principle. The resulting concurrence of empathic affect and moral principle (justice) 'creates a bond between them', a bond that – if all goes well – is strengthened by future concurrences. Thus, the empathy–justice bond transforms justice into an emotionally charged 'hot cognition' (ibid., pp. 14–15 and ch. 9).

It should be noted here that when Hoffman first introduces justice, he seems to think of it primarily in terms of reciprocity or desert ('good deeds should be rewarded, bad acts punished'). For him, such reciprocity is not 'inherently' pro-social, but it becomes pro-social precisely when associated with empathy. When that happens, the abstract justice principle intensifies the observer's empathic distress and transforms it into an empathic feeling of injustice (ibid., p. 16). Thus Hoffman tries to show how the mixture of essentially diverse elements (hot affect and cool principle) can eventually lead to a happy end, namely, a mature moral sense in a well-developed person. This is, admittedly, a somewhat simplified version of the story of the developmental marriage of empathy and justice that Hoffman wants to tell us, but it is still, I hope, one that suffices as a starting point for a critique of Hoffman's theory: a critique that also gives us a chance to fill in some of the missing details.

Critique of Hoffman's Theory

Let me single out for consideration *three* aspects of Hoffman's theory that I think might benefit from some philosophical (conceptual and moral) reflection. They concern (a) the meaning of empathy, (b) the meaning of justice and (c) the nature of the alleged congruence between empathy and justice. While my observations will not, neither individually nor collectively, amount to a sustained, comprehensive assessment of the theory in question, I hope they may help the reader both to appreciate the strength of Hoffman's theoretical approach and to recognize some of its potential weaknesses.

(a) What exactly does the term 'empathy' denote? It seems to me that two different senses can be gleaned from the historic literature on empathy. Sometimes, 'to empathize with someone' means having the capacity to discern/understand another's psychological states, that is, being able to view things from someone else's perspective and imagine how that person feels. This sense of empathy is sometimes referred to as *perspective-taking*. In another and stronger sense, however, 'to empathize with someone' means identifying with another's emotional set-up, that is, in a sense, to feel that person's own feelings. In setting forth his theory, it is plain that Hoffman has in mind this second and stronger sense of empathy: empathy as emotional *identification*. He thus defines an empathic response as the involvement of psychological processes that make a person have feelings congruent with another's situation (ibid., p. 30). In other words, the empathizer does not merely discern them or imagine what they would feel like, but actually *has* the relevant feelings.

Neither in this sense nor in the weaker one can empathy, however, be understood as a specifically moral notion. It may well be *the spark of* moral concern but it is surely not by itself *a moral concern*. The obvious reason for this, which I explained in Section 3.2, is that this same capacity, namely the capacity to discern or even identify with another's suffering, is also a necessary condition for taking pleasure in, rather than bemoaning, that suffering – for example through pure malice or *Schadenfreude*. This is why it is difficult to make sense of the common claim that a child's empathy gradually develops from a pre-moral kind of empathy to a moral (or pro-social) one. Empathy can never be more than a necessary condition of moral concern. Dyed-in-the-wool Kantians might even deny that it is a necessary condition; Goldie does so also for a non-Kantian reason, namely that sympathy can be evoked even when empathy in both of its senses, as perspective-taking and as emotional identification, is impossible: in situations where we, for instance, sympathize with the suffering of a dog or a whale (2000, p. 216). Now I am not a Kantian, and I do believe that sympathy with an animal requires the belief that the animal's suffering is sufficiently similar to ours to be understandable (to us) as suffering. Nevertheless, empathy is only a necessary condition, not a sufficient one, of sympathy or other moral concerns. However much the capacity for empathy develops in depth and scope, the moral aspect does not set in until the empathizer does not merely identify with the suffering but also experiences a *desire to alleviate* it rather than, for example, a sadistic desire to intensify it. Neither can the difference between immature and mature empathy be seen as the difference between a non-emotion (a mere 'feel') and a full-blown emotion, for empathy, in whatever stage of development, is simply not an emotion at all. It does not uniquely pick out a certain cognitive-conative/affective combination, as a genuine emotion does. That it may easily, *qua* psychological capacity, lead to emotions – and, fortunately, often pro-social ones – is another, if no less interesting, story.

These observations about the meaning of empathy are not invoked here as a direct criticism of Hoffman's theory. I am not even sure that he would take exception to any of what has been said so far. The fact is that when he claims that beginning with the third empathy stage, children's empathic distress is transformed in part into a feeling of 'sympathetic distress or compassion' for the victim, and that from then on, we can speak of a fully pro-social motivation (2000, pp. 87–8), it is unclear whether he is referring to a qualitative transformation of one (immature) kind of empathy into another (more mature) kind, or saying, more plausibly – and as I have decided to understand him in the following – that empathy is transformed into sympathy and that it is the latter which yields the fully pro-social motivation. Now sympathy is, I take it, whereas empathy is not, clearly a moral notion; it involves not only the sympathizer's understanding *of* or identification *with* the sufferer's pain but also pain *at* the sufferer's pain, that is, the wish that the latter did not suffer (and additionally, under certain conditions, a decision to take positive action to relieve the suffering). Also, sympathy is an emotion with its own distinctive beliefs and desires. When Mill speaks of the 'tender plant' of noble feelings, so easily killed in youth by want of sustenance (1931, p. 9), as the core of all morality, he is surely thinking of sympathy rather than mere empathy.

All this makes Hoffman's terminological decision to continue, for convenience of exposition, to use the term 'empathic distress' – even after empathy stage (3) – somewhat inconvenient substantively; he should have distinguished more systematically between empathic and sympathetic distress. This is particularly true if my reading of him, as considering sympathetic distress the first pro-social motivation, is correct. As a matter of fact, his book would have benefited enormously from a more careful and fine-grained distinction not only between 'empathic distress' and 'sympathetic distress' but also between the very terms 'empathy' and 'sympathy'. Again on my (sympathetic!) reading, one of the most important parts of Hoffman's theory is his exploration of the relation between sympathy and justice, not between empathy and justice. In what follows, I will take Hoffman at his word, that his terminological decision 'should be understood by the reader' (2000, p. 90), and talk about his view of sympathy, rather than empathy, in relation to justice.

(b) Unfortunately, there is also some terminological confusion surrounding Hoffman's use of the justice concept. As we saw in the previous subsection when the topic was first introduced, the kind of justice which seems to interest Hoffman and is relevant for his developmental theory is justice as desert or, as he calls it, 'reciprocity'. This is later reiterated in his claims that reciprocity pertains to the perception of balance or harmony, for example, earning what one deserves, being rewarded for good deeds and punished for bad (ibid., pp. 228, 241). Elsewhere, however, he suggests various components of justice, such as need, equality, effort, productivity and competence. It is somewhat moot what work this latter idea of justice as a grab-bag of diverse components is supposed to do in Hoffman's theory. He maintains that reciprocity 'underlies' all of them, except equality (ibid., p. 228). That clashes, at least in the case of need, with received philosophical wisdom (see, for example, Miller, 1999). For one thing, sensitivity to others' needs already involves a caring aspect, and this fact, even if not positively fatal to Hoffman's subsequent thesis about the bonding of sympathy and justice, makes it at least less interesting. Let us, at any rate, in order to give Hoffman's bonding thesis the required bite, understand it as a thesis about the bonding of sympathy and justice in the narrower sense of justice as reciprocity/desert (that is, not justice as entitlement, need, equality or anything else).

(c) We are now approaching the crux of my concern about Hoffman's exploration of sympathy and justice and the connection between the two. To begin with, when Hoffman starts to explain in detail the transformation which makes sympathy ensue from empathy, he stresses that sympathy is kindled 'if the victim's pain or discomfort is clearly due to natural causes or is otherwise beyond the victim's control' (2000, p. 95). What Hoffman seems to be describing is the evocation of Aristotle's famous emotion of *eleos*: pain at someone else's undeserved suffering. However, this emotion is best rendered in modern parlance by the term 'compassion' (see my earlier discussion in Section 3.2), and indeed Hoffman seems to use 'compassion' interchangeably with 'sympathy'. That is somewhat worrisome because it leaves no space in Hoffman's theory for the less specific emotion of sympathy – which we might, for clarity's sake, call sympathy *simpliciter*, pain at someone else's suffering as such, whether deserved or not – nor for pity, pain at someone else's deserved suffering. One would have thought that sympathy *simpliciter* was developmentally prior to compassion: that children would learn to feel pain at someone else's suffering before they started to distinguish between the origin of the pain in natural causes, on the one hand, and in the sufferer's own folly, on the other. Indeed, this also seems to be Hoffman's view, for he acknowledges that sympathetic distress may 'also' be evoked if the victim's distress is 'salient' but its cause 'unclear', and that this is what originally happens in the developmental transformation of empathic into sympathetic distress, in the third stage of empathy (2000, p. 95). That is all well and good, but nowhere does Hoffman make clear the distinction between these two emotions (sympathy *simpliciter* versus compassion), nor does he give us any clues as to when children start to differentiate between the two.

This leads us to a more damaging point to be made against Hoffman's discussion of sympathy/compassion and its gradual bonding with justice. To recount and flesh out in more detail his view, Hoffman claims that abstract moral principles, such as justice, learnt in 'cool' didactic contexts (lectures, sermons and so forth), lack motivational force. Sympathy's contribution is to transform them into pro-social hot cognitions: 'cognitive representations charged with empathic affect'. Thus the cognitive preference for reciprocity adds an injustice component to the person's sympathy, while gaining (pro-social) motivational strength from being associated with the emotion. In this way, while sympathy does not make a 'structural contribution' to justice, it may provide a motive for rectifying violations of justice (ibid., pp. 228, 239, 243).

The critical point that I would raise against this developmental story is threefold. First, if the sympathy to which Hoffman refers is actually compassion, it is wrong that the emotion does not make a structural, but merely a motivational, contribution to justice. Compassion is essentially a justice-structured emotion: it involves pain at undeserved suffering, as Hoffman himself has indirectly noted (when talking of the victim's pain being beyond the victim's control). Remove the justice structure from compassion and you remove the emotion. Second, if Hoffman is talking about the bonding of sympathy *simpliciter* and justice, for instance in children at his third empathy stage who may not yet distinguish between pain at deserved suffering and pain at undeserved suffering, it would be singularly implausible to describe that as the bonding of a hot affection with a cool principle. Justice concerns in children do not, as has repeatedly been pointed out in this book, start with lofty insights about abstract principles, or with Humean 'artificial virtues', but arise precisely from the promptings of basic emotions, such as anger and indignation (see Section 3.1). It is difficult to imagine children at Hoffman's third empathy stage cherishing any abstract philosophical principles about justice at all, and it seems reasonable to conclude, therefore, that at that stage, if there is any bonding between sympathy and justice at work – as I believe there is – it is between sympathy, on the one hand, and justice-based *emotions*, on the other: for instance, where sympathy would temper the child's satisfied indignation (pleasure at someone else's deserved misfortune). Third, Hoffman is not very precise on timings here, but if we are to take him at his word that children do not show signs of reciprocity until eight to ten years of age (2000, p. 242), and that justice primarily means reciprocity (see earlier), then it would seem that the bonding process does not actually start until the age of eight and that before that time, children are devoid of justice concerns. But that sounds implausible, to say the least. So either the bonding process described by Hoffman is dispensable (if sympathy means compassion, which is already a justice-based emotion), would be better described in different terms (for instance, as the mutual balancing of emotions), or takes place much too late to constitute a plausible explanation of the origin of justice motivations in children.

All in all, Hoffman's overly rationalist view of justice blinds him to the fact that what is most plausibly set in motion when sympathy begins to interact with justice is a process of balances and trade-offs between different emotions, not a process of an emotion giving motivational force to an abstract principle. In the average child this probably happens from somewhere around the age of two. Moreover, justice-based emotions such as compassion and indignation do not need any external cognitive input for motivating justice: *qua* emotions they are already inherently justice-motivating.

4.2 The Input from Social Psychology: the Belief in a Just World

This section aims to subject to philosophical scrutiny a well-known theory in social psychology, the theory of belief in a just world (hereafter, for brevity's sake, BJW theory) and to explore its implications for justice theory in general and moral education/schooling in particular. I am interested in its implications both in a weak sense, relating to its compatibility or incompatibility with certain philosophical positions, and, even more so, in a strong sense: that is, in questions of BJW theory's substantive relevance to moral and educational issues. The essential question that I would like to be able to answer at the end of this section is this: should parents and teachers discourage or encourage children to believe in a just world, in the sense given to such a belief in this theory?

The BJW theory (or simply 'just-world theory') is one of those empirically based theories of justice which has met with stony silence on the part of most philosophers. Yet it is touted in many current psychology textbooks as one of the key theories in social psychology. Originally the brainchild of the psychologist Melvin J. Lerner, who claims to have spent the greater part of his professional life 'trying to understand why people care about justice' (2002, p. 10), this theory has, over the years, generated a formidable body of literature in which Lerner himself still occupies a central role, although various researchers on both sides of the Atlantic have given further form and substance to his ideas. As we shall soon see, BJW theory may have various moral and educational implications, but references to those implications, or to BJW theory in general, are almost non-existent in the writings of not only most leading moral and political philosophers, but also philosophers of education.

To start with as bare an outline of the theory as possible – to be fleshed out in what follows – the theory maintains that people have a basic, intrinsically motivated desire to believe that the world is a just place and that this so-called 'justice motive' is somehow rooted in the near universal, emotionally driven, childhood realization that immediate gratification of desires can and should be delayed in favour of long-term gain. The force of this internalized mechanism is allegedly such as to induce people to engage in wide-ranging pro-social activities in order to bring perceived unjust states of affairs into line with the desired ideal of justice or, alternatively, to engage in cognitive distortions in order to explain away unjust states of affairs as fundamentally just. Three caveats are in order at this point to avoid possible misunderstandings: (a) The alleged belief in a just world not only involves the belief that the world *should be* just – which, however commendable, would count as somewhat platitudinous from a moral point of view (who would not want that?) – but also the more controversial belief that the world at present *is*, in some sense, essentially just. (b) Additionally, it should be noted that the theoretical claim is not that everybody believes equally in a just world; despite the near universality of the justice motive, it is supposed to vary in strength between individuals. BJW theorists have, thus, devised scales for measuring the relative strength of the motive in different persons and groups (see further below) and for exploring its relations to other cherished beliefs and concerns. (c) Finally, BJW theory must not be confounded with the nativist position in the natural-law tradition, with which some readers may be acquainted, that postulates an innate and universally valid *Rechtsgefühl*: a sense of proper law. The latter is more concerned with the workings of certain societal institutions than is the alleged belief in the world as a just place, and also has more to do with how things should ideally be rather than how they actually are (see (a) above).

The belief in a just world has been found to cause, or at least correlate with, various other psychological states, beliefs and dispositions. To take but a few examples, strong believers in a just world report more life satisfaction than weak believers, they are healthier mentally and have more self-esteem (see references in Bierhoff, 2002, p. 191). They also respond with less frustration to their own negative outcomes and are less likely to blame others when things go wrong for themselves (Hafer and Correy, 1999). Additionally, in a school setting, pupils with a strong belief in justice feel less stressed in the classroom, less pressed towards achievement and generally exhibit less school aversion. They have more trust in their teachers and tend to interpret their school experiences in meaningful and positive ways (Dalbert and Maes, 2002). Finally, strong justice believers react more acutely to perceived injustices: either, as has already been mentioned, by acting pro-socially on behalf of sufferers of injustice or, more harmfully perhaps, by cognitively reconstructing the relevant situations in such a way that they appear just. More will be said about that latter possibility in the next subsection.

BJW theory is a theory in social psychology, yet its potential relevance for concerns typically addressed in other distinct literatures is clear. For instance, readers will not have failed to notice how philosophically salient many of its implications might be. From the point of view of moral and political philosophy, BJW theory is potentially useful in understanding the nature and origins of justice, and, at least for those of us sympathetic to Miller's contention that 'empirical evidence should play a significant role in justifying a normative theory of justice' (1999, p. 51), also provide grist for the mill of substantive theorizing about justice (cf. my earlier discussion in Section 1.2). From the point of view of philosophy of education, or, more specifically, its sub-branch moral education, interesting questions arise about whether the belief in a just world – to the extent that it is responsive to coaching – should be encouraged and inculcated in children by parents and educators, given the fact that it apparently has a positive impact on their achievement in and attitudes towards school and, even more importantly, helps them cope better with life in general. After all, the recent invocation of 'emotional intelligence' as an educational goal in many Western countries and, *inter alia*, as a topic to be pursued in ethics and life-skills classes at school has, no doubt, had more to do with the proposed link between EQ and general life success than with the more elevated goal of creating morally and emotionally developed moral agents. If BJW works as soundly as EQ in this respect, why not go for it too?

In light of the much-discussed conceptual distinction between justice as desert and justice as entitlement, the obvious first question to ask about BJW theory is in precisely *what kind of* justice are strong believers, more than weak believers, supposed to believe? Unfortunately, the answer to this is not entirely clear. In the first place, BJW literature contains, in general, disturbingly little reference to the historical literature on justice – and offers (with the exception of Feather, 1999, 2002, who takes a somewhat different tack) scant evidence of acquaintance with it. And in the second place, Lerner has chosen to employ 'entitlement' as the umbrella term of BJW theory, a term that is supposed to cover equity, fairness, desert, and procedural as well as retributive justice (Lerner, 1981, pp. 12–13; see also Feather's critique of Lerner's terminology, 1999, p. 25. Feather not only distinguishes clearly between desert and entitlement, he also presents a formidable empirically based theory of people's understanding of the former, as we saw in Section 2.3.)

Now, this terminological decision by Lerner is problematic for two reasons. On the one hand, it seems to inflate the concept of entitlement beyond good sense, as well as being out of line with the general philosophical consensus on what that notion implies. On the other hand, it detracts from the philosophical significance of the whole idea of a belief in a just world by making it potentially susceptible to simple factual errors. For instance, if a person living under a tyrannical regime, where trials had been abolished and crime or innocence decided merely on the dictator's whim, claimed to believe in a just world as a world where entitlements (in Lerner's wide sense) are honoured – and such entitlements would *ex hypothesi* have to accommodate entitlements in the more narrow, philosophically relevant sense, including the moral right to (fair) trials – the person could simply be written off as deluded or duped. It seems evident, however, from the essence of Lerner's writings, that the belief in a just world is not a simple factual belief but rather a complex evaluative one. In other words, mere non-evaluative facts, such as the proportion of criminals apprehended and tried in a given society, cannot resolve the issue of the reasonableness or unreasonableness of the belief in question.

In fact, choosing 'entitlement' rather than, say, 'fairness' as the umbrella term seems for Lerner to be a matter of mere convenience, for he thinks that although 'there may be slight differences in nuances' in the way in which people construe different judgements of justice, 'it is probably safe to consider them all equivalent in terms of social-psychological processes' (1981, p. 13). Does Lerner, then, mean that all the subtle distinctions drawn by philosophers over the centuries are either wrong or irrelevant? That would be an uncharacteristically frivolous view by an academic of Lerner's standing. More plausibly, Lerner might be taken to mean that despite the theoretical value of such distinctions in philosophical or political debate, they are irrelevant from the point of view of recording laypeople's opinions about the world as a just or unjust place since those distinctions are not part of their intellectual repertoire. That view, however, may also be questioned. Feather (2002), for example, has recently shown how nurses are acutely aware of the desert–entitlement distinction, explained above, when reflecting upon conflicts between their own conceptions of the responses which different patient groups (schizophrenic patients and personality-disorder patients) deserve on the one hand and are entitled to on the other.

In spite of their reliance on Lerner's original work, most recent writings about BJW theory seem, deliberately or not, to be moving away from his wide and over-inflated conception of justice towards a more narrow one, in which the justice belief in question is construed as being that 'individuals get what they deserve and deserve what they get' (Reichle and Schmitt, 2002, p. 127). A person who believes in a just world could, then, more helpfully than in Lerner's formulation, claim that even under conditions where legal justice (*qua* entitlements) does not reign, the world is still essentially just since bad people will somehow get their comeuppance in the end and good people their deserved good rewards. This narrower conception of justice in BJW theory, makes it arguably more, rather than less, philosophically topical. What, for example, explains (psychologically) and justifies or fails to justify (philosophically) children's common belief in the 'good guys' and the 'bad guys' eventually getting what they deserve? Or – to take a question on which the post-Feinbergian jury among philosophers is still out (see Section 2.1) – how can we strike a balance between the claims of entitlement, on the one hand, and desert, on the other hand, when the two part company? What is, in such circumstances, *the* just state of affairs?

Philosophers often complain about the lack of conceptual rigour in social-science research and sometimes with good reason, as we have seen above. I hope it will not be deemed an example of the opposite error, namely the alleged conceptual fetishism of philosophers, to maintain that the narrower understanding of justice in BJW theory is more theoretically serviceable than Lerner's own conception. If the narrower understanding is true, however, some amendments of the scale most commonly employed to measure the strength of people's beliefs in a just world seem to be required. Rubin and Peplau's (1975, pp. 69–70) so-called Just World Scale is a self-report instrument where respondents indicate the extent to which they agree or disagree with each of twenty statements by circling a number on a six-point scale, ranging from Disagree (1) to Agree (6). Of those twenty statements, sixteen seem to focus on deserts in the traditional philosophical sense, statements such as 'I've found that a person rarely deserves the reputation he has' (no. 1), 'People who get "lucky breaks" have usually earned their good fortune' (no. 2), 'Students almost always deserve the grades they get in school' (no. 6), 'By and large, people deserve what they get' (no. 11), 'People who meet with misfortune have often brought it on themselves' (no. 18) and so forth. Four statements, however, concern time-and-place-relative entitlements and should, I submit, be omitted in order to make the scale more valid as an instrument measuring belief in the world as a place where people generally get what they deserve: 'It is a common occurrence for a guilty person to get off free in American courts' (no. 5), 'It is rare for an innocent man to be wrongly sent to jail' (no. 9), 'In professional sports, many fouls and infractions never get called by the referee' (no. 10) and 'It is often impossible for a person to receive a fair trial in the USA' (no. 17). A person could easily agree with (5), (10) and (17), and disagree with (9) while believing that people in our world normally get what they deserve in the end. Surprisingly, I rarely see doubts about the validity of this widely used instrument being entertained by those who have adopted a desert conception of justice in BJW theory, which perhaps indicates that, even for the majority of those theorists, it may not yet be sufficiently clear what kind of justice beliefs are being measured. Claudia Dalbert (1999), however, constitutes a notable exception here: she has (with her colleagues) developed two new scales for assessing *personal* belief in a just world, and *general* belief in a just world, respectively, beliefs which she claims must be explored separately. It is hoped that BJW theorists are slowly realizing that Rubin and Peplau's commonly used scale is both flawed and outdated.

Now BJW theorists tell us a specific developmental story about the internalization of the justice motive, a process which can be traced back to early childhood. We are, incidentally, told in just as much detail what this process (originally) *is not*, namely the process of learning that it is to one's own advantage to apply standards of justice, as we are told what it *is*, namely developing a genuine concern for justice itself. BJW theorists are thus eager to distance their theory from the economic rational-choice model of moral internalization, outlined in Section 4.1, according to which children learn to believe in justice in order to attain some other goals both prior and external to justice. What is missing in such a model of human beings as profit-maximizers is, so we are told, 'the normative, prescriptive core' of the justice concept: 'Justice is an ought, a moral imperative for social life. It is not a means for attaining personal aims, but an end in itself' (Montada, 2002, p. 44). Justice judgements are at bottom non-egoistic, rather than egoistic, automatic rather than trained, compelling rather than conditional, and they emerge spontaneously from basic cognitions rather than being derived from them later (see, for example, Lerner, 2002, p. 19). To describe this essential nature of the justice motive, different BJW theorists use different phrases, all of which come down to more or less the same thing: the motive is a 'categorical', 'primary' or 'primordial' one.

There is good reason for BJW theorists to set their view of moral internalization in sharp relief to older theories, especially the economic one. The dominant idea there is, as we saw earlier, of the idealized *homo economicus* who is motivated basically by self-interest when interacting with others, but who gradually codifies a justice system for mutual benefits – a system that each person is, however, more than ready to abandon as soon as it does not satisfy his or her self-serving interests any longer. These theories differ as to the conditionality of the adherence to the 'social contract' about justice: some claim that as long as the original conditions remain more or less unchanged, people do not question the need to respect justice; others (for example, so-called 'equity theories') hold that the terms of justice are constantly being negotiated and manipulated as each agent tries to enhance his or her social power and get every edge possible in an ever-continuing war of all against all. Lerner thinks that these differences matter less than the fact that all such rationalist models are open to the same objections: one specific and one general. The specific objection is that there are various situations in which most people are motivated to do 'the just thing' irrespective of any personal gain, be it short-term or long-term: for example, when we feel that children or the 'stricken' justly deserve to have their needs met. The general objection is that people do not normally think of justice (*qua* getting what they deserve) as a secondary resource, an instrumental device to facilitate the acquisition of other more basic resources, but rather as being itself the most 'desired resource'. For, Lerner claims, according to the available evidence, 'there is no amount of desired resources – money, prestige, power, and so on. – that is sufficient to be considered an acceptable fate, if it is less than people believe they deserve' (1981, p. 21).

To enlarge our insight into exactly what the justice motive is for BJW theorists, as opposed to what it is not, it is interesting to note that they typically acknowledge the existence of a contract-driven, 'received' (didactically learned) motive to *adhere to* justice principles. They also assume that children's rational processes play a large part in shaping their behaviour. They do, however, believe that such processes are radically altered very early in the child's moral development, and that the social contract to behave justly supervenes on an emotionally driven 'emergent' (naturally learned) motive to *believe in* a just world. The key explanatory concept here is that of a 'personal contract'. To quote Lerner himself:

> My best guess was based on the work of Freud and others who had observed that children typically learn to delay indulging the immediate gratification of their

> desires and instead engage in time and tension binding so that they can ultimately obtain more desirable outcomes. In order to do that, I thought, the child would have to participate in the more or less conscious self-dialogue of making a promise to him- or herself that the anticipated delayed outcomes would, in fact, occur, and that they would be worth the costs of both the sacrifice of immediate pleasures and the necessary additional efforts. In order to adopt this 'reality principle', the rational part of the child controls the impulses to seek immediate gratification by adopting what I term the 'personal contract'. (2002, p. 11)

The Freudian element of Lerner's 'best guess' is pellucidly clear, but as he acknowledges (ibid., p. 13), it also draws on the ideas of Gestalt psychology and – more significantly – Mead's symbolic interactionism. One would not have been surprised to find a further explanation of the personal contract in terms of its 'adaptive value', but for some reason BJW theorists generally avoid employing the language of evolutionary theory.

Three elements seem to be central to the process of the personal contract and its ensuing justice motive: first, the child's early visualization of the *cause–effect* link (the notion that a certain input will reliably produce a corresponding output); second, the idea of *desert* coming to symbolize and represent the relationship between immediate deprivation (cause) and subsequent satisfaction (effect); and third, the *transference* of this symbolization to other people inhabiting the same world: 'Were we to believe that they do not [also] get what they deserve, our confidence that we will get what we deserve would be shaken'. Thus the 'justice motive is born' (Batson, 2002, p. 93).

The Strange Case of Victim Derogation – and the Theory Assessed

A plausible corollary of the justice motive, as described in BJW theory, would be to induce people to alleviate the troubles of, or provide some sort of compensation to, those suffering under an injustice – or, at least, in the case of desert-loving children and others who through lack of resources are unable to take positive action, to facilitate the experience of compassion for the undeserved suffering of the victims. Lerner admits that this is, indeed, often the case; such emotions and ensuing pro-social actions frequently do occur. Equally frequently, however, believers in a just world are said to react to contrary evidence through psychological rationalizations such as blaming victims for their misfortunes and derogating their characters, identifying them as bad or unworthy persons (Hafer, 2002, p. 109). This phenomenon, referred to in BJW theory as 'victim derogation', was first introduced by Lerner as a theoretical 'hunch': an inference from the idea of belief in desert being a harmony-balancing psychological mechanism, a mechanism based on a desire strong enough to call for the maintenance or restoration of the envisioned harmony through either fair means or foul. In Lerner's analysis, witnesses to a victim's undeserved suffering are likely to reject the victim in proportion to the degree of injustice associated with the victim's fate or, more accurately perhaps, in proportion to the degree of difficulty involved in restoring real justice to the victim. Lerner seems to have left it mostly to his disciples to provide direct evidence for this 'hunch'; one of those recalls the 'excitement generated' by the first set of experiments demonstrating the reality of victim derogation (Darley, 2002, p. 314). That 'excitement' seems to have gradually eclipsed their expectations of strong justice believers ever batting an eyelid – let alone raising a hand in help – when confronted with cases of undeserved outcomes; the emphasis in BJW rhetoric is now all on the alleged rationalizing inference warrant: 'if the world is such that people get what they deserve, then if they get a positive or negative outcome, they must have deserved it' (ibid.).

A recent anthology by BJW theorists, dedicated to Lerner as the theory's founding father (Ross and Miller, 2002), contains accounts of studies aimed at confirming his 'hunch' about victim derogation. One set of studies describes the reactions of respondents to an edited television news clip portraying a victim of robbery and physical assault. Strong BJW believers (as measured by Rubin and Peplau's 1975 scale) were more willing to 'derogate the victim's character' by seeing him/her as an irresponsible and careless person (Hafer, 2002). Another study is based on questionnaires, answered by German university students and groups of employed citizens, about differences in the quality of life between (West) Germans and people in developing countries, Turkish migrant workers living in (West) Germany, and unemployed (West) Germans. The participants who 'rationalized' or 'downplayed' the lower quality of life of the disadvantaged groups as partly self-inflicted (owing to lack of effort, rather than simply to bad luck or adverse treatment by others) turned out to have stronger beliefs in a just world than those who did not (Reichle and Schmitt, 2002). Similar, older study results seem to abound (see, for example, Rubin and Peplau, 1975). What exactly we should make of those results is another story, to which I will return later.

At this point let me just note that social scientists, who typically claim to be non-evaluatively recording people's beliefs and dispositions, refraining from any moral verdicts about the results – including the rationality and/or moral justifiability of belief in a just world – seem to be quite willing to cast off the mantle of neutrality when it comes to the case of victim derogation. Rubin and Peplau state bluntly, as their 'personal view', that it is based on a factual error (1975, p. 66). Others, who do not reveal their preferences as directly, still see it as some kind of (rational or moral) malfunction. This can be divined from their interpretations of the available data and the conceptual framework in which those interpretations are cast. For example, the 'hard fact' of the matter here seems to be, simply, that people who believe in a just world, according to the given scale, are more likely than others to think that the victims of certain negative outcomes (muggings, economic hardships and so on) are at least partly to blame for their own sufferings. By describing the victims as 'innocent', as the researchers frequently do in their interpretations (see, for example, Hafer, 2002, p. 115) although this label does not figure in the original questionnaires or study scenarios, they unambiguously give the reader to understand that strong justice believers are factually or morally wrong. Moreover, by terming this attribution of responsibility or blame to the victims 'victim derogation', the researchers have reinforced this impression by choosing a value-laden term that conveys the sense of illicit scapegoating. If person *P* is really blameworthy, we would not normally describe a negative attitude towards *P* as *derogatory* (unless the derogation were seriously out of proportion to the blame); calling *R*'s attitude towards *P* 'derogatory' is a way of saying that *R* is putting down a *blameless P*. It might be objected that the social scientists in question have simply operationalized the term 'derogatory' and given it a (new) non-value-laden meaning. After all, their use of the term does not *by itself* exclude the possibility that the respondents may rationalize (and even satisfactorily justify) their described attitudes towards the victims. However, as I noted above, there is ample subsidiary evidence of the scientists' conceptualization of those attitudes as a rational and/or a moral malfunction: for example, the common references in the BJW literature to 'innocent victims' being stigmatized by strong just-world believers.

I have, in fact, no complaints as such about social scientists engaging in normative considerations, as long as those are as well argued for as the non-normative considerations; I am merely pointing out that in this case of so-called victim derogation, normative labels of 'innocent victims' and 'misconceived culprits' seem to be quickly and unhesitatingly invoked – without any recourse to arguments – by the very same people who otherwise take great care and pride in avoiding such labels.

The aim of this section was to subject BJW theory to philosophical scrutiny and to explore some of its moral and educational implications. The philosophical relevance of those implications hinges in strong measure, of course, on the question of whether the theory is true or at least plausible. For a complex theory of this sort, however, that question hardly admits of a simple, unilateral answer. Let me in the following single out for further consideration a few aspects of the theory, (a)–(d), and then offer some concluding suggestions.

(a) The developmental story, told by Lerner, about the internalization of the 'justice motive' seems to have been well received in psychological circles and appears plausible to a non-psychologist such as the present author. It is, to be sure, at least a reasonable guess that children's early interest in deserved outcomes comes about through their learning to postpone the gratification of their own desires to a later 'time of reckoning'. This would, among other things, help to explain the emotional underpinnings of justice *qua* human virtue, pointed out by a number of philosophers from Aristotle onwards, as we saw in the foregoing chapter. Through a plausible psychological explanation of the genealogy of at least one facet of morality, BJW theory would then offer indirect evidence for a naturalist moral theory – rooted, such as Mill's utilitarianism or Hume's moral outlook, in the existence of certain 'natural feelings' – and against a purely formalist moral theory, be it of a rationalist or a proceduralist kind. After all, naturalists typically believe that psychological facts about human beings help to justify not only morality as a whole but also specific moral claims.

All that said, it must be admitted that BJW theorists have not given much consideration to alternative – in particular, social-learning – explanations of the origin of the justice motive (I am here referring to the justice motive as based on a primary 'personal contract', as opposed to the secondary, supervening, 'social contract'; the role of social learning in constructing the latter is helpfully discussed in various articles in Montada and Lerner, 1998). These theorists seem to take it for granted that all the lessons learnt through fairy tales, religious myths and soap operas, about people getting what they deserve in the end, merely reinforce rather than create the primary belief children have in due rewards. Furthermore, relativist and postmodern misgivings about the belief in a just world being a historically located, culture-bound phenomenon – for example, an outgrowth of a socio-historically relative Protestant work ethic, or Enlightenment illusions about progress – have not been sufficiently answered. As with many of Lerner's original 'hunches' and 'guesses', the idea of a personal contract as an anthropological constant evidently lends itself more easily to confirmations than to potential Popperian refutations.

(b) Apart from adding some backbone to the naturalist view of morality, it is difficult to assess what contribution BJW theory can make to moral/political theory, in general, and to the justice debate, in particular. The main problem here is the theory's conceptual laxity and the failure of its proponents to take account of the underlying philosophical issues. While the conflation of justice with desert can perhaps be redeemed by rereading the theory as being only about the belief in ultimate deserts (see earlier), there is also some confusion abroad in the theory about the role of justice in moral development. Some BJW theorists speak as if they have discovered the key to moral internalization in general, not only to justice (or desert) internalization, and thus replicate the famous Kohlbergian error of collapsing all judgements about morality into judgements about justice.

There is a long tradition in philosophy, harking back at least to the thirteenth-century Franciscan thinker Duns Scotus, of distinguishing between two kinds of justice motivation: an intrinsic affection for justice (*affectio iustitiae*) and an affection for advantage (*affectio commodi*) which can, indirectly, become an extrinsic motivation for justice (Scotus, 1968, d. 2, q. 2). The dualism of the *intrinsic* and the *extrinsic* has, however, come under polemical fire, in psychology as well as philosophy, in recent times, and so has another distinction on which Lerner evidently relies in his separation of the child's primary 'personal contract' from the subsequent 'social contract': the distinction between a person's *experiential system*, which houses articulable but unarticulated construals or quasi-beliefs, and a person's *rational system*, which is the home of fully fledged beliefs (see Feather, 1999, pp. 8–11; for a critique, see Kristjánsson, 2002, pp. 30–36). In default of any critical engagement with theoretical issues when such problematic distinctions are invoked, it is, I repeat, not entirely clear what to make of the potential substantive contribution of BJW theory to moral theory or even, more specifically, to the lively ongoing debate among philosophers and psychologists about the emotional foundations of justice and other moral virtues.

(c) The question which might seem of most practical importance is whether the belief in a just world *can* and *should* be encouraged through moral education in the home and at school. Before that question can be answered, however, some remaining puzzles need to be solved.

BJW theorists talk about the justice motive as an 'anthropological constant' (Montada, 2002, p. 56). Nevertheless, it emerges from their own research that the belief in a just world, as measured by the prevailing instrument, varies across individuals (and perhaps also across cultures and social contexts). We are not given any explanation of such differences. Why does the alleged 'personal contract' work better for some than for others? Has it something to do with the different psychological make-up of different children during the early acquisition of the justice motive, or with its subsequent stimulation/repression during upbringing? Can parents and teachers do something to discourage or encourage the strength and direction of this motive?

Even if that last question were, in principle, answered in the affirmative, the earlier question remains of whether the justice motive *should* be discouraged or encouraged. Social scientists typically fight shy of moral evaluations of their gathered data although such evaluations sometimes shine through, as in the case of the standard interpretation of 'victim derogation'. As we saw above, strong belief in a just world seems to have beneficial implications for students' school work and school attitudes and, indeed, for their self-image. Are those later offset by the pernicious implications of inducing young people to derogate innocent victims and to write off as self-inflicted all of the trials and tribulations people endure? If that is the case, the remedy of trying to stimulate a child's belief in a just world in order to enhance self-esteem and school achievement may be worse than the disease.

(d) It has long seemed to me that the implication of *victim derogation* is the Achilles' heel of BJW theory. I referred earlier to this as 'the strange case of victim derogation'. It is, indeed, strange in that most current accounts of moral development presuppose that children's natural disposition to empathy and sympathy is the cornerstone of their progressing moral sense (see, for example, Damon, 1988; Hoffman, 2000). On an Aristotelian account, as I have repeatedly stressed, this original disposition gradually distinguishes itself into, on the one hand, compassion – pain at others' undeserved suffering – and, on the other, pity – pain at others' deserved suffering. According to the recent emphasis in BJW theory on victim derogation as the typical response to perceived injustice, however, the fount of compassion in strong justice believers seems to dry up; they can, at best, feel some kind of condescending pity when witnessing other people's hardships. Given the role that compassion normally plays in naturalist moral theories, strong justice believers become, on this reading, strangely immoral creatures. It seems, indeed, that the moral and educational implications of a belief in a just world could not have any real substantive appeal unless it were possible to interpret the case of victim derogation in a more favourable light.

What can we then say about the educational implications of BJW theory? One would perhaps, at first glance, be tempted to give a rather pessimistic answer to that question. Evidently, little effort has been made by the BJW theorists themselves to draw out any relevant educational conclusions. And in default of an answer to the fundamental pedagogical question of whether the psychology behind the belief in a just world admits of external regulation in the first place, educators might have some reason to shrug off BJW theory as a body of research that, from an educational perspective, is opaque and inconclusive. Such a response would, however, be somewhat out of line with recent Aristotelian-inspired optimism about emotional control and redirection (see, for example, Kristjánsson, 2002, ch. 6). Surely something can be done in children's upbringing to regulate the strength and direction of the 'justice motive', as can be done with other parts of their emotional make-up. Another pessimistic response – in a more substantial sense of 'pessimistic' – would be to say that given the fact that the belief in a just world involves a strong tendency to unsavoury 'victim derogation', the natural growth of this belief should be systematically discouraged by parents and teachers. Moreover, the belief in question – the sceptic could add – is not only immoral but foolish; we only need to turn on the next TV news programme to realize that fact, which is why the gut reaction of many of my university colleagues, when they first hear of the results of BJW research, is to write off the apparently vast number of strong justice believers as fools. After all, the best thing that BJW theorists themselves say about the belief in a just world is that it a 'positive illusion' (Dalbert, 1999, p. 80).

These pessimistic responses might, however, be somewhat too quick. One needs, I believe, to be wary in general of any interpretation of extensive social-science research into people's beliefs that considers the respondents immoral or foolish/deluded creatures. A person's belief in a just world is, morally and existentially, a significant belief that must be understood and evaluated against the background of his or her general value system. The just-world belief is, as Dalbert correctly observes, an indicator of a fundamental 'world theory' (ibid., p. 80). This is why I think there would be good reason to step back a little at this point and ask how children and adults who score high on the BJW scale would *justify* their belief in a just world, given their more fundamental world views. As far as I know, no questionnaire has been devised for testing that. In the Eastern parts of the world, one might expect to see references to karmic powers at work, indicating belief in a universal, spiritual governing force that ultimately delivers deserts in this world.

Supernatural explanations of that kind would, I presume, be less likely in the West, where religious and quasi-religious beliefs inform everyday attitudes to a lesser degree than in the East and where the predominant religions are also non-karmic. Notably, the idea of 'cosmic justice', defended in Section 2.1, obviously need not imply the idea of 'karmic justice': that good people will get good rewards in the end and bad people bad rewards, the moral qualities of their actions somehow having the causal power to award persons their deserts (on the latter notion, see French, 2001, pp. 71ff.). The answer that I would expect to hear more often in the West is that 'virtue pays off in the end'. The belief in a just world is, after all, essentially a belief in just deserts, and desert is arguably best understood – as was the message of Chapter 2 – as a matter of a fit between, on the one hand, certain outcomes and, on the other, specific moral qualities and actions of individuals which are generally held in high regard because they are moral.

Hypothesizing that the so-called belief in a just world is simply, at least in our part of the world, an instantiation of the belief that virtue pays off in the end may help us find a more subtle way of interpreting cases of 'victim derogation' than by radically assuming that strong justice believers conclude, unhesitatingly, that all sufferers of injustices must deserve their sufferings. The idea would rather be that strong justice believers doubt more than others – and often reasonably so – whether the victims of the described hardships have exercised their moral virtues to the full. Was the mugging victim perhaps not *careful* enough in wandering through that park at night? Were the unemployed people lacking perhaps a little in *diligence* and *perseverance*? And so on. If this 'modest' interpretation of the attitude of strong justice believers towards the described (and notably often, in research scenarios, *under*-described) victims were more correct than the 'radical' one of recent BJW theory, then one would expect strong justice believers to react with even stronger compassion than weak believers towards victims in fully described cases, where the victim's moral character had obviously nothing to do with his or her plight. Tellingly so, this seems to be precisely the case. In a study where a car accident was sufficiently described such that the blame fell only on driver *A*, but driver *B* was the one who suffered injuries, strong justice believers evaluated *B* more favourably than did weak justice believers; the former reserved their wrath for driver *A* and 'showed extra sympathy for the victim by contrast' (Rubin and Peplau, 1975, p. 72). This also shows that it is, at least partly, misleading to refer to the belief in a just world – as commentators often do – as a 'conservative' belief. If by 'conservative' we simply mean 'tending to the maintenance or reinforcement of the *status quo*', strong just-world beliefs seem, by contrast, often to call for change, in particular radical shifts from existing practices of moral non-commitment and emotional apathy.

Let us thus suppose that the recorded belief in a just world is simply one expression of a much broader belief: the belief that the locus of control for a person's 'fate' is largely in that person's hands and that virtue generally brings happiness. The belief in a just world, then, starts to sound agreeably Aristotelian. While Aristotle did not share Plato's optimism about virtue's invulnerability to bad luck, he believed that virtue is conducive to, and constitutive of, well-being and that although 'great misfortunes' may 'oppress and spoil' the blessedness of the virtuous, they will at least accept those with equanimity and good temper, and never become wholly miserable (Aristotle, 1985, pp. 25–6 [1100b–1101a]). Note that I said 'agreeably Aristotelian' above, for much of contemporary naturalist moral thought – in particular, of course, the currently popular virtue ethics – is more or less directly derived from Aristotle.

I have now presented a certain suggestion about the possible grounding of the belief in strong justice in a more general moral outlook, a suggestion which explains, *inter alia*, why strong justice believers may, reasonably, be more wary than others of accepting that people are at the mercy of external forces as an explanation of their hardships, although strong justice believers will be more compassionate than weak justice believers towards those persons once the fact of pure bad luck has been established. Let it be clear that I have not simply – as a possible objector might complain – substituted the strong justice motive with another, more appealing, motivational belief. Rather, I have tried to restore and reconstruct the possible reasonableness of the belief in a just world. I have done so, not by offering a logical analysis of that belief in BJW theory, but rather with a suggestion about its moral genealogy. The suggested moral grounding of the belief in question turns out to be in full accordance with leading strands in contemporary moral thought, rather than being some kind of a moral or factual aberration. I admit, however, that this is simply a 'hunch', resting on theoretical considerations rather than empirical evidence, since the latter is evidently not available at present.

To recapitulate, the 'essential question' that I posed at the beginning of the present section was this: should parents and teachers discourage or encourage children to believe in a just world, in the sense given to such a belief in BJW theory? If my hunch is correct, the answer is that adherents of virtue ethics and other Aristotelian-inspired moral outlooks (such as Millian utilitarianism) would be well advised to try to *encourage* the belief in question. This is obviously a doubly conditional answer, depending on both the plausibility of my hunch and on one's adherence to a broadly Aristotelian naturalist ethics (or even triply so, if we also consider the condition of whether such a belief *can*, in fact, be encouraged). As we have seen above, however, without adding some normative and factual interpretative conditions of this kind, BJW theory remains opaque and unilluminating, both morally and educationally.

4.3 A Utilitarian Justification of Desert and Desert-Based Emotions

However much the wiser we may be about the nature of desert-based emotions after Chapter 3 and about their psychological origins after the first two sections of the present chapter, and however much we might welcome the recent philosophical trend towards exploring justice via desert-based emotions and productive intercourse with the social sciences, no moral justification of those emotions has yet been provided. As I have pointed out before, it could be that the desert-based emotions themselves are morally neutral, or even immoral, and that there are other (perhaps institutional) aspects of justice which make it all-in-all virtuous. We still need, in other words, that independent moral justification of desert and desert-based emotions called for at the end of Chapter 3. After all, Strawson did not morally justify desert-based or other 'reactive attitudes', although he did posit them as 'essentially natural human reactions', the absence of which would be practically inconceivable in this world (1962, pp. 195–7). Thus questions still linger as to whether desert-based emotions are rational and morally proper, as well as to what extent they should be allowed to shape our actions and allocation decisions.

The odds may seem to be stacked against the enterprise of justifying the experience of desert-based emotions – and, more generally, the salience of desert in distributive justice – from a utilitarian standpoint. Despite the fact that empirical research has found a kind of truncated utilitarianism (maximizing total welfare subject to a floor restraint on individual welfare) much more popular among the general public than Rawls's 'difference principle' (Frolich and Oppenheimer, 1992), received wisdom still views justice, in general, and desert, in particular, as hard cases for the utilitarian. Liberals, for instance, commonly take heart in the contention that however problematic desert is for them, utilitarians have even more difficulty accommodating desert within their moral theory. Nevertheless, I will not be deterred by the received wisdom here but, rather, take on the challenge in what follows of articulating and defending a utilitarian justification of desert in distributive justice. I first argue against the liberal partners-in-crime manoeuvre by showing that while there may be ways of accommodating desert concerns in liberal theory, this cannot, in the view of liberals themselves, be done without considerable cost to the ideals that are closest to their hearts. In contrast, I suggest that a deceptively simple utilitarian defence of desert can be made to work. Utility need not, as Fred Feldman claims in his somewhat tortuous defence of desert, be 'adjusted' or 'discounted' for desert as a separate intrinsic value; as Mill pointed out, desert is, in fact, one of the essential goods conducive to the sole intrinsic value: utility (or pleasure). The area in which utilitarianism is supposed to encounter one of its severest trials, is, I propose, on closer inspection fertile ground for utilitarians. Finally, in this section, I attempt to surmount various possible objections that might be raised against my 'deceptively simple' defence.

The standard liberal position on distributive justice is to have no truck with desert. On that point neo-liberals concur with libertarians and liberal egalitarians. Even a liberal thinker as highly critical of recent trends in liberal thought as Susan Hurley refuses, in her recent book, to make any room for distribution in accordance with desert: an option she finds 'deeply unattractive' (2003, p. 202). The reasons behind this liberal antipathy to desert are well known and were summarized in three theses in Section 2.1: the plurality-of-the-good thesis, the non-responsibility thesis and the equal-worth thesis.

Notwithstanding these three theses, it might be worth considering whether making some allowance for desert – or, more specifically perhaps, for people's desert-based reactive attitudes – could help lead liberalism out of the political isolation about which some of its advocates are concerned (see Section 3.1). The question of whether a theory that is at least in some minimal sense sensitive to desert can be derived from liberal theory is one which I will only skirt. Let me mention here, though, that in a somewhat surprising twist, Martha Nussbaum, one of the staunchest opponents of the liberal plurality-of-the-good thesis, has recently gestured towards Rawlsian liberalism by acknowledging that her objectivist human-capabilities view might be reconcilable with a basic political form of liberalism (2000). Liberals, moreover, may overestimate the extent to which a strict conception of personal responsibility underwrites desert. It is common for a person to deserve an outcome without being responsible for it (the villain may deserve to be crushed in a landslide, to revert to an earlier example, although he is not responsible for the landslide). Desert only requires, in most cases, as I argued in Section 2.3, a minimal Aristotelian conception of responsibility for character formation – for having allowed ourselves to become the persons we are – and it is not clear that a concession in that direction must involve any radical rupture with the liberal tradition. Finally, it does not seem that granting the original equal worth of humans as moral persons excludes the possibility of subsequently considering them of unequal moral worth as persons, depending on their demonstrated level of moral attainment, nor does it require us to treat them equally in all respects (see my brief elucidation of this point in Section 2.1).

Nevertheless, it is clear from the current literature that liberals are loath to make the concessions necessary for incorporating desert concerns in their theories of distributive justice, fearing that this might jeopardize fundamental liberal values and even imperil the whole liberal project. This reluctance may be considered somewhat odd given that they seem willing to make rather similar concessions with regard to retributive justice. Liberals as distinct as Rawls and Scheffler thus hold an 'asymmetry thesis' with respect to retributive versus distributive justice, denying the role of desert in the latter but accepting it in the former (see, for example, Moriarty's deft analysis and critique of this thesis, 2003). While slightly embarrassed by the practical consequences of the liberal inability to make sense of desert in distributive justice, Scheffler appears to take some comfort in the contention that utilitarianism fares even worse, since 'no form [of it] treats desert as a basic moral concept' in any justice discourse (1992, p. 304). In what follows, I want to resist this partners-in-crime manoeuvre and argue that Millian utilitarianism is, in fact, far better equipped than liberalism to give desert its due.

Let us start by recalling a commonly made complaint about utilitarianism. The first thing which is typically noted is that whereas desert is a backward-looking notion, referring to a person's past actions or characteristics, utility is determined only by the future benefits an action brings. Thus utilitarianism is unable to take account of the essential retrospective character of desert. Now, I do not concur with those who hold desert to be exclusively, or even essentially, a backward-looking notion. Rather, I would agree with Miller, who points out that while desert claims are never justified on the basis of states of affairs to be created in the *future*, they can be justified on the basis of both *past* and *present* facts about persons (1976, p. 93). We might, for instance, want to increase proportionally our positive estimation of a man's deserts in light of his present admirable efforts in turning away from past error, as in the biblical parable of the prodigal son (cf. my earlier discussion of this point in Section 2.2).

Fred Feldman goes even further, however, and claims that desert claims can be based on future states of affairs: such as the claim that a child who has caught a fatal disease deserves special treatment now in virtue of its future sufferings, and the claim that a soldier who has volunteered for a suicide mission deserves gratitude and honours now in virtue of his future sacrifice (1995b). I think Feldman's examples put unnecessary strain on the notion of desert; it seems more natural to say that the child deserves special treatment in virtue of the present fact of its having (undeservedly) contracted the terrible disease, and the soldier in virtue of his already-taken action in volunteering for the mission in question. For even if a cure were miraculously found before the disease ran its course, or the soldier died of a heart attack before he could accomplish his feat, those unforeseeable *future* events would not compromise our verdicts about the treatment they *presently* receive having been deserved. To this Feldman might counter that for a desert claim to be forward-looking, it need not be based on future events, but only on reasonable expectations of future events, and that we would, for instance, be inclined to revise our judgement about the deservingness of the sick child if we reasonably expected a cure to be found for the illness before it led to the child's death. My rejoinder would be to say that all moral discourse (including desert discourse) takes place, in some minimal sense, against the background of future expectations. If we knew that the world were going to perish in a couple of hours, the point of most moral concerns would vanish; even the point of a simple desert-based emotion such as 'satisfied indignation', pleasure at another person's experiencing – at this very moment – some deserved bad fortune, would be lost, for there would be no time for the consequences of the bad fortune to sink in. On the other hand, if we want to understand the reference to future expectations in a fuller sense, a sense required for desert to be substantively forward-looking, we not only end up with an idea that is conceptually awkward (in the same way as is the idea of paying back a debt that has not yet been incurred), but also one which would make desert-based allocation decisions hopelessly impractical and desert-based emotions irredeemably hypothetical.

More importantly, however, we should reject the claim that an action's utility is necessarily forward-looking. Since utilitarianism is concerned with the maximization of pleasure, then if it should be the case that taking account of backward-looking concerns increases pleasure, utilitarianism must, other things being equal, commend it. In other words, if people are really naturally constituted in such a way that they feel a warm glow of pleasure when confronting cases of a deemed proper fit between certain (desert-conferring) states of affairs, on the one hand, and specific esteemed or disesteemed actions or characteristics of individuals in the present or past, on the other, then utilitarianism will take this natural fact into consideration even if the sentiment is not conducive to any further (future) pleasures – especially since it would take more to change the sentiment than to accommodate it. And Strawson's claim about (desert-based) reactive attitudes – notably recorded and acknowledged by Scheffler – was precisely that, that such attitudes could not be uprooted from human beings if they were, in fact, to remain human. I will exploit this point further in the following subsection.

This response, however, will not satisfy those sceptical of utilitarianism's ability to deal properly with desert. A further, and potentially more damaging, point can be made, namely that it is central to our belief about desert that a person may deserve a benefit or burden even if receiving it will *not* maximize pleasure (see, for example, Sher, 1987, p. 12; Feinberg, 1970, p. 82). In contrast, we are told, the utilitarian does not really understand the separate value of desert or, more generally speaking, of justice: an action or policy is deemed just (or, for that matter, deserved) if and only if it maximizes utility/pleasure in society (see, for example, Sabbagh, 2001, p. 241). The utilitarian is thus seen as playing an unrewarding game of nothing-buttery: justice is 'nothing but' the maximization of utility/pleasure. Too many theorists of a naturalist, consequentialist bent seem to me to acknowledge this reductionist claim as a legitimate point made against utilitarianism and to respond by trying to save consequentialism via tortuous side-routes at the expense of (pure) utilitarianism. Feldman provides a case in point. Examining his strategy may help us defuse some common misunderstandings and also shed light on some options which are actually open to utilitarians, but to which many of their sympathizers remain blind. Note that in what follows I will, for simplicity's sake, use 'pleasure' as a shortening for Mill's 'pleasure and the absence of pain, as experienced to the greatest extent by the greatest number', rather than talking, more cumbersomely, about 'utility in the Millian sense' (the term 'utility' having nowadays been hijacked by subjectivist preference utilitarianism and welfare economics) or 'welfare/happiness' (which need not be understood along Millian lines).

Feldman is deeply worried about possible-world scenarios of the kind where one imagines in world 1, on the one hand, 'a million happy saints and a million sad sinners' and in world 2, on the other, 'a million happy sinners and a million sad saints'. The 'welfare fanatic' (read pure utilitarian) will have to say that the two worlds are of equal intrinsic value. That, however, is an entirely unsatisfactory conclusion for anyone who believes in the value of justice – justice, for Feldman, being equivalent to desert (2003b, p. 147; recall from Section 1.1 that Feldman is one of the few current advocates of a desert-monistic theory of justice, although that fact is not germane to my criticisms in the following of his pleasure-adjusting strategy). Feldman takes on the task of adjusting utilitarianism in order to make it immune to counter-examples of this sort I say 'adjust utilitarianism', rather than 'propose a new consequentialist theory', for Feldman normally takes utility/pleasure as his starting point and then starts to 'discount' or 'adjust' it for *x* or *y* in ways he deems necessary, rather than constructing a completely new axiology in line with what he considers the central consequentialist doctrine: 'An act is morally right if and only if it maximizes intrinsic value' (1995a, p. 569). Yet it must be borne in mind that Feldman has gradually developed and reformulated his proposals in a number of articles and it is by no means clear that all the formulations are logically equivalent. For instance, Feldman originally entitled his salvaging proposal 'justicized act utilitarianism' – stating that an act is morally right if and only if it maximizes universal justice levels (1992, pp. 185ff.) – a formulation which made him rather easily susceptible to a utilitarian accusation of 'justice-worship' (see, for example, Vallentyne, 1995, p. 216). Feldman has subsequently dropped the reference to 'act utilitarianism' and refined the formulation of his proposal in various ways.

Feldman explains, at one point, that he wants to do for justice (desert) something similar to what Mill did in discounting for quality the lower-rated pleasures. According to Feldman, Mill gives the lower-rated pleasures a quality-discounted value such that, say, low sensual pleasures would count as 20 per cent of the highest (moral) pleasures. In other words, if you have a moral pleasure containing 10 'hedons', then its quality-discounted value is 10 (100 per cent of its raw value), whereas a low sensual pleasure containing 10 'hedons' would yield a discounted value of just 2. Feldman then suggests that we do something similar for desert, so that in the end we discount twice, once for quality and then once again for desert: if a pleasure contains 10 'hedons' but the person experiencing it is only partially deserving of it (say, 50 per cent), then the desert-discounted value of the pleasure is just 5 'hedons' (2003a).

In yet another place, Feldman explains his proposal along the lines of the enhancement and mitigation of positive and negative desert upon (a) the intrinsic goodness of pleasure and (b) the intrinsic badness of pain, so that positive desert enhances (a) and aggravates (b), negative desert mitigates both (a) and (b), and neutral desert neither enhances nor mitigates either (a) or (b) (1995a). These enhancement and mitigation effects are worked out in more mathematical detail in Feldman's latest exploration of this issue (2003b).

I have a number of difficulties with Feldman's proposal (or perhaps I should say proposals). One problem lies in some of its technicalities, which seem to engender counter-intuitive conclusions in a number of instances. These have been pointed out by other writers and will not be further discussed here (see, for example, Vallentyne, 1995; Cooley, 2000). Another is the sheer, and steadily increasing, complexity of his axiology. First, we are given to understand that Mill himself discounted pleasure only for quality, then we get a further adjustment for desert, and even more recently, a suggestion that a similar adjustment is theoretically possible for equality (although not endorsed by Feldman himself), leading to 'desert and equality adjusted aggregate welfarism' (2003b). In the end, there seems no fixed limit to those states which have intrinsic value and need to be adjusted for (see Cooley, 2000, p. 365): why not also freedom, knowledge, truth, intelligence, virtue or whatever else happens to fit into one's bag of values? Now Feldman is free, of course, to construct any consequentialist value theory he likes, however complex. What is evident, however, is that Feldman's efforts to salvage desert along consequentialist lines take him ever further from the simple elegance of Mill's utilitarianism, where pleasure (and the absence of pain) is the sole source of intrinsic value. This observation leads directly to the crux of my dissatisfaction with Feldman's project in so far as it is supposed to be based on a Millian precedent (of discounting for quality). In point of fact, I do not think Mill discounted for quality in the way Feldman describes, nor do I think that utilitarianism need, or even should, be 'adjusted' in order to take account of higher-quality pleasures, desert, or any other good, in the way he suggests.

As I understand Mill, those suitably acquainted with the cultivation of a higher-quality pleasure will place it so far above the cultivation of a lower-quality one that they will resolutely prefer the former and not relinquish it for *any quantity* of the lower-quality pleasure. Thus the possibility, in Feldman's schema, of an x-number of discounted lower-quality 'hedons' outweighing, through sheer quantity, a lower y-number of non-discounted moral-pleasure 'hedons' would never come up. The core of the matter here is that Mill upholds a theory which distinguishes between essential and non-essential goods instrumental to the sole intrinsic value: pleasure. Those two kinds of goods are incommensurable: that is, although we may have to make choices in weighing different non-essential goods (such as chocolate biscuits versus hamburgers) against one another and, similarly, in weighing different essential goods (such as truth versus kindness) against one another, there will never be a real choice for a wise chooser between a non-essential and an essential good. (This claim is, of course, subject to various contextual provisos. Eating a hamburger might, in principle, be essentially inferior to listening to a good philosophy lecture; yet a wise chooser might opt for the former if he happens to be starving, or if the philosophy lecture takes place far away from his home, and so on.) The essential goods, which give rise to the higher-quality pleasures, are things that we ought to value, whether or not we do, and the evidence for that is an exclusively empirical one, namely, the experience of competent judges who are equally acquainted with both and on whose judgements we must rely as rational beings, just as we rely on other empirical evidence which time and experience has proved sound (I draw here on Mikael M. Karlsson's excellent exploration, 2001, of how one can countenance a distinction between essential and non-essential goods, for instance along purely empirical Millian lines, without venturing into Kantian metaphysics).

Desert is for Mill, as we shall see presently, an essential good in this sense, and that is why Feldman's original example of the two possible worlds is, just like many examples of that ilk, quite misguided. There could never be two worlds of that kind, inhabited by human beings as we know them, containing equal pleasure – for no quantity of sin-induced pleasure (pleasure stemming from a non-essential good: the attraction of sin) could, *in natural fact*, equal or outweigh the pleasure of saintly induced pleasure (stemming from an essential good: virtue). This does not mean that various vexing choices will not remain between competing essential goods (desert versus kindness, for example), but it puts a completely wrong construction on the matter, from a Millian perspective, to describe such a conflict as involving some kind of adjustment of pleasure. We need not adjust pleasure for desert or any other essential goods; rather, we use desired pleasure (valued by competent judges) to adjudicate between such goods, which is quite another matter. It is, of course, equally wrong to say, as many foes of utilitarianism do, that for a utilitarian desert simply *means* pleasure. Desert is an essential good, as we can see from the fact that its satisfaction is valued as a higher-quality pleasure by competent judges, and is (as are other essential goods and also, to a lesser, incommensurable, degree, non-essential ones) not *reducible* to, but (other things being equal) *instrumental* to, pleasure. Let me try to spell this out in a little more detail and, consequently, to articulate more clearly the 'deceptively simple' utilitarian justification of desert that I promised.

Utilitarianism continues to be a badly understood moral theory, particularly by its opponents but, sadly, sometimes also by its own proponents (see Kristjánsson, 2002, s. 2.3). Utilitarians allegedly do not, according to the received wisdom mentioned above, understand either desert or justice, nor take them seriously enough. If we look at what Mill says about justice, however, a radically different picture appears. He understands justice perfectly well: *logically* as a combination of legal/moral rights and deserts (it being 'universally considered just' that each person receives what 'he deserves'), and *psychologically* as a 'powerful sentiment'. So far is it from being the case that he does not take justice seriously enough that it would seem more accurate to accuse him of the opposite error: of taking it too seriously. He says, let us recall, that justice is 'incomparably the most sacred and binding part' of all morality, it being a name 'for certain classes of moral rules, which concern the essentials of human well-being more nearly, and are therefore of more absolute obligation, than any other rules for the guidance of life'. A little later he rephrases and reiterates the same claim by saying that 'justice is a name for certain moral requirements which, regarded collectively, stand higher in the scale of social utility, and are therefore of more paramount obligation, than any others; though particular cases may occur in which some other social duty is so important, as to overrule any one of the general maxims of justice' (1931, ch. 5).

Mill has various things to say about the different 'maxims of justice'. Let us hold those remarks in abeyance here and rely simply on Feinberg's less fine-grained (and hence less controversial) classification, according to which justice involves a combination of entitlement claims and desert claims, where the focus is sometimes on the former, sometimes on the latter. While these are the basic ingredients of any sound theory of justice (with small letters), as I noted in Section 2.1, they do not amount to a full-fledged Theory of Justice (with capital letters). For that, we need much further elaboration on the ingredients of justice and, in particular, their relative weight. Such a theory, I submit, would have to take into account, among other things, the strong intuition that entitlements should be allowed to reign as long as they do not involve, or lead to, glaringly undeserved states of affairs. The reason behind such a privileged status for entitlements is society's practical need to abide by consistent rules and guidelines (for example, in Western democracies, rules of private property and free exchange of goods), the just or unjust nature of which it would, simply, not be feasible to question in each particular case. After a certain threshold of serious undeservingness is crossed, however, we become more than ready to deem a state of affairs unjust in virtue of its being undeserved, even if it arose through legitimate entitlements – although that does not mean that it is morally wrong, all things considered, or should be overturned. Similarly, before a certain threshold of serious moral inappropriateness is reached, we tend to accept a state of affairs as morally in order, without further ado, as long as it is just, but after that threshold has been crossed, the relevance of justice considerations starts to wane. Where do these two thresholds lie?

Let me now sketch what I have called a 'deceptively simple' utilitarian answer to that question. Classical utilitarians of the Millian kind do not work with some idiosyncratic conceptions of desert and justice that somehow reduce those notions to pleasure; *contra* some common misinterpretations, a person may, for utilitarians, deserve a benefit or burden even if receiving it will *not* maximize pleasure: a desert-based emotion can be rational and a desert claim have normative (moral) force in default of any pleasure maximization. Such utilitarians would, however, claim that pleasure is the criterion by which to *adjudicate* between competing claims of desert and entitlement, and also between competing claims of justice and other moral values. In other words, they would say that pleasure defines the two above-mentioned thresholds, between entitlement and desert, and between justice and other moral concerns. Let entitlement claims prevail over desert claims so long as the pleasure of abiding by the former is greater than that of overruling them in favour of desert (here, Mill's rule utilitarianism comes into play); and similarly, let justice claims prevail over other moral claims as long, and only as long, as that promotes pleasure. Mill's empirical contention is that, after such calculations have been made, justice will turn out to be the overriding concern in the vast majority of cases, since it is, after all, an essential good, 'guarded by a sentiment not only different in degree, but also in kind' from the sentiments which guard the non-essential goods conducive to the lower-quality pleasures. Yet he also warns against an unmitigated primacy-of-justice thesis, the origin of which he explains as stemming from people's natural reluctance to let go of the 'indefeasibility attributed to justice' and what he calls a 'useful accommodation of language' according to which the few cases where justice is actually overruled are described in terms of a particular kind of justice having taken precedence over the ordinary (1931, ch. 5).

This, then, is the utilitarian theory that I promised: (1) While justice is a virtue, it is not tantamount to moral rightness, (2) desert forms an important element in justice as an essential good conducive to pleasure, and (3) sometimes desert outweighs entitlement and sometimes it does not. Moreover, (1) pleasure is a reasonable criterion for deciding when the just is also the morally right and when it is not, (2) pleasure is a reasonable criterion for deciding when desert should prevail over entitlement and vice versa, and (3) after a certain threshold of undeserved outcome is reached, desert will prevail over other considerations of justice in our judgements about – if not necessarily in our actions regarding – what is, on the whole, just and what is unjust. Justice, in general, and desert, in particular – the latter being my main focus of concern here – are not weak links in the utilitarian programme; rather utilitarianism provides a sound and plausible moral justification for both of them.

Objections and Rejoinders

Various objections to the moral justification of desert above which I have culled from Millian sources will no doubt have occurred to the reader. Is my justification perhaps simplistic rather than simple? The aim of this subsection is to examine, and to respond briefly to, some such objections.

Objection of distributive holism 'Distributive justice is a *holistic* notion in that the justice of any assignment to an individual depends on the larger distribution of benefits in society. This applies to utilitarianism, in so far as it focuses on the allocation of benefits and burdens, as well as to Rawlsianism and other well-known theories of distributive justice. Desert claims are, in contrast, *individualistic*; their legitimacy can be established without looking at what others are receiving. Therefore, desert cannot be taken seriously as a principle of distributive justice (as opposed, perhaps, to retributive justice) in utilitarianism, any more than in other moral theories.'

This objection draws on Feinberg's earlier distinction between distributive justice as an example of *comparative* justice, and desert as a principle of *non-comparative* justice (1980). Recently, however, as I pointed out in Section 2.1, serious criticisms have been raised to this distinction, criticisms where it is most commonly claimed that desert has a comparative as well as a non-comparative element. I went even further than that and argued, convincingly I hope, that it is simply a mistake to talk of what individuals deserve non-comparatively, because the extent to which what one receives satisfies what one deserves must depend on what others receive compared to what they deserve. *All* desert claims are comparative because they all must involve an implicit reference to a baseline of expectations. Objection (1) is, thus, based on a false premise and fails to hit the mark.

Objection of universalism 'Your utilitarian defence of desert rests on the alleged fact that desert is generally cherished by human beings and that they entertain desert-based emotions, potentially instrumental to pleasure. This, however, involves an illicit assumption of universal values and emotions.'

Millian utilitarianism is a naturalist theory *par excellence*. By 'naturalist' I mean that all moral properties and relations are considered natural properties/relations, and that any moral theory must ultimately be answerable to empirical findings about human beings as biological, social and moral creatures. If the point of objection (2) were correct, it would, indeed, spell trouble for a naturalist theory. Let me emphasize here that I have not been defending a subjectivist theory of pleasure (such as most forms of preference utilitarianism are) but rather an objectivist one, where the evidence for the essential desirability of a (higher-quality) pleasure lies in the experience of wise, competent judges. This makes my justification of desert even more sensitive to the relativism implied by objection (2).

The truth of the matter is, however, that recent social-science research reinforces, rather than undermines, the assumptions of utilitarian naturalism, as was amply demonstrated at the beginning of this chapter. Justice, in general, and desert, in particular, have been shown to be universal concerns across cultural groups, and recent research in developmental and social psychology implicates 'reactive attitudes' (Mill's 'powerful sentiments') more and more in the experience and development of a sense of justice. While the dispositions to such attitudes are not yet virtues, and their exact origin presents something of an enigma to psychologists (see Section 4.1), neither need worry the utilitarian, who can simply say that these dispositions become virtues when cultivated within the framework of a general moral outlook, namely utilitarianism, and who can – from a justificatory perspective – ignore with impunity the intractable debates in psychology about the exact origin of the justice motive. What matters for the utilitarian is that the desert-based emotions and values are there, universally, from childhood: that people feel happy, other things being equal, when desert is done, and that ways to change the fundamental emotional make-up of human beings seem neither feasible nor desirable.

Objection of genetic fallacy 'The naturalist argument of universality, extracted from research in the social sciences and presented above, falls afoul of the "genetic fallacy": a theory cannot be evaluated merely on the basis of its causal (psychological and/or historical) genesis. What we need is a reasoned assessment of the moral value of desert, rather than an irrelevant account of the origin of the belief in such a value.'

Is committing the proverbial 'genetic fallacy' the besetting sin of my utilitarian justification of desert? For a start, that alleged fallacy may not always be as fallacious as it is commonly made out to be. May it not matter for the food inspector to know *how* the food he is inspecting was produced? While such knowledge will not substitute for a check on the quality of the food itself, it seems untrue to say that it is irrelevant for the inspection. Indeed, much recent literature on the 'genetic fallacy' acknowledges that the causal history of a belief or position is sometimes highly relevant to its epistemic status or even its truth or falsity (see, for example, Klement, 2002, who correctly notes, among other things, that 'according to many contemporary theories of meaning and reference, the causal history of a word or concept in part determines the semantic content of the statements or judgments in which it plays a part', p. 386). To show that a real genetic fallacy has been committed, it needs to be established that certain information about the source of a claim is taken to be relevant for its evaluation when it is, in fact, *not* relevant. Conversely, when the context of origin is incorporated into the context of justification in a theory, it needs to be shown that there is an objective connection between the given aspect of its origin, on the one hand, and the evaluation of the theory, on the other (see further in Crouch, 1993). And this is precisely what utilitarian naturalism does. It identifies certain features of the way in which the belief in the value of justice comes about that are relevant to assessing the quality of that value. Furthermore, it locates this value within a system of essential and non-essential goods instrumental to the ultimate source of intrinsic value: pleasure. The evidence for the intrinsic value of pleasure is obtained through empirical research into the choices of experienced, competent judges. Utilitarianism would not, by contrast, commend, say, the value of *Schadenfreude* (pleasure over someone's undeserved suffering), even if that emotion can, perhaps, be given an evolutionary explanation: a certain roughness of mind being optimal for adaptation. *Schadenfreude*, however it came about, would certainly not be compatible with the attainment of the higher-quality pleasures.

I suspect that the accusation of 'genetic fallacy' often masks a deeper antipathy to naturalist moral theories and explanations: an antipathy that could be expressed such, by irreverently paraphrasing Nietzsche, that theories for the world are always foul-smelling theories, with the smell of small people clinging to them. Is not the heavenly alchemy missing here? Do we not need a justification of desert that replaces or transcends people's natural attitudes for it to be genuinely a *moral* justification?

I have elsewhere tried to provide a sustained defence of naturalism and will not repeat that here (Kristjánsson, 2002, s. 2.3). Let me rather emphasize how strictly naturalist Millian utilitarianism is. It is a substantivist, foundationalist theory with its foundation in human nature as it really is. The scattering of *other-worldly* counter-examples typically thrown at utilitarianism (as, for instance, Feldman's example above of the two worlds) misses the mark, for utilitarianism is not a theory about possible worlds where the inhabitants are radically different from human beings as they appear in daily experience and observation, and as they manifest themselves through (social-)scientific findings. It is, without exception, a *this-worldly* moral theory. It is thoroughgoingly foundationalist to the extent that it considers natural facts sufficient to account not only for psychological factors, such as the existence of the desert-based reactive attitudes, but also for the existence of morality itself (cf. de Sousa, 2001, p. 119). A person lacking those attitudes is seen as lacking fundamental capacities that are part of our notion of humanity: of being, as it were, morally defective. The expectations of interpersonal regard implied by these reactive attitudes are, as Strawson (1962) argued so forcefully, simply part of what it is to participate in a normal human relationship. These attitudes form part of the bedrock of human sentiments, relating to our evaluations of ourselves and of others, in which all moral concepts and principles are rooted. Any moral theory that ignores them is doomed to failure.

Let me, as a final comment on the alleged 'genetic fallacy', offer the timely reminder from David Wiggins that there are 'things that we need reasons to opt out of rather than things that we have to look for deep reasons to opt into' (1987, p. 307). Perhaps an acceptance of our naturally generated reactive attitudes and their moral implications is a case in point.

Objection of the inferiority to virtue ethics 'Everything that utilitarianism can do for the justification of desert from a naturalist standpoint, virtue ethics can do better. It is also a naturalist theory, which takes its cue from natural facts about what human beings need to function and flourish, but it does so without importing the repugnant hedonism and the misconceived demand for maximization which mar the utilitarian project.'

It is true that, like utilitarianism, virtue ethics is a substantivist (as opposed to a formalist) and a foundationalist (as opposed to a non-foundationalist) moral theory. Utilitarians, however, consider the merits of virtue ethics to be overwhelmed by two daunting weaknesses. The first is its self-centredness, which makes the moral agent the focus of self-concerning attention, hence obscuring the essential other-concern of morality. By contrast, irrespective of the ultimate motivation for being a utilitarian, it is clear that the overarching virtue of utilitarianism is a kind of a generalized benevolence toward others. Thus other-regarding acts and emotions will naturally take precedence over self-regarding ones, and there is no hint of the virtue ethicist's inclination toward settling for what there is.

This weakness of self-centredness manifests itself in Tara Smith's otherwise enlightening exploration of justice (including desert) as a personal virtue. The reason for treating others as they deserve is, in her view, to promote *one's own* well-being by expressing one's ideals and enhancing one's own future gain: 'The point is simply that a failure to treat others as they deserve where desert is applicable is contrary to one's interests' (1999, p. 367). For the utilitarian, the reason for treating others as they deserve it that they deserve it, and that a world where people get what they deserve is, other things being equal, a better world than one in which they do not.

The other well-rehearsed weakness of virtue ethics is its failure to provide a decision procedure, instructing us what to do in cases of conflict between the demands of different virtues. I have elsewhere argued that this weakness of non-action-guidance comes to the fore with redoubled force in virtue ethics' inability to tell us what to *feel* in the case of conflicting emotions. As regards possible conflicting actions, we are guided by various types of indications and warnings: social norms, contextual conventions and practical considerations. In the case of potentially conflicting emotions, contextual conventions offer less help, and without a moral decision procedure at hand, we would, for instance, be at a loss whether satisfied indignation or pity would be the morally right thing to feel when, for example, a dear friend suffers deserved misfortune after getting himself into trouble (see Pugmire, 1996, on the logical impossibility of feeling both emotions simultaneously). Utilitarianism would here enjoin us to feel the emotion that is most instrumental to the world's happiness, thus offering us some guidance in dealing with hard emotional choices (see further in Kristjánsson, 2002, s. 2.2).

It must be remembered, however, that when responding to the objection of the inferiority to virtue ethics by recalling the commonly invoked weaknesses of the latter (self-centredness and non-action/emotion-guidance), I am relying on the tenets of contemporary virtue ethics. If we go back to the teachings of Aristotle himself, the father of virtue ethics, there would be less for utilitarians to criticize. Although Aristotle was neither a pleasure-maximizer (since he did not believe in the original equal worth of persons) nor a hedonist, some of his remarks about pleasure are remarkably similar to those that a utilitarian would be inclined to make. No one can experience happiness without also experiencing pleasure, since the latter 'completes' virtuous activities 'like the bloom on youths' (1985, pp. 20–21, 278 [1099a, 1174b]). More importantly, however, there is no hint in Aristotle of the thesis that each human virtue is simply one among others of either equal or incommensurable standing. Rather, 'the greatest virtues' (including emotion virtues) 'are necessarily those most useful to others', for instance justice and courage (1991, p. 80 [1366b]). In other words, if someone preferred to justify desert and desert-based emotions by reference to Aristotelian virtue ethics (as opposed to its contemporary counterpart), rather than by reference to Millian utilitarianism, advocates of the latter would have little to quarrel with.

Objection of non-action-guidance 'Utilitarianism prides itself on its action-guiding abilities, in which respect it pretends, *inter alia*, to be superior to virtue ethics. It is, indeed, exclusively – whatever we may think of its moral credentials – an action-guiding moral theory. Desert is, however, a "cosmic" concept, in the sense that it often carries no implications for human action (as argued in Section 2.1). We may legitimately feel that a sick child deserves not to die of a fatal disease although there is no cure for the disease and nothing anyone can do about it. But this is completely alien to the utilitarian spirit of action-guidance.'

As can be gathered from my response to objection (4) above, I believe that the present objection runs counter to the spirit of utilitarianism. It is not true, as Feinberg claims, that utilitarianism remains silent on our responsive attitudes and 'at last' enters in when questions start to arise as to whether and how to translate our emotions into action (1970, pp. 82–3). It is, on the other hand, quite true that many desert claims entail no obligations about steps that must be taken to provide what is deserved. The fact is that an able student failing to get a deserved grade in an exam, while another one gets an undeservedly high one through serendipity, provides no good reason for raising the first one's grade and lowering the second's. Entitlement rules should in this case prevail over desert claims. But it is a mistake to think that utilitarianism must remain silent on such issues of deservingness. Irrespective of the (separate) question of whether a desert claim should be translated into action, such a claim has *normative force*. It tells us that the deserving party's having what is deserved (or the undeserving party's not having what is not deserved) would, other things being equal, be a good thing (see Sher, 1987, p. xi, on the normative force of desert claims).

There are two sound reasons why utilitarianism enjoins us to feel the proper emotion in such cases, irrespective of the possibility or performance of any action. The first is that it is characteristic of the good person (the person who makes the world a happier place) to take pleasure in the contemplation of people receiving what they deserve. Persons who experience this kind of moral pleasure exhibit their virtue in their emotional responses, without necessarily performing any actions (cf. Roberts, 1989, pp. 302–3). T. M. Scanlon has claimed that the possibility of a justifiable reactive attitude (such as indignation) without the implication of a further propensity to engage in desert-restoring (for instance, blaming, punitive) behaviour shows that the notion of responsibility underlying our reactive attitudes need not be understood as entailing desert (1998, pp. 274–7). But in the light of what I have just maintained, this claim of Scanlon's appears to involve a *non sequitur*. Reactive attitudes can indeed be (although not all are) desert-entailing, in the sense of having a desert-based normative force, without either the possibility or the desirability of their being translated into action. The other, and even more obvious, reason for the utilitarian to feel proper emotions is that it is well documented in the empirical literature that various emotional and motivational states have a positive general effect on moral behaviour (see, for example, Montada and Schneider, 1989, on emotions as positive predictors of pro-social commitment). A person who feels pain at someone else's undeserved suffering, even when unable to do anything about it, is more likely to do something about such suffering when possible (cf. Adams, 1976, on 'motive utilitarianism').

Objection of impracticality 'Utilitarianism is allegedly a practical moral theory; that is supposed to be one of its main assets. If, however, it countenances desert in the ways described above, little remains of the practicality asset. Not only is it initially difficult to measure the extent to which people deserve different benefits and burdens, trying to distribute them according to individual deserts would, given the complex and cooperative nature of most human enterprises, be a hopelessly impractical and arbitrary endeavour.'

Catherine Wilson (2003) has made a careful division into categories of the alleged practical difficulties: These are (a) the *sweep limitations*, which entails there often being more people deserving of a benefit than there are slots open for them, (b) the repeated evidence from the social sciences of *misattribution*: of people consistently overestimating their ability to judge the performance of others objectively, (c) the strong element of biased *conventionality* or historicity in the determination of what is a valuable performance and (d) the proven competence for *mimicry* that people have, for devising ingenious ways of displaying the surface features of deservingness without really being deserving. Rather than attending systematically to all these possible sources of difficulty, which would take up too much space, let me sketch a more general utilitarian response to the problem at hand.

First, as this objection customarily stems from liberal thinkers, utilitarians may accuse them of inconsistency. Since most prominent liberals hold an asymmetry thesis on the role of desert in distributive versus retributive justice (see earlier), it seems odd to think that the difficulties which are supposed to bar us from using desert as a principle of distribution somehow evaporate when we use it to mete out deserved punishments. Second, to repeat an earlier point, even if a desert claim is justified, it does not mean that anyone (including society as a whole) is obligated to provide what is deserved. Hence, what the objection considers unworkable need often not be worked at all (see, for example, Sher, 1987, pp. 137–8). This response, however, only pushes the objection back one step because the impracticality then becomes that of determining the proper desert-based emotion. Third, the problem of measuring people's performance, for instance in the workplace, may be overestimated. To make sense of the common practice of employers giving their employees bonuses for exceptional work, we must suppose that the former feel they can adequately measure the contributions of the latter.

Otherwise, this practice would simply be a farce (see, for example, Moriarty, 2003, pp. 529–32). Fourth, the present objection can be seen as a direct descendant of other more general problems, such as that of other minds and of knowing the real virtues of one's neighbours, about which there is a much longer-running literature. Needless to say, in all these areas there is room for doubt and uncertainty, but there is no good reason for considering the task of justifying desert claims any more absurd than that of justifying claims in other areas. Indeed, numerous sociological studies indicate that people's opinions across societies and cultures converge to a considerable extent on questions of just distribution (see Sadurski, 1985, pp. 140ff., for a general discussion). I am inclined to agree with Pojman, who claims that crude as our measures may be, we have a good enough idea of what and how our neighbours are doing, both morally and in terms of well-being, to give us a basis for making justifiable desert claims about them: 'The more we know the other person, the more confident we can be about these judgments, though perfect knowledge may elude us' (2001, p. 107).

All in all, I conclude that none of the objections canvassed above confutes the simple utilitarian justification of desert that I have tried to hammer out in this chapter. But let me end with a final caveat. My aim has been to defuse common misunderstandings about the utilitarian view of desert and to flesh out a coherent, reasonable justification of desert along utilitarian lines. I am fully aware, however, of the fact that the move of placing desert among the 'essential goods' which give rise to the higher pleasures will do little to appease those who reject the very idea of a single intrinsic value, pleasure, and/or those who believe in impersonal moral values, that is, moral values which do not necessarily make life better for anybody. To be sure, in utilitarian theory, although desert does not mean pleasure and is not reducible to pleasure, desert is of value only to the extent that it produces pleasure. In other words, for the utilitarian, desert is only of instrumental value: it is extrinsically but not intrinsically valuable, nor is its value impersonal, independent of the good it produces for the persons who experience its satisfaction. What I hope to have shown in this section is the plausibility, along classical utilitarian lines, of the view that desert, as an ingredient in justice, is the bearer of a highly important (if sometimes overridable) extrinsic value, and that the fact that persons get what they deserve is (other things being equal) extrinsically good. This would also mean that a general disposition to experience desert-based emotions is essentially, if extrinsically, good and constitutes a virtue, and that particular occurrences of such emotions are (all things considered) essentially, if extrinsically, good, that is, when they are rational and morally proper (pleasure-maximizing). However, such occurrences can be rational and carry normative force even when they are not pleasure-maximizing.

Some might claim that the real challenge for the utilitarian would be to handle the common-sense intuition that desert, or justice, has an intrinsic, impersonal value. I do not, as a matter of fact, believe that this is a commonsense intuition, but that is beside the point, which I unabashedly grant: I have not attempted in this section to justify utilitarianism itself – I have merely tried to make out a case for the viability of a utilitarian defence of desert for those of broadly naturalist sympathies.

Chapter 5

From Theory to Practice: The Schooling of Justice

5.1 Values Education and Justice

Having established that our sense of desert can, from the naturalist standpoint adopted in the previous chapter, indeed be considered virtuous, the question which naturally arises next is how it is to be cultivated and coached. Unfortunately, even those previous accounts of desert which have been sympathetic to its role in distributive justice have tended to be long on theoretical and conceptual considerations, short on practical advice about what fosters and what stifles its development in moral education. That is a pity since, at least for a naturalist, the value of desert must have educational ramifications at all levels of engagement. In the remainder of this book, I will address those ramifications and attempt to explore justice education in the context of recent discourse on values education. This is a particularly apt and pressing task for a classical utilitarian, such as the present author, for although utilitarianism is not a 'practical', 'action-guiding' moral theory in the narrow sense invoked by our imagined interlocutor at the close of the previous chapter, utilitarianism does hold that knowledge of the good and the right has, as such, little moral value unless it is reflected in our actual reactions and actions towards fellow human beings. We are, from the utilitarian perspective, all jointly responsible in caring for the inculcation of proper moral dispositions in the young, with moral education being seen – to adapt a common aphorism – more as a (proper moral) *condition* than as a specific *profession*.

In the present section, after giving a brief overview of the rising optimism about the possibility of early moral schooling of the young, I will focus on some recent trends in values education, making use of the felicitous terminology of 'non-expansive' versus 'expansive' character education. I argue that the essential characteristics of non-expansive character education are moral cosmopolitanism and methodological substantivism. I call special attention to salient differences between the views of non-expansive character education, on the one hand, and a particular brand of expansive character education, namely citizenship education, on the other, concerning values education in general and justice education in particular. I suggest that citizenship education, with its overarching ideal of democratic justice, politicizes values education beyond good reason by assuming that political literacy and specific (democratic) social skills, rather than cosmopolitan moral and emotional 'basics', are the primary values to be transmitted. I show how this objection is based on three major moral and political disagreements between advocates of non-expansive character education and citizenship education.

In Section 5.2, I then go on to consider various remaining educational – in particular, didactic – concerns. While my sympathies lie with non-expansive character education, with its broadly Aristotelian view of moral schooling, such character education has recently been the subject of harsh criticism which stands in need of rebuttal. I take on that defensive task, with special reference to two canonical works of the contemporary character-education movement by Lickona and Kilpatrick. Non-expansive character education stands out, in the end, as a reasonable middle-ground proposal with neither too little nor too much meat on its bones. I also consider and reject the complaint that the Aristotelian position is somehow less salutary in the case of emotion education than in instilling character traits relevant for proper action. At the end of Section 5.2, I do, however, point out that a mere panegyric to Aristotle is not enough: some of his practical guidelines may be faulty and stand in need of amendment from modern sources, for instance from Hoffman's cogent line of argument for moral induction. In the end, I hope to have said something important about the practicalities of both justice education, in particular, and moral education, in general. Finally, in Section 5.3 I draw together not only the major strands of the present chapter but also those of the whole book.

A Brief History

Let us start, then, with some historical observations about moral education in its most general sense. It has become more or less *de rigueur* to initiate discussions of such education with a nod back to its halcyon days when character-building and moral tutelage formed an integral part of any educational programme: a period which lasted, almost uninterrupted, from the time of Plato and Aristotle to the middle of the twentieth century. A fair diversity of individual reasons, or a combination of such reasons, tends to be given to explain why the belief in direct moral and emotional formation, at least at school if not also in the home, then crumbled. These range from the effects of bleak research findings about how context-dependent and chameleon-like children's virtues and qualities of character are, to increased personalism and relativism, growing fear of paternalism and indoctrination (encapsulated, for instance, in the basic tenets of humanistic psychology), the general anti-traditionalism of the hippie period, *Sputnik*-inspired emphasis on technology and science at the expense of 'soft' disciplines such as morality, the mounting antagonism of religious groups toward secularized moral teaching, less optimistic views than before (based on Kohlberg or at least on some stock interpretations of Kohlberg's research) about children's capacity to engage rationally with moral questions, and last, but not least, to general cold-war pessimism about the possibility of a genuine moral dialogue and moral consensus.

How much relative weight to ascribe to each of the particular reasons above remains controversial. Beyond controversy, however, is their cumulative effect in sidelining moral concerns from mainstream educational discourse in the Western world and marginalizing, if not wholly extirpating, references to the cultivation of the character of children via school curricula and other school processes. Beyond controversy also is the fact that over the last decade or so the tide has turned dramatically, and with astounding swiftness, in favour of moral education in general, and character education in particular, at the school level. A groundswell is currently evident among the general public in support of more direct character formation of the young. Its origins are less evident than its existence; when pressed, however, parents cite with familiarity such buzzwords as 'multiple intelligences' and 'emotional intelligence' as grounds for their new-found enthusiasm. Since the emphasis of today's rhetoric on character education, particularly in the USA, is on character education as the cultivation of personal *virtues* of action and reaction (emotion), it might seem reasonable to suppose that its reappearance has something to do with the upsurge of virtue ethics in academic circles. After all, virtue ethics is all about the flourishing (*eudaimonia*) of humans *qua* natural beings, to whose flourishing the virtues are conducive and of which they form constitutive parts. Nevertheless, 'virtue ethics' is in many ways a misleading category, given the fact that many other historical moral outlooks, such as those of Aristotle, and of Mill, the classical utilitarian, are also essentially virtue-based (Nussbaum, 1999; recall also my discussion in Section 4.3), and, as I point out in the following section, character education may do itself no good by embracing all the insights of modern-day virtue theory.

So why has values education become such a hot topic in educational discourse of late, given that it was almost consigned to the educational scrapheap a quarter of a century ago? There is a 'pessimist' explanation here to hand, as well as an 'optimist' one. Moral pessimists will insist that what finally convinced educators of the need to instil pro-social values in students, not only in the home but also at school, was the eroding moral fabric of modern society, increased crime and drug abuse, voter apathy and the propensity of the young to be taken in by racism and other extremist views. Moral optimists will not endorse such a 'moral-declivity' thesis; their point is rather that the decline in values education after the middle of the twentieth century was rooted in undue pessimism concerning the potential positive effects of moral schooling; now that psychologists have demonstrated the possibility of modifying the human personality for the better at an early age, both emotionally (e.g., Goleman, 1995) and morally (e.g., Damon, 1988), educators have, reasonably enough, shed their earlier misgivings and followed suit. As Shaffer emphatically puts it in a widely used undergraduate textbook in developmental psychology, the experts on child development, who until recently would have claimed that well-intentioned adults trying to stimulate moral concerns in young children were simply wasting their time, 'were wrong!' (2000, p. 313). Careful scholarly analyses of the common misgivings about the viability of moral education have found most of these to be unfounded (for an overview, see Kristjánsson, 2002, ch. 6), and as a result we have taken a roller-coaster ride into the world of post-Kohlbergian hopefulness about the ability of schools to make children both 'smart and good' (Lickona, 1991, p. 6). Children's moral character is, indeed – the story now goes – amenable to schooling, its affective, as well as its purely intellectual side, educable. In my home country, Iceland, for instance, old-style character education has suddenly reappeared in the state school curricula from pre-school to secondary school levels under the rubric of so-called 'life-skills' classes. And a currently influential educational think-tank in Iceland openly proclaims moral character-building as the alpha and omega of *all* its educational efforts and plans to model its school ideology on that of the successful, and highly moralistic, City Montessori Schools in Uttar Pradesh, India (Cottom, 1996). That, in itself, must count as a somewhat defiant gesture in an age which speaks so easily about the essential heterogeneity of cultural values.

Interestingly enough, for our present purposes, some of the criticisms levelled at Kohlberg's now much-maligned results about children's moral maturity – apart from the most obvious methodological ones which denounce his use of far-fetched dilemma stories in measuring such maturity – focus on his lack of engagement with children's moral emotions and his implicit primacy-of-justice thesis: his conflation of a sense of the morally right with a sense of justice, the latter being narrowly understood by him as formalist, proceduralist fairness. By implication, these mounting criticisms open the way for a reappraisal of children's emotionally driven sense of desert.

Some Recent Trends in Values Education

'Values education is the hottest topic in education today', Lickona says (1991, p. 5), and that is hardly an exaggeration. Although I began my educational exploration with some historical observations about the swiftly changing fortunes of moral education, my goal is not to probe more deeply its genesis. Nor is this section meant to defend values education against those who still view the general project of transmitting moral values to the young at school with a suspicious eye. Rather, my main aim is to explore some recent trends in so-called character education, since that constitutes the 'hot topic' of the day to which Lickona refers. Character education is, furthermore, highly germane to questions of justice education, where justice is understood as a personal value as well as a social one. I call attention to certain tensions within the pro-character-education camp (in its broadest sense) and, more specifically, propose a classificatory schema that affords a theoretically useful way of distinguishing between competing factions within the camp and of clarifying their relations to other trends in values education. My classificatory schema takes its cue from McLaughlin and Halstead's (1999) helpful labelling of character-education accounts as either 'non-expansive' or 'expansive', although it departs substantially from their specifications of those terms.

The view put forward under the banner of 'character education' in the USA and elsewhere in recent years is more often than not synonymous with a *specific* conception of character education, espoused by thinkers such as Lickona, Kilpatrick, Wynne and Bennett, a conception that I will, following McLaughlin and Halstead's (1999) lead, term 'non-expansive'. Nevertheless, there are other more 'expansive' conceptions of character education abroad, some of them prominent and powerful, and indeed it is from the proponents of those, rather than from old-fashioned opponents of any kind of direct moral formation in the schools, that non-expansive character education has recently taken the most flak.

What distinguishes non-expansive character education (hereafter, for brevity's sake, NECE) from expansive character education (hereafter ECE)? McLaughlin and Halstead characterize these two conceptual categories in the following way (ibid., pp. 137–8): (i) The rationale given for NECE is limited and superficial (involving mainly the allegedly deteriorating moral condition of modern society), whereas the rationale for ECE is more elaborate and broader; (ii) NECE concentrates on basic and fundamental virtues and values, whilst ECE goes 'beyond the fundamental and the basic' to more complex qualities of character and virtue; (iii) in NECE emphasis and priority are given to sound moral habits rather than to abstract moral reasoning, while in ECE the nature and scope of moral reasoning and discourse are emphasized.

McLaughlin and Halstead's categorizations are, I suggest, unnecessarily broadly sketched, as well as begging important questions in favour of common criticisms of NECE. As examples of the latter, I take exception to the claim inherent in (iii) that a characteristic of all NECE accounts is 'their neglect of moral reasoning, however conceived' (ibid., p. 138), and also to the claim inherent in (i) that NECE is necessarily seen by its proponents as a remedy for a particular kind of envisioned 'social deterioration and crisis' distinctive of our times (ibid., p. 140). I will in the following propose an alternative classificatory schema for making sense of the difference between accounts of character education that can aptly be labelled 'non-expansive' and 'expansive', respectively. I will compare and contrast my classifications with those of McLaughlin and Halstead in due course, but meanwhile let me simply state the two conditions which I take to be jointly sufficient for characterizing accounts of NECE and distinguishing them from ECE.

I will refer to the two (allegedly) sufficient conditions of NECE as, in the first place, *moral cosmopolitanism* (as opposed to *moral perspectivism*) and, in the second, *methodological substantivism* (as opposed to *methodological formalism*). Moral cosmopolitanism and moral perspectivism differ on the question of the *content* of character education. According to the former, there exist cosmopolitan moral values that transcend the boundaries of time and geography. Because we are human beings inhabiting a common sphere of existence in our material world, certain virtues of character – manifested in action and emotion – will rightly be cherished in any society and at any time, and it is precisely on those virtues that we should focus in character education. Although the lists of the cosmopolitan virtues differ somewhat between different NECE theorists, virtues such as reliability, honesty, self-respect, responsibility, truthfulness, compassion, indignation, (proper) shame and, most generally, justice as a personal virtue figure on most lists. Compiling such lists of moral universals is not to deny the possibility of conflicting cultural values, nor the actual existence of ever-increasing pluralism in modern societies. Quite the reverse: it is precisely against the background of such pluralism that it becomes reasonable to confine character education to the 'moral basics' (Bennett, 1991, p. 137) which can appeal to every reasonable person, irrespective of cultural identity, political affiliation or religious creed. For while every field has 'its complexities and controversies', of which we become increasingly aware as we grow in age and experience, it is also the case that 'every field has its basics' (ibid.) – and it is on the latter that the schools should naturally concentrate. Moral cosmopolitanism, the first fundamental characteristic of NECE, distinguishes NECE from *moral perspectivism*. According to the latter, the virtues espoused in NECE are too narrow, too underdetermined, or even, simply – *qua* cosmopolitan values – non-existent. These need to be complemented, if not simply replaced, by a set of perspective-sensitive virtues, reflecting more specific moral concerns of a society, culture or religion than allowed for by the generalities of NECE's alleged moral basics.

It is important that the reader keeps these particular specifications of 'moral cosmopolitanism' and 'moral perspectivism' in mind in what follows. The two terms are simply invoked here for the sake of exposition and will, I hope, be useful as such, although they have elsewhere been used for other purposes. For instance, common connotations notwithstanding, moral perspectivism in the present sense is not the same as – and does not, as I explain later in this section, necessarily imply – moral relativism, the theory that the truth of moral judgements is relative to a specific group at a specific time.

According to *methodological substantivism*, the second defining characteristic of NECE, the content of the moral truths that are transmitted to students in character education is more important than the process or method by which they are taught. This does not mean that the methods are not themselves subject to moral considerations. Methods matter, but only in so far as they tend to the general development of basic moral character in students. It is wrong to lean, like Hope on her anchor, on some one particular strategy; if called for, let us use as many strategies as necessary to make students smart and good. The contrasting view here is *methodological formalism*, of either a cosmopolitan or a perspectivist kind, which claims that moral education is to be restricted to the development of ways of thinking about moral issues. These two methodological stances obviously draw on more deep-seated philosophical views of how morality itself is to be justified, namely moral substantivism (including naturalism), and moral formalism (including rationalism), respectively (cf. Gunnarsson, 2000, chs 2 and 5), but that kinship will not be pursued further here.

McLaughlin and Halstead (1999) concentrate on the kind of 'non-expansive' character education which tends to be referred to as 'character education' *simpliciter* in the USA (e.g., Lickona, 1991; Kilpatrick, 1992). Notably, however, other trends may fall into the same category (of moral cosmopolitanism and methodological substantivism), for instance the recently fashionable movement of 'socio-emotional learning' in the USA (e.g., Elias et al., 1997, based largely on Goleman, 1995). While that movement draws more directly on psychological research into so-called emotional intelligence than does character education *simpliciter*, and has, mostly through a historical accident, become associated with left-wing values rather than the right-wing values commonly, if controversially, ascribed to 'character education' (Mayer and Cobb, 2000), both movements advocate the inculcation of a similar set of cosmopolitan values and virtues (the above-mentioned 'moral basics'). Whenever I mention 'non-expansive character education' in the following, this should be understood to refer to *any* trend in values education that falls under the rubric of moral cosmopolitanism and methodological substantivism concerning the cultivation of moral character, rather than exclusively the Lickona/Kilpatrick-inspired kind.

Although proponents of ECE typically have stronger opinions on the pros and cons of different didactic methods than their NECE counterparts, they are not methodological formalists either. What essentially distinguishes them from the NECE movement(s) is their insistence on the cultivation of an expansive set of perspectivist virtues. The proponents of ECE adhere to perspectivist substantivism rather than cosmopolitan substantivism; they want us to come down from the generalities of the latter to the particularities of the former. This means, however, that they do not form as unified an alliance as does NECE, for they differ widely on the question of what *kind* of perspectivist virtues should be included in the character-education curriculum. Three main factions of ECE will be distinguished here: *religious-based character education, citizenship* (or *civic*) *education* and *liberationist pedagogy* (including, most prominently, critical postmodernism).

Let 'religious-based character education' refer, for our present purposes, to the view that religious beliefs are fundamental to a justified moral outlook, and that those need to be reflected in the character-education curriculum. Proponents of this view, who are *religiously fundamentalist* in this particular sense (although they may or may not be 'religious fundamentalists' on a more common reading of the term), will then object to the 'watered-down' secularized teachings of NECE for either or both of two reasons, namely (a) that without a divine law-giver the idea of moral truths lacks rationale and authority and (b) that NECE illicitly implies that ultimate moral salvation is possible outside of a religious community. On this view, in proper character education, NECE's 'moral basics' need to be replaced or at least complemented by more specific religious virtues, and justice, in particular, must not be severed from its ultimate transcendental sense of divine retribution.

Citizenship education forms a more tangled skein. This particular term refers to a set of values that have recently been espoused by a somewhat motley group of theorists, including both traditional liberals and people of a more politically conservative bent. The idea behind citizenship education is that 'we' happen to live in Western democracies, in whose fundamental ideals we presumably believe, and that this fact needs to be reflected in the content as well as (to some extent) in the form of character education at school. What should primarily be taught are the democratic virtues: virtues such as self-control, tolerance, compromise, critical thinking and various aspects of proceduralist justice, such as acceptance of majority rule, respect for property rights and freedom of speech.

In so far as the cry of citizenship education is for a thicker, more 'embedded' and more perspective-sensitive set of virtues than that of NECE, one might consider it – at least when coming from liberals – as a cry from a group of poachers turned gamekeepers, for a well-known criticism of the liberal theory of the good focuses precisely on its thinness and disembeddedness, when compared, for instance, to a thicker Aristotelian conception (Nussbaum 1990/1992; for an interpretation, see Kristjánsson, 2002, s. 2.1). Because of its insistence that the goods promulgated by the state, notably in state schools, must be restricted to bare essentials in order to make room for an endless array of equally valid ways of living, political liberalism has historically produced little in the way of concrete advice about which particular virtues to teach. The emphasis has, rather, been on teaching students formally *how* to choose without telling them *what* to choose (see, e.g., Gutmann, 1982), which tallies more with the Kohlbergian or values-clarification formalism of the 1960s and 1970s than with methodological substantivism. The argument for citizenship education seems, however, to go much further than this formalism, calling for the inculcation of a kind of 'liberal patriotism' (Callan, 1997, ch. 8) which involves many of the substantive democratic virtues listed above, as well as an eagerness to 'defend democracy' (Gutmann, 1987, p. 58) and justice (in its institutional sense) through, so to speak, thick and thin.

The explanation for this apparently conflicting message coming from different liberal thinkers (and sometimes even from the same thinker at different times, witness Gutmann) seems to be that some are working within a strictly Kantian-inspired deontological, rights-based kind of liberalism, which understands morality in terms of procedures and principles rather than virtues of character, while others are, by contrast, more influenced by a virtue-based type of liberal thought. The former kind of liberalism, which inspired the methodological formalism of Kohlberg and 'values clarification', falls under the rubric of 'moral formalism' (cf. Gunnarsson, 2000) or, more specifically, 'enlightenment rationalism' (Carr, 1998), with 'its prescinding of the formal from the substantive features of ethical life' (ibid., p. 118), and its assumption that emotions are basically irrelevant to moral deliberation. The latter kind of liberalism is, on the other hand, a version of 'moral substantivism' (cf. Gunnarsson, 2000), and it is from the ranks of this latter kind of liberalism that the call for citizenship education, as an expansive liberal ideal of character education, typically comes.

To complicate matters even further, most of the advocates of NECE agree that in 'our' schools a 'host of democratic values' should be taught in addition to the cosmopolitan moral basics (see, e.g., Lickona, 1991, p. 45); similarly, many of the citizenship-education enthusiasts would not be unsympathetic to the idea that good citizenship also implies a commitment to personal, non-institutional core values (e.g., Tomasi, 2001). But, someone might ask, if moral cosmopolitanism and methodological substantivism together are sufficient for an approach to be categorized as NECE, and citizenship education not only defends the transmission of substantive values but also the moral basics, is citizenship education not then, in my schema, simply a form of NECE? Admittedly, at this point, the distinction between NECE and ECE becomes porous, but it is still far from being negligible. NECE views the cosmopolitan moral basics (for instance, justice in its personal-virtue sense) alone as *essential* – that is, as morally sufficient ingredients in character education in democratic or non-democratic societies – although the *specifically democratic* virtues cherished in modern Western societies (such as acceptance of majority rule, respect for private property rights and other democratically grounded justice-based entitlements) are important add-ons which should, for prudential reasons, also be taught there, just as we teach children in detail about the geography of their own country. The advocates of citizenship education, by contrast, consider the democratic virtues essential for the development of moral agents in a democratic society, and thus of at least the same, if not greater, importance in 'our' schools as the moral basics. That is why those theorists are more usefully described as perspectivist than cosmopolitan substantivists, in the previously explained sense. It must not be forgotten here either that most of the prominent advocates of citizenship education are dyed-in-the-wool *liberals* for whom what NECE terms 'moral basics' involves substantive personal values that are irredeemably non-neutral with regard to conceptions of the good life, and must thus be considered secondary, from a political and (formal) educational point of view, to the public values that sustain society.

Liberationist pedagogy distinguishes itself more sharply from NECE than does citizenship education. In liberationist pedagogy, there is no toying with the idea of non-expansive virtues, such as a natural sense of desert, as necessary, if insufficient, ingredients in character education; rather, those alleged virtues are seen as common sources of (Western) hegemony and (diverse kinds of) domination. The most emphatically proclaimed form of liberationist pedagogy since the mid-1980s is that of the politically engaged critical postmodernism which developed out of the early irreverent and uncritical pastiche postmodernism of the 1970s. The emphasis in critical postmodernism is on 'difference and otherness in all aspects of life' (Nash, 1997, p. 113), amounting to a much more radical form of pluralism or 'politics of difference' than is meant to be suggested even by the thinnest rights-based liberalism. In so far as talk of common virtues and a shared socio-moral identity makes any sense at all, it is at the local level where the limited scale makes some kind of mutual understanding and a notion of mutual interests possible (West, 1993). 'Local' here refers to the values of different cultures and, especially, subcultures (blacks, women, homosexuals and so on), and the different socio-moral perspectives and justice conceptions of those groups must, according to critical postmodernism, be identified and transmitted through expansive character-education programmes within each group. To what extent the values and virtues of a particular subculture can and should be explained to members of other subcultures is not entirely clear. Sometimes critical postmodernists emphasize the need for making others familiar with the different moral norms of each individual group in a multicultural society; at other times, they despair that – given the lack of any inter-human denominator – the search for such familiarity is an illusion, since no one who does not belong to a particular subculture can even, in a minimal sense, understand, let alone appreciate, its specific moral code. He or she is bound to remain an opaque 'Other' (see further in Kristjánsson, 2002, s. 2.1).

The strongest and most sustained attack mounted so far against the tenets of NECE from an ECE perspective is that expounded in Robert J. Nash's book, *Answering the 'Virtuecrats'* (1997). I will explore the deconstructive side of his writing, in particular some of the specific animadversions he directs against NECE, in the following section. Those are clearly stated and deserve serious attention. The constructive side of his book presents more of a puzzle, which I cannot even begin to resolve here. First of all, the title of the book seems rather misleading, namely the derogatory use of the term 'virtuecrat', as Nash himself appears in it as a 'virtuecrat' *par excellence*: a person deeply concerned with 'hustling' (to use one of his favourite words) a particular agenda of expansive virtues; a veritable 'minister of morality' if ever there was one. Second, the virtues he aims to promote make rather strange bedfellows, for he proposes not only the fostering of a liberal 'democratic disposition', but also 'a sensitivity to the postmodern realities of incommensurability, indeterminacy, and nonfoundationalism' (ibid., p. 11), as well as to the liberationist notions of oppression/oppressed, colonialism, sexism/racism, hegemony/counter-hegemony and so forth (ibid., pp. 103–4). One might conjecture, at first glance, that Nash wanted to show how the thinness of the rights-based liberal conception of the good is ultimately bound to collapse into a more radically relativized postmodern conception (see, e.g., Kristjánsson, 2002, s. 2.1). That, however, is not Nash's point at all; rather, he champions simultaneously the democratic virtues of justice, liberty, authority, political equality and so on (1997, p. 11) typically advanced by proponents of citizenship education, and the insights of postmodernism – apparently forgetting that those very virtues are an anathema to postmodernists, who see nothing in them but the remains of one more oppressive foundational 'grand narrative'. Either Nash is using 'postmodernism' in a new, idiosyncratic and unhelpful sense, or the constructive part of his book is little but an eclectic mixture of ill-sorted elements. As previously noted, however, that does not prevent us from taking his critique of NECE seriously.

The reader might, at this point, find it helpful to look at Figure 5.1, which, I hope, gives an illuminating, if a bit simplified, overview of some basic trends in values education over the last forty years or so.

I deliberately talk about trends in 'values education' here rather than in 'character education', for the accounts of *values clarification* and *moral reasoning/development* were not historically connected to the ideal of cultivating 'character'. Neither the former, which aimed at the internal clarification and consistency of each individual's set of subjective preferences, nor the latter, which concentrated on the development of a formal capacity of moral reasoning in line with certain (Kohlbergian) fixed developmental stages, were *virtue-based* – in stark contrast to the whole of contemporary character-education ideology, be it of the expansive or non-expansive kind (witness again the misleading connotation of Nash's term 'virtuecrat'). A few more clarifications and caveats concerning Figure 5.1 are in order.

		VALUES TO BE TAUGHT	
		Perspectivist	*Cosmopolitan*
EMPHASIS IN TEACHING	*Substance*	*Expansive character education*, e.g.: • Religious-based character education • Liberationist pedagogy/critical postmodernism • Citizenship education	*Non-expansive character education*, e.g.: • Character education *simpliciter* • Socio-emotional learning
	Form	• Values clarification	• Philosophy for children • Moral reasoning/ developmental approach

Figure 5.1 Overview of trends in values education

(a) Substantivism does not imply the irrelevance of form/process. For instance, proponents of citizenship education (and, arguably, also NECE advocates) may hold that a certain form/process is indeed required (in particular, critical thinking and training in moral discussion) for instilling certain virtues. That, however, does not change the fact that their main emphasis is on the given substantive virtues being fostered in students, which clearly distinguishes, for instance, the citizenship educationists' idea of justice and democracy from that of the formalist Kohlberg who, at least until 1970, considered the organized cultivation of any particular set of virtues (his famous 'bag of virtues') indoctrinatory and undemocratic.

(b) Perspectivism does not necessarily imply moral relativism in the ordinary sense. To take religious-based character education (as already specified) as an example, although considering one's religious beliefs fundamental to one's moral outlook does not necessarily imply the belief that the whole of mankind should do the same, it does not necessarily imply either that the truth of those beliefs is and must remain relative to a specific group of people. Indeed, religious people typically believe that their particular set of moral and religious values should, ideally and ultimately, be adopted by the whole of mankind; until then, however, virtues should be taught to believers of their credo from the perspective of that credo (and some would add that this can only take place in separate schools). Citizenship education, based on virtue-based liberal ideals, is here similar in the sense that liberals who believe in such ideals normally think of democracy as *in fact* the only morally sustainable (the best, or at any rate the least faulty) form of government, which in the end will be disseminated to the rest of the world. Before that, democratic countries should lead the way by adopting citizenship education as the main perspective of character education in the common school. Here, virtue-based liberalism distinguishes itself once again from the more philosophically mainstream rights-based liberalism of the Rawlsian kind which accepts, in addition to Western liberal democracies, the lasting existence of other 'well-ordered' but non-democratic 'hierarchical' societies, that is, societies which guarantee their citizens some basic human rights, such as freedom from slavery and forced labour, but not necessarily the freedom to vote or freedom of thought and expression, enforcing instead some authoritarian doctrine. As long as such states remain peaceful and do not threaten to attack others, they should not be criticized in international forums, for such criticisms would assume the privileged access of Western liberals to scientific and moral truths, and undermine the liberal neutrality with regard to conceptions of the good life. In other words, we have, according to Rawls (1993), no rational means at our disposal for convincing non-liberals of the superiority of liberal justice and democracy, or, for that matter, of citizenship education as the core of character education. In contrast to the *modus vivendi* perspectivism of virtue-based liberalism, but similar to the permanent perspectivism of Rawlsian rights-based liberalism, postmodern perspectivism does, however, imply full-blown moral relativism (see Kristjánsson, 2002, s. 2.1).

(c) Philosophy for children (the P4C-movement) is something of an outsider in the figure. Its uniqueness rests on the fact that P4C advocates are not so much interested in the cultivation of moral character *per se* through the use of a certain formal technique (the 'community of inquiry') as they are in the adaptation of this technique to the *whole* of classroom practice. In so far as character education is on the agenda, however, most leading P4C enthusiasts would suggest cosmopolitan formalism as the way to make it work. Nevertheless, there are also individuals within the movement, particularly at the grassroots level, who reject moral cosmopolitanism, and whose ideas have, as a result, more resemblance to the method of values clarification (perspectivist formalism).

(d) It should be noted, in speaking of values clarification, that the perspective adopted there is not the perspective of a particular culture or subculture, but simply of an individual and those individuals who may, coincidentally, share his or her personal preferences.

(e) Not included in the figure are the ideas of those who totally reject the direct cultivation of *any* set of moral values in children at school, considering such cultivation inevitably harmful (for instance, indoctrinatory) or irrelevant ('mumbo-jumbo'), taking valuable time away from 'real' school subjects. Such ideas still persist although they are not as commonly expressed in mainstream educational and moral discourse as they were during the period from the 1950s through the 1970s.

Let me now say something about the differences in nature and merit between my classificatory schema of character education and that of McLaughlin and Halstead. By stating that NECE is typified by (a) moral cosmopolitanism and (b) methodological substantivism, whilst ECE is typified by (a) moral perspectivism and (b) methodological substantivism, I have dropped two important characteristics that McLaughlin and Halstead present, namely (i), concerning the nature and extent of the rationale offered for the respective conceptions, and (iii), concerning the nature and extent of the role given to appropriate forms of moral reasoning on the part of the student, and have added another feature, namely (b), methodological substantivism. In McLaughlin and Halstead's view, (i), (ii) and (iii) function as distinguishing criteria of NECE and ECE; for me, on the other hand, only (a) marks the difference. In other words, in my schema, there is one criterion that distinguishes between the two positions, namely (a) moral cosmopolitanism versus moral perspectivism. While (a) corresponds substantially to McLaughlin and Halstead's (ii), there is good reason to ask whether the subject of my specifications and that of McLaughlin and Halstead's is really the same (as I suggest by using the terms they coined) and, hence, whether these specifications can be seen as *competing*. If not only the subject but also the way the terms NECE and ECE are used are different, then *both* specifications might, for instance, be adequate.

In response, let me point out that both of these classificatory schemas take as their starting point certain accounts of character education prominent particularly in the USA (by Lickona, Kilpatrick and so on), and term them 'non-expansive'. The aim in both is, then, to suggest specifications that uniquely pick out those accounts and distinguish them from others. In this sense, both classificatory schemas are clearly about 'the same thing'. It is, however, well known that two different conceptual schemas can, in principle, carve up the same theoretical terrain in equally sound ways. Nevertheless, as long as one is not a follower of certain popular non-objectivist philosophies of modernity and postmodernity, one has good reason to consider factors such as respect for pre-theoretical facts, and usefulness or serviceability, in order to assess the relative merits of different schemas (cf. Carr, 1998). With those factors in mind, I would argue that my specifications of NECE and ECE are superior to those of McLaughlin and Halstead for at least three different reasons: (1) It is simply not in accordance with the facts to claim that all NECE accounts neglect moral reasoning, and offer primarily a naïve moral-declivity rationale for the enterprise of character education. This I aim to show in my rejoinders to objections (2) and (4), respectively, in the following section. (2) McLaughlin and Halstead's classifications fail to make room for certain important expansive accounts of character education, such as religious-based character education and postmodernism, which may for different reasons doubt the value of critical reflection as being either essentially biased against the infallibility of religious authority, or 'logo-centric'. Since McLaughlin and Halstead posit that in ECE the nature and scope of moral reasoning and reflection is emphasized, religious-based character education and postmodernism seem to fall by the wayside, fitting into neither ECE nor NECE although they are indisputably concerned with the transmission of qualities of character; in my schema, however, they usefully fit into the ECE framework. (This difficulty seems to be anticipated by McLaughlin and Halstead, 1999, p. 147.) (3) McLaughlin and Halstead limit themselves to formulating excluding features, that is, the differences between NECE and ECE, while my specifications are not only meant to divide character-education accounts among themselves, but also to distinguish them from other (non-character-education oriented) accounts of values education, for instance to distinguish both NECE and ECE from methodological formalism. I take this also to be a useful feature of my schema.

Non-expansive Character Education versus Citizenship Education on Justice

So much for taxonomical considerations. In the remainder of this section, I will concentrate on certain differences between NECE and the kind of ECE which has gained such prominence in recent educational discourse, not least in Europe, namely citizenship education. My exploration will bring to the fore crucial (actual or potential) disputes about justice education. Proponents of both NECE and citizenship education care deeply about justice as an educational value, but they do not share a common understanding of what justice is nor how it should be taught. Salutary lessons may, I believe, be learnt from their differences in this respect.

Some time ago, a high-school-level teacher phoned me for advice: 'I would like to teach my students something about the nature and value of justice. How would I best do it: European citizenship-education style with emphasis on just democratic skills and practices, or US character-education style with emphasis on justice as a personal virtue?' I was, admittedly, somewhat baffled by this question. My gut reaction at that time was to reply to my interlocutor that he was employing a somewhat misleading dichotomy, since citizenship education had as venerable a history in the USA as in Europe, and that he would, in any case, do best by emphasizing, at different stages in his teaching, both elements of justice. After this conversation, I was left with a lingering sense of dissatisfaction with the response I gave, and the following discussion may perhaps be seen as an extended attempt to come to terms with my own discontent. In fact, the teacher had put his finger on a distinction that, though oversimplified in the terms in which he couched it, nevertheless exists: a distinction that has, I believe, been given inadequate attention in the recent literature on citizenship education.

First a simple question: should schools help bring up students as good democratic citizens? If formulated in these somewhat vague terms, and allowing a broad enough conception of democracy as any form of government in which the ultimate source of power lies in the hands of the people, a positive answer to this question would meet with wide approval in most corners of the world. Even the leaders of a seemingly authoritarian regime, such as the People's Republic of China, might well insist that their single-party system constitutes, in this respect, a highly developed form of democracy, encompassing superior principles of democratic justice that students should learn to understand and appreciate.

The question of whether 'citizenship education' – in the familiar sense which has been developing gradually in education discourse – should be introduced into school curricula as a distinctive element is likely to meet with a more diverse, and less compliant, response. Although the notion of citizenship has, since the early 1990s, topped the charts for topic popularity in political theory (cf. Enslin and White, 2003, p. 110), and significant agreement exists 'in many quarters' that introducing citizenship education into the national curriculum – as has recently been done in England – is a 'positive step' (McLaughlin, 2000, p. 542), there are other 'quarters', political, philosophical and educational, where people remain more sceptical of, or even openly antagonistic to, such an introduction. The actual and potential sources of contention here are varied. Some object to citizenship education as a special school subject for pedagogical reasons; others point out, indeed correctly, that the conception of democracy and democratic justice implicit in the ideal of citizenship education is narrower, and more specific to Western (liberal) democracies, than the broad conception invoked in the foregoing paragraph and involves *inter alia* the regular transfer of power between elected representatives according to certain established justice procedures, as well as the invocation of a plethora of allegedly 'democratic' rights and responsibilities. Some critics would consider those to be essentially consumer-oriented and to presuppose a controversial Enlightenment idea of the primary role of the nation-state; they might then take exception to such a politically loaded conception for a number of distinct reasons.

Citizenship education constitutes, as I have already explained, a quintessential programme of ECE. It advocates the cultivation of perspective-sensitive (specifically, democratic) rather than cosmopolitan values – although its proponents may think that those democratic values should, ideally, be adopted by all human societies in due course, which is another story – and it is methodologically substantivist rather than formalist in that it does not confine itself to a single teaching method, even though it prioritizes critical thinking.

A quick look at guidelines for the teaching of citizenship education (e.g., DfES, 2002) brings more clearly to light the perspective-sensitive values it endorses. What should be noticed first is that citizenship education is concerned primarily with the transmission and inculcation of democratic values, not merely the teaching of facts about what such values involve. What is on offer is not mere 'civics', as it used to be known in some quarters, but an extensive programme of character moulding. The three main strands of citizenship education in England, for example, are said to be 'social and moral responsibility', 'community involvement' and 'political literacy'. The aim is to create thoughtful, just, critical, responsible and active democratic citizens who are able to reflect on moral and social issues, participate in discussions and reach informed decisions. Actualizing this ideal requires not only an awareness of the basic human rights and responsibilities underlying society, including a belief in human dignity and equality, but also a more specific commitment to particular democratic values such as democratic justice, tolerance, multiculturalism, majority rule, respect for private property and freedom of thought and speech. Furthermore, the best way to achieve this is through critical discussions in the classroom, although other didactic methods are not excluded.

Rather than outlining the content of citizenship education in more detail, I will assume that the reader is sufficiently familiar with the subject to appreciate the thrust of the ensuing exploration, and turn instead – again, rather briefly – to a rehearsal of the most commonly presented objections. Some of these are not so much objections to citizenship education *per se* as objections to any systematic programme of values education at school; others are pointed more directly at the proposed content of citizenship education. I will divide the objections at hand into 'conservative' and 'radical' ones. By 'conservative' I simply mean 'tending to the maintenance or reinforcement of existing practices in the given field of inquiry', while 'radical' here means 'tending to an important shift from existing practices in the given field of inquiry'. This distinction is politically neutral with respect to the distinction between 'right' and 'left' a dichotomy that in our times may be of dubious relevance.

The typical *conservative* objections to citizenship education can be divided, roughly, into those of *pedagogical* conservatism and *political* conservatism. Pedagogical conservatives think of citizenship education – as, indeed, of any form of values education *qua* special subject matter – as being at best useless and at worst harmful in that it takes valuable time away from core subjects and thus wastes school resources. There are no pedagogically accepted, sustainable ways of teaching values at school, but even if there were, values education is simply not the role of the school; rather, it is the responsibility of the family and other outside institutions (e.g., Tooley, 2000). Political conservatives go further in their criticisms by not only rejecting citizenship education as useless and/or uncalled for, but also as positively harmful, incapacitating individuals and undermining the social fabric. The methods customarily suggested for values education, not least the critical discussions championed by devotees of citizenship education, are said to make students easily liable to intellectual intoxication (plus, quite likely in its wake, political bias), and stimulate an overly critical frame of mind which constantly questions, and gradually erodes, traditionally proven forms of practice (e.g., O'Hear, 1981).

The most commonly heard *radical* objection to citizenship education stems from critical postmodernists and others sharing a similar orientation, for instance post-feminists. While applauding citizenship education for its sensitivity to moral perspectivism, these objectors claim that the perspective suggested there is too wide. There are no homogeneous notions of democratic justice or citizenship abroad which can and should be transmitted to all citizens in Western democratic societies, irrespective of gender, class and race – unless, that is, it is our intention to perpetuate and reinforce the middle-class, white, male image. Rather, in order to take account of the full range of cultural diversity and fragmentation, we need to identify and transmit more local-scale values which will help strengthen the self-identity of various subcultures (Hall, 2000; see also references to feminist critiques of citizenship education in Enslin and White, 2003, pp. 119–20).

There is, however, another and equally important – although rarely stated – radical objection to citizenship education and the ideal of democratic justice that it incorporates, implicit in the teachings of NECE, although rarely made explicit, and it is to this particular objection that I now turn. I hope that filling this lacuna in the literature may aid us in putting the idea of citizenship education to the test: 'us' in this case referring particularly to those who share McLaughlin's intuition of the initial plausibility of the claim that students should be entitled to some form of education in democracy and democratic justice at school (2000, p. 546), but who are also concerned, from a more general perspective, that schools should set the right priorities in values education.

In broad outline, the potentially radical objection directed at citizenship education from the NECE camp would maintain that citizenship education *politicizes* values education beyond good reason by assuming that political literacy and specific (democratic) social skills, rather than the cosmopolitan 'moral basics', are the primary values to be transmitted. One does not, of course, necessarily exclude the other: in England, for example, the older goals of Personal, Social and Health Education still remain, alongside those associated with citizenship education, which has been introduced as a foundation subject. Nevertheless – advocates of NECE might claim – the emphasis on this new foundation subject runs the risk of overshadowing and sidelining the necessary core of all values teaching, including justice teaching: namely, the inter-human psychological capabilities and moral virtues which lay the basis for social and political skill. To put it bluntly, the danger is that the cart will be put before the horse.

'Discovering' this objection does not require much philosophical excavation; the objection is, in fact, inherent in the very belief that distinguishes NECE from citizenship education, according to the earlier categorization in the present section. NECE theorists are, after all, moral cosmopolitans concerning core values, whereas citizenship education highlights a set of perspective-sensitive, if not necessarily morally relative, values. What is perhaps puzzling is why this objection has been at most hinted at, rather than carefully explored and expounded, in the teachings of NECE. I will analyse this objection in more detail presently, but let me first suggest a number of possible reasons for its absence from the overt NECE agenda.

(a) The breeding ground of NECE has been in the USA, while the debate about citizenship education as a special school subject has taken place mainly in Europe. This does not mean that theorists in the USA have been less enthusiastic about democratic values than their European counterparts; some of the most influential writings about citizenship and democracy education stem precisely from there. Since, however, citizenship as an educational goal has been more evenly mixed with various other psychological, moral and social goals in the American discursive tradition about values education than in the European one, there has, perhaps, been less room for potential conflict between basic and non-basic values in the former than in the latter.

(b) The chief aim of (at least earlier) NECE writings has been to slay the subjectivist dragon, witness Lickona's (1991) *bête noire* of 'personalism'. NECE theorists have, in general, been more concerned with arguing against those who oppose any systematic character cultivation at school rather than with deprecating attempts to initiate alternative values programmes, as long as those aim at transmitting positive values to students. In other words, to avoid internal dissension, NECE theorists seem to have chosen to stand together, as much as possible, with other substantivist trends in values education, rather than inviting factious dispute. What matters most for NECE is the ultimate goal, that is, creating morally better persons, and not quibbling over the methods or the order through which this is best achieved.

(c) What must not be overlooked either is that NECE theorists have taken up various insights from recent citizenship discourse. Lickona explicitly claims, as I noted earlier, that 'a host of democratic values' should be taught at school in our Western democratic societies, in addition to the cosmopolitan 'moral basics' (1991, p. 45). There seems to be a difference of emphasis here, rather than a difference in essence, but it is still a difference worth noting. For NECE, in our society, the democratic values constitute an important addition to a foundation of 'moral basics'; but if the latter has not been firmly secured, the former will be doomed to float in thin air. For example, it is, psychologically speaking, hard to imagine what could induce people to establish and sustain just democratic institutions if they were not driven by a personal virtue of justice as a motive. Citizenship is a valued activity in a person's life, but it is not the most valued activity, or, more accurately put, the democratic values do not penetrate as deeply to the core of a person's self as do the emotional and moral basics, incorporating, for instance, our desert-based emotions.

(d) Another reason, to the surprise of some readers, why NECE theorists seem to have refrained from trenchant criticism of the idea of citizenship education is that many of their writings are lacking in philosophical bite and rigour. Without such rigour, subtle differences and taxonomical nuances may easily be overlooked. It is not only the case that the canonical works of NECE have been written by non-philosophers, while citizenship education has boasted a number of prominent philosophical spokesmen (e.g., Gutmann, 1987; Callan, 1997), but also that the psychologists and educationists who have been at the forefront of NECE (be it the socio-emotional learning, or the slightly older character-education *simpliciter*, movement) have been science journalists, like Goleman, or educational activists, like Bennett, Lickona and Kilpatrick, rather than academics. The canonical works of NECE (e.g., Lickona, 1991; Kilpatrick, 1992; Goleman, 1995) are best-sellers, written for the general public, rather than monographs for fellow academics: works whose style of argument reflects, at times, the Emersonian point that a scream is sometimes better than a thesis. Furthermore, although NECE has, as I noted at the beginning of this chapter, gained momentum parallel to the upsurge of virtue ethics in academic moral philosophy and is similarly virtue-based, there seems to have been little direct rapport between the two. The frontrunners of NECE apparently did not arrive at their convictions by reading Anscombe, Foot or MacIntyre, and although their works tend to be interspersed with the odd nod to Aristotle, especially on the importance of childhood moral habituation and the recognition of the moral salience of the emotions, their ideas lack an explicit philosophical basis. In contrast, the citizenship-education movement has developed through an active dialectic with the citizenship debate in political philosophy, inspired by the works of Kymlicka and others. This is perhaps the chief explanation of why NECE theorists have been ill equipped – or have simply not cared – to criticize the idea of citizenship education from a theoretical standpoint.

Let me now, on behalf of NECE theorists, take a closer look at their putative radical objection to citizenship education. What precisely is the bone of contention? I think it is helpful, by way of analysis, to delineate here three major disagreements on which the objection rests.

(1) Disagreement about the good and the right Although the philosophical roots of NECE are not always easy to untangle, the sympathies of NECE theorists clearly lie with a teleological virtue-based ethics which considers the good prior to the right. What is right, socially or morally, is what makes people psychologically competent and morally good, wherever they live and at whatever time. The philosophical heritage of citizenship education is more deontologically oriented, with what is good being considered subservient to what is right, in virtue of institutional entitlements or general human rights. The citizen is, first and foremost, a *rights bearer*, whether of property rights or welfare rights (see Enslin and White, 2003, p. 112). The good citizen is 'a person who is skillful at the art of exercising her rights' (Tomasi, 2001, p. 75).

This must not be understood to mean that citizenship education is a kind of applied Kantian formalism. Quite the contrary, as I mentioned earlier. With respect to the well-established distinction within the liberal tradition between a 'thin' notion of citizenship based on Lockean entitlements or Kantian formalist procedures, and a 'thicker' notion harking back to Rousseau's positive-liberty republicanism or Mill's liberal virtues, citizenship education clearly attaches to the latter. The emphasis is, for example, on citizenship as an exercise concept – an 'active', 'maximal' notion – rather than merely an opportunity concept – a 'passive', 'minimal' notion – (see, e.g., McLaughlin, 2000, pp. 549ff.; Enslin and White, 2003, pp. 112–14). This does not change the fact, however, that the fundamental 'civic virtues' espoused in citizenship education, such as democratic justice and tolerance (Enslin and White, 2003, p. 123), are understood as social virtues whose ultimate justification rests on the *right* to be treated justly or to have one's way of life tolerated, rather than on a *human capabilities* view (e.g., Nussbaum, 1988), according to which human beings simply need justice-based (or, more specifically, desert-based) virtues, among other things, to function successfully. The ultimate grounding of NECE's virtues in the psychological and moral notion of the transcultural human good is, by contrast, more in line with the latter kind of justification, a point which relates to what I say about disagreement (3) below.

Given this disagreement about the good and the right, it is easy to understand why citizenship education's understanding of justice is first and foremost one of justice as a *social* virtue, grounded in procedural, democratically grounded rules, and dealing with institutional entitlements. For NECE, on the other hand, justice is at bottom a *personal* virtue, emotionally grounded in early childhood experiences, and dealing with pre-institutional deserts that are historically and developmentally prior to institutional entitlements – although they may ultimately be morally outweighed by such entitlements, which, as I have repeatedly pointed out in previous chapters, is quite another matter.

(2) Disagreement about pluralism The core belief of NECE is in one sense less, but in another sense more, pluralist than that of citizenship education. It is *morally* less pluralist in being less sympathetic to the notion of an endless array of good ways of living: a notion rooted in the famous liberal claim to neutrality with regard to the content of the good life as long as civic rights are carefully adhered to. Tolerance, for instance, seldom figures as a fundamental virtue in NECE lists of 'moral basics'. It is, however, *politically* more pluralist than citizenship education in refusing to consider active participation in a democratic society a necessary condition of human well-being. There is nothing in the tenets of NECE which excludes the possibility that such well-being can be achieved under some other form of government, as long as people there are able to actualize their 'emotional intelligence' and 'moral basics'. Moreover, it would be in line with NECE's view to say that while a just society is logically and psychologically impossible without just persons, persons can, in principle, remain just although democratic justice does not happen to be the 'first virtue' (in the Rawlsian sense) of political institutions in the society in which they happen to live.

(3) Disagreement about the connection between the political and the moral There is a long tradition in philosophy, harking back to the ancient Greeks, which maintains that politics supervenes on morality, both logically and psychologically. In the order of books in Aristotle's corpus, the *Politics* follows naturally on the heels of the *Nicomachean Ethics*. For it is only after the soul of the student has been properly habituated for noble joys, and our conception of human *eudaimonia* has been firmly secured, that it becomes logically appropriate and psychologically possible to ruminate over questions of legislation and statesmanship (Aristotle, 1985, pp. 291–8 [1179b–1181b]). The ideas of NECE – in particular of the socio-emotional learning movement – are heavily influenced by this line of thinking, and this is reflected in the objection under scrutiny. When talking about the danger of the cart being put before the horse in values education, the underlying thought is, precisely, that the correct logical order of morality and politics will be reversed, namely, that justice as a moral concept will be thought to supervene on justice as a political concept, rather than the other way round – a view that could allegedly have harmful pedagogical implications.

Various reasons have now emerged which explain why the virtue of justice, while espoused in both citizenship education and NECE, would be viewed from radically different perspectives in the two values-education programmes. These differences obviously have ramifications for what should be taught about justice in values education and how. NECE would, for instance, emphasize that while justice education should be provided to all children, it should not be provided to them primarily *qua* upcoming citizens but rather *qua* human beings, suiting them not merely for their public, political functions, but more importantly (or at least more fundamentally) for their private, domestic ones. Justice would, then, first have to be cultivated as an *emotional virtue*: as the capacity to feel the right *desert-based* emotions, such as compassion, indignation and so on, at the right time, in the right proportion, towards the right people, until this capacity had seeped into the child's character like dye into wool (cf. Reeve, 1998). Only thereafter could critical inquiry about questions of *political* justice start to have a useful educational function.

Interesting and important as the curricular implications of NECE and citizenship education, respectively, are for justice education, as well as for all values education, we must not forget the more pervasive implications of those two values-education programmes. All theories of education need to be understood in relation to certain fundamental conceptions of the human being and of the human good. As we have seen, NECE's essential misgiving about citizenship education rests on the latter's vision of human beings as fundamentally rational choosers and as bearers of social, democratically grounded, rights. Proponents of NECE also champion democratic rights and justice, but they ask us to remember that a human being is not only a political being, at least not in a narrow sense of 'political': it is a physical, emotional and moral being growing up in a natural world. We need to understand democratic justice and teach students about its workings, but we also need to look *beyond* (see Tomasi, 2001) – or to put it more accurately here: *beneath* – democratic justice to the kind of emotional sense of justice that originally shapes us as human beings. It is, thus, not enough, although important, to acknowledge that there are vital issues about human relationships 'that are not reducible to concerns about justice but instead arise *after* [institutional] justice has been freely affirmed' (ibid., p. 34); it needs to be acknowledged that such issues arise *prior to* the affirmation of institutional justice.

To sum up, I have now located the crux of what I have called 'NECE's radical objection to citizenship education' in three interrelated disagreements: about (1) the good and the right, (2) pluralism and (3) the connection between morality and politics. The next logical step would be to ask whether the suggested objection is defensible. Given my earlier moral justification of desert-based emotions, the reader will know that my general sympathies lie here with NECE, whose basic tenets I will, furthermore, defend against various misfired objections in the following section. But this is not the place to argue that point further. Let me close this discussion, rather, by anticipating and answering a likely misgiving about my characterization of this objection.

A possible interlocutor might claim that I have misidentified NECE's objection as a radical one when it is simply a conservative objection in disguise. Conservatives like to attribute moral or immoral characteristics to individual accomplishments or failings rather than to societal factors. Is that not precisely the point of the objection that I have explored, namely, that citizenship education cannot, allegedly, succeed in improving the workings of society because it does not penetrate deeply enough to the locus of the individual's free will which alone decides whether he acts justly or unjustly? And in that case, have I not confirmed the old suspicion that the proponents of NECE – at least those belonging to the movement of character education *simpliciter* in the USA – are, overtly or covertly, pursuing a 'neo-conservative agenda' in values education (see, e.g., Nash, 1997), an agenda which tells us to let well enough alone?

In response, I would like to explain why this misgiving fails to show that the objection in question is a *conservative*, rather than a *radical*, one, given the 'literal' understanding of those two labels invoked earlier. First, NECE wants to implement an extensive programme of values education at school, rather than 'letting well alone', and it does not share the conservatives' fear of indoctrination. NECE's objection to citizenship education is not, like the conservative ones, that citizenship education sets unrealistic and/or potentially harmful goals, but rather that its goals are not far-reaching enough. Second, NECE does not, in fact, disagree with the introduction of citizenship education and democratic justice into school curricula, as true conservatives do (e.g., O'Hear, cited in McLaughlin, 2000, p. 553). NECE simply wants citizenship education to be kept in its proper place as a supplement to, but not a replacement for, the 'moral basics', and democratic justice as a supplement to justice as a personal, emotional virtue. Third, NECE is not only concerned with individual moral improvement; its aim is to effect an eventual change in society, a change of which schools would become one of the main engines (Lickona, 1991, pp. 320–21; Kilpatrick, 1992, p. 226; see further in the following section). This is hardly the expression of a conservative position.

Perhaps NECE's radical objection to citizenship education can best be summarized by saying that programmes of citizenship education are not ambitious enough in changing people for the better: in making them, for instance, as they should be, more righteously indignant of ill-gotten gains, more compassionate towards undeserved sufferings and so forth. Now, it may well be that the claims of NECE are themselves too ambitious; the odds are obviously stacked against an enterprise whose aim is not only to improve people's morality but also to radically alter character traits which might predict up to 80 per cent of success in life (see Goleman's somewhat exaggerated original claim, 1995). Some early research shows improvements in classroom behaviour (better mood and less violence) after the implementation of NECE programmes, but more ambitious claims about NECE's ability to make students both 'better and smarter' in the long run have yet to be borne out in research results (see Mayer and Cobb, 2000). So, whatever our view of NECE's objection to citizenship education, it is obvious that an extensive evaluation of NECE's own claims and programmes is needed before we can determine whether it stands a chance, in actual practice, of achieving those very goals that it blames citizenship education for not setting.

5.2 Some Further Educational Concerns

Non-expansive character education (NECE) is a direct heir to the Aristotelian legacy of moral education. Although this is rarely stated explicitly in the writings of what tends to be referred to as the character education *simpliciter* movement in the USA, that is, by people such as Lickona and Kilpatrick, the Aristotelian spirit of moral cosmopolitanism and methodological substantivism animates their whole project. Aristotle famously highlighted the common inter-human denominator through his observation that 'in our travels we can see how every human being is akin ... to a human being' (1985, p. 208 [1155a]), and his suggested moral pedagogy was a multifaceted one, building on young people's nascent moral and emotional sensibilities not only through verbal instruction or dialogue but also through poem recitals and musical performances. Perhaps a young person's sense of proportionality, needed among other things for a proper sense of desert, would, as Aristotle and many of the other ancients suggested, be better cultivated through music rather than through discussion classes. This kinship to Aristotle is clearly brought out in the works of Goleman, the guru of the socio-emotional learning movement – another NECE variety, as we recall. He acknowledges that the whole idea of 'emotional intelligence' is but a response to Aristotle's challenge 'to manage our emotional life with intelligence' so that we can feel the right emotions towards the right persons, at the right time and in the right proportion – all in order for us to function well as moral and social beings (Goleman, 1995, p. xv; see further in Kristjánsson, 2002, pp. 177–8). When trying, in the present section, to expand the discourse about NECE by exploring some of the objections that have been raised against it, it does well to recall this historical kinship. Indeed, a person's general sympathies with, or reservations about, the Aristotelian view of moral education are likely to be carried over into an assessment of the pros and cons of NECE. It is, therefore, paramount to begin by rehearsing briefly some of the main underpinnings of the Aristotelian view.

Enter Aristotle

For Aristotle, the very point of moral development is to help the young to acquire a personal character exemplifying true moral virtue. As already noted (in Section 1.3), virtue, for Aristotle, is about both actions and emotions. Virtue, as other character traits, arises through *repeated practice*: we become just by performing just acts; or we grow a disposition to *Schadenfreude* if we indulge in *Schadenfreude* often enough. But what is meant by saying that to be just, we must first act and feel justly? If we do what is musical, we must already be musicians. In the same way, if we choose what is just, must we not already be just? (1985, p. 39 [1105a]). This objection is invoked as a rhetorical question by Aristotle himself, and his answer to it is very much to the point. Cultivation of the virtues starts (as the cultivation of any other capacity or craft) by *habituation*: 'It is not unimportant, then, to acquire one sort of habit or another right from our youth; rather, it is very important, indeed all-important' (ibid., p. 35 [1103b]). The moral educator must make sure that the child performs the right actions, feels the right emotions. However, if this is so, are we really responsible for our character traits? Are they not then attributable to our parents and other educators, who train us in youth to acquire the right or wrong habits, and hence beyond our control?

We must hold in view here the fact that Aristotle is not talking about or addressing brainwashed people, people systematically inculcated with vicious beliefs, or imbeciles. His audience comprises normal, autonomous persons who have enjoyed average or better upbringing. Such persons not only acquire a whole gamut of virtuous dispositions through habituation – with pursuits assiduously followed becoming by and by ingrained habits – but equally importantly, they also grow their own intellectual virtue of practical reason (*phronesis*): the capacity to evaluate and choose between courses of action and reaction through gradually developing discernment of which of the courses accords best with the human *telos* of *eudaimonia*. (Contrary to some of the recent educational literature on Aristotle, e.g., Dunne, 1993, Aristotle was not a moral intuitionist or particularist, but rather a naturalist foundationalist, with the foundation of morality resting firmly on the ideal of human flourishing.) Gradually, habituation plays a less significant role in people's character formation; more and more dispositions become established as a result of their own deliberations and choices. Concomitantly, they also become capable of reassessing and gradually refining those traits with which they were originally inculcated. This is a process of natural transformation from habituated internalized virtue to full virtue, the lifeblood of the whole moral developmental process, as children learn to channel their habituated responses into streams of true moral awareness and motivation.

In this way 'we are ourselves in a way jointly responsible for our states of character', as Aristotle famously put it (ibid., p. 70 [1114b]). The unjust person or the person prone to *Schadenfreude* may not be able to get rid of these traits now, but is still responsible for them since it was originally open to that person to take the steps necessary for not acquiring such a character (see ibid., p. 68 [1114a]). Once the relevant disposition has taken root through this natural reappraisal process and become, so to speak, second nature to the person, it will not be necessary for practical reason to dictate every act or every experience of an emotion – the person will simply act and feel in accordance with his or her character. It is, then, in a sense true that a just act may be defined as one that a just person would do, and a just emotion one which a just person would feel. But if you are an adult and wish to be considered just, you will not be considered so merely on the basis of doing just actions or feeling the right justice-grounding emotions; rather, it is only if you perform those acts and feel those emotions *in the way* that just people do (ibid., p. 40 [1105b]), that is, *only if*, first, you act or feel justly as a direct or indirect result of your own *choice*; second, you are *reflectively conscious* of what you are doing or feeling; third, you choose to act or feel virtuously because you have a personal appreciation of the *essential worth* of the relevant action or emotion, the value of which you have taken to heart; and, fourth, you take *noble pleasure* in the given activity or emotional experience. Being taught to act or feel correctly in youth is, therefore, only a necessary but not a sufficient condition of eventual virtue. Practical reason must still be called upon, if needed, to justify and sustain an act or an emotion in each particular instance, and also to adjudicate between the competing claims of competing acts or emotions in times of conflict (see further in Reeve, 1998; Curzer, 2002; Kristjánsson, 2002, pp. 172–3).

NECE: Objections and Rejoinders

With this Aristotelian background in mind, we are now better equipped to deal with some of the *negative* arguments commonly brought against NECE. In rebutting them, as I aim to do, two strategies are be open to me. One is to claim that although many criticisms of existing accounts of NECE are valid, it is possible to formulate a more sophisticated account, for example one drawing more explicitly on Aristotle, which circumvents those criticisms; I avail myself of such a strategy, to a limited extent, in what follows. My main strategy, however, will be to argue that the criticisms typically levelled against NECE do not apply to two of the most famous canonical works of NECE, namely Lickona's *Educating for Character* (1991) and Kilpatrick's *Why Johnny Can't Tell Right from Wrong* (1992), and that many of the criticisms seem, in fact, to be based on a misreading of those books. What stands out at the end of my defence of NECE will, I hope, be a view of NECE as a reasonable middle-ground proposal in values education, avoiding both the underdetermination of formalism and subjectivism, and the overdetermination of more expansive accounts. While the former have too little substance to give children a proper moral grounding, and the latter too much to account for a justifiable plurality of values – religious or non-religious; in one political system or another – NECE seems more or less right. Human beings, from whatever background they come, form a single species that cannot thrive without a minimal set of common virtues – including, in my view, justice as a personal virtue incorporating proper desert-based emotions – and schools need to occupy an active role, rather than being moral bystanders, in cultivating these virtues.

In order to keep the length of the present section within reasonable limits, I will try to summarize the main objections against NECE as briefly as I can and also to keep my rejoinders, as much as possible, to the point.

Objection 1 'Grounding a character education programme in the alleged "moral basics" of NECE is both infeasible and unfair (to various cultures and subcultures) since all the virtues it espouses are time-and-place-relative. NECE falsely creates the appearance of standing above the fray when, in reality, it simply pursues the virtues of a certain controversial world view. More specifically, (a) the virtues advanced in NECE are based on an "obsolete" view of human nature as fixed and agreed upon (Nash, 1997, pp. 15; 40–41); (b) there is, as a matter of fact, "no universal moral standard" today for evaluating the worth of those virtues (ibid., p. 15); (c) they make scant room for difference but push rather for conformity like some kind of "moral police" (ibid., pp. 10–11); and (d) they are, in any case, too "underdetermined" (McLaughlin and Halstead, 1999, p. 145) to serve as a guide to correct action and emotion in particular cases.'

Rejoinder 1 When Lickona stakes out the opposite view, namely that there 'are rationally grounded, nonrelative, objectively worthwhile moral values' (1991, p. 230), he does not spend much time meeting the specific complaints listed above; neither does Kilpatrick. What could, however, be said is that (a) when contemporary moral objectivists most plausibly utilize the notion of a human *telos*, they do so without invoking any controversial metaphysical, biological or theological conception of human nature, and without taking a stand regarding the perennial nature–nurture debate. What they invoke is simply a conception derived from the 'human experience of life and value', the shared identities of people, which cut across time and place, about what it means to be a human being rather than a beast or a god (Nussbaum, 1988, p. 177). This is what Nussbaum terms 'empirical' or 'internalist essentialism' (1992, p. 208), and it is precisely to that kind of 'essentialism' that I implicitly referred in my naturalist justification of desert in Section 4.3. Such essentialism can hardly be considered a narrowly fixed 'antiquarian' view of human nature. In response to (b), it may well be that when we consider the far-fetched quandaries with which students tend to be presented in ethics classes, we come to think of all virtues and vices as inherently context-dependent and problematic (see Kilpatrick, 1992, p. 85). However, once we focus on the core virtues, such as respect and responsibility (Lickona, 1991, p. 43) or our basic sense of desert, and consider everyday this-worldly, rather than contrived science-fiction, scenarios, we realize that there are, indeed, moral values which – when clearly analysed and argued for – should appeal to all rational persons, irrespective of their philosophical/political orientation. These values are what they are in virtue of what human beings need in order to thrive and what human societies need in order to function properly. The critics of NECE, who deny the existence of any transcultural values, it should be noted, cheat when they themselves make use of precisely one such value, namely the *undeservingness* involved in discriminating against other cultures. Interestingly, Goodstein (1993) reports that in September 1993, representatives of more than 125 different religions signed a 'Declaration of a Global Ethic'. The consensus reached on general moral issues was such that 'there was no objection to any important point', which indicates, in line with Lickona's reasoning, that the extent of not only philosophical, but also religious, disagreement on moral issues tends to be overemphasized. And as to (c), contemporary moral cosmopolitanism makes do with a conception of human beings and their good that, while being 'thick' as compared to the ultra-thin one of rights-based liberalism, is also 'vague' in that it admits of as many different manifestations as there can be ways to lead a good human life (Nussbaum 1990, p. 205). It allows for a great deal of – albeit not endless – latitude with regard to individual and cultural differences, and highlights the variety, as opposed to the single uniformity, of ways in which one can be a good person. NECE thus need not be 'conformist' at all, in the objectors' sense of the term.

The opponents of NECE seldom set out in detail precisely what they mean by (d), the underdeterminacy of NECE's core virtues. Perhaps three sub-complaints can be disentangled here: that (d1) possessing the proper virtues does not remove the need for moral reflection on particular situations, (d2) definitions of virtues versus right actions 'tend to be circular' (Nash, 1997, p. 15) and (d3) it is impossible to determine which virtue on the basic list should take priority in times of conflict (ibid., p. 40). In answer to (d1), no serious virtue theorist has ever claimed that moral virtues can simply be 'carried out' unreflectively, like eating a cone of ice-cream with one's mind somewhere else. Ever since Aristotle, as we saw above, the need for practical reason (*phronesis*) as a specific (meta-) virtue, or as a tool of the other virtues, has been strongly underlined. As regards (d2), it is true that virtue-based accounts define an action or emotion as morally right if and only if it is an exercise of a moral virtue, but to avoid circularity the virtues are not simply defined as those dispositions which lead to right action/emotion, but rather as those character traits a human being needs to flourish or live well (in the Aristotelian sense) and/or to enjoy the higher-quality pleasures (in the Millian sense). And finally, in respect to (d3), perhaps modern virtue theory *à la* Foot and Hursthouse does fall prey to a non-action/emotion-guiding objection, as is frequently charged (see Section 4.3). NECE, however, does not necessarily presuppose that kind of virtue theory. It can easily avail itself of a more comprehensive moral framework, and a stricter decision procedure, such as that provided by older, virtue-based theories like classical Millian utilitarianism or, for that matter, Aristotle's own brand of virtue ethics. In sum, there is no reason to doubt that the set of virtues championed in NECE can guide action and emotion, even in dilemma situations.

Objection 2 'NECE is "dangerously antidemocratic" and "anti-intellectual" (Nash, 1997, p. 10) in its "relative neglect of the development of reasoning and critical independence in students" (McLaughlin and Halstead, 1999, p. 144). By emphasizing habituation over moral reasoning, it creates intellectually impoverished, uncritical moral agents and is conducive to the nebulous ways in which bias and prejudice are perpetuated. If character education is a remedy for the underdevelopment of students' moral faculties, then NECE is worse than the disease.'

Rejoinder 2 At least three points are pertinent in response here. First, (a) one must not forget that, historically, NECE serves as an antidote to the emphasis on form over content inherent in the earlier accounts of moral development and values clarification. If some proponents of NECE (I am thinking of Bennett and Kilpatrick in particular) go a bit further than is reasonably required in the opposite direction, that may have been needed, for historical reasons, to rectify the imbalance. Second, (b), as Nash for one concedes (1997, p. 40), Aristotle – on whom it would be natural for NECE theorists to draw in their arguments for the necessity of early habituation – never thought of habituation as a sufficient form of moral training. Of equal importance for him is, as we saw earlier, to help students gradually develop their own practical reason: the capacity to evaluate and choose between different courses of action and reaction. In the third place, (c) the claim that NECE theorists underestimate the importance of moral reasoning seems unfounded; Lickona, for example, emphasizes its importance in a chapter about moral reflection which could have been written by Kohlberg in his heyday (1991, ch. 12). It would be singularly inapt to say about Lickona that he wants 'uncritical acceptance of ready-made truths' (Kohn, 1997, p. 160). Even Kilpatrick, who is more wary than Lickona of the perils of moral-reasoning classes turning into 'bull sessions' (1992, p. 16) or nugatory chatter – at worst, fostering the capacity for artful self-deception, rationalization and hypocrisy (see also Puka, 2000, p. 141) – still thinks that the moral-discussion method, if 'used judiciously and in an age-appropriate way', can constitute a 'useful teaching tool' (1992, p. 88). For instance, although a virtuous character trait, such as the general sense of desert, need not be called into question in our teaching, there is room for exploring its proper application (cf. ibid., p. 239). There is also an important distinction here between exploring and questioning. Perhaps the best way to teach students to appreciate the virtue of justice is to let them reflect morally upon what human society would be like without such a virtue. That is, however, not the same as putting the virtue into question in class (except perhaps for rhetorical purposes).

Admittedly, the charge of 'relative neglect of the development of reasoning' in NECE accounts is not adequately met simply by producing a few places in a couple of books where reasoning is advocated, although it shows that such accounts do not necessarily incorporate this 'neglect'. More generally speaking, however, presenting habituation and moral reasoning as mutually exclusive *alternatives* seems to be nothing but an exercise in intellectual browbeating, a typical example of the detrimental either–or kind of pedagogy against which Dewey so memorably warned in his later work. Surely, as McLaughlin and Halstead themselves concede, children 'need to receive initial training in the virtues and it is incoherent to object to such training as involving illicit influence' (1999, p. 149), reflecting the Aristotelian point that the palace of moral reasoning must be entered through the courtyard of early habituation; surely also, moral maturity cannot be reached without the cultivation of one's moral-reasoning skills. It is the old truth about the hard-working Martha as well as the inspiring Mary of education. In so far as habituation and reasoning involve competing emphases, NECE – built as it is on a broadly Aristotelian virtue-based foundation – seems admirably equipped to accommodate both of them (cf. Puka, 2000, p. 132). Nevertheless, one must never forget the *Euthypro*-type message that a moral statement does not become true simply *because* of its having been arrived at in a certain reasonable way, such as through moral discussion and reflection, and that this holds even if the only way to arrive at its truth is through such methods. Rather, it will then be arrived at through such methods *because* it is true.

Objection 3 'The virtues proclaimed by NECE are too methodologically and morally individualistic, anti-social and hence politically conservative. The concept of virtue is reified as the attribute of a distinct individual and as separable from its socio-cultural context (Purpel, 1997, p. 143). Vice is thus considered rooted in individual failings rather than in social, economic and political structures, and improvement is sought through personal change, rather than the change of societal factors.' Different strains of ECE suggest different alternatives. Citizenship education, for example, proposes the creation of virtuous citizens (Callan, 1997, p. 3), while liberationist and postmodern accounts demand the active overthrow of institutionalized injustices and social domination.

Rejoinder 3 My answer is again fourfold. First, (a) NECE is, at least, not individualistic in one common sense of the word, namely it cannot be accused of being subjectivist. Lickona, among others, is highly critical of all types of subjectivism and personalism which he sees as causing the erosion of moral values, and also strongly opposes the 'new selfishness' of contemporary commercialism (1991, pp. 9ff.). Moreover, he is well aware of the fact that even if personal virtues are conceptually prior to social ones (see below), the former must rely on social relationships and social settings for their nurture and sustenance (see also Puka, 2000, p. 131). Second, (b) proponents of NECE are not opposed to the cultivation of social virtues and political awareness. They seem, however, to believe that charity must start at home and that political education begins with 'personal works' (Lickona, 1991, p. 320). This is not a stance that can simply be dismissed as 'conservative'. For instance, non-politically engaged philosophers have argued that a developed sense of *social* justice gradually develops as a generalization and, eventually as a rationalization, of a *personal* sense of injustice, awakened by perception of undeservingness (see my discussion in Section 3.1). In other words, an important social virtue is parasitic on a personal one, without which the former can be neither developed nor sustained. More radically, (c), as I noted in Section 5.1, Lickona and Kilpatrick suggest not only that the personal virtues are conceptually prior to the social ones and *can* ensue in social action, but also that they *should* do so. Kilpatrick wants schools to be 'one of the main engines of social change' (1992, p. 226), and Lickona approvingly cites examples of specific schools having a tradition of developing 'social-political awareness as a source of social action', concluding with the German educator Michael Miller that 'moral education must include political education' (1991, pp. 320–21). These are hardly statements of conservative individualism. It may well be that, unbeknownst to me, Lickona happens to be a spokesman for conservative politics, just as William Bennett happened to be Secretary of Education in the Reagan government; but reading such a message out of Lickona's book would be an exercise in *ad hominem* argumentation. Finally, (d) it should be pointed out that the political implications of the kind of Aristotelian empirical essentialism which underlies many of the NECE accounts seem to be anything but conservative. Such essentialism requires the state to take a firm, even radical, stand on many educational and cultural issues eschewed by liberal authorities. The state will, for instance, have to support educational programmes aimed at fostering the basic human capabilities, and it must make sure that the content of these programmes is conducive to human flourishing (Nussbaum, 1990) and/or the Millian higher-quality pleasures.

Objection 4 'NECE is too apocalyptic, nostalgic and anachronistic. We are considered to be in the midst of a moral crisis, caused by a deteriorating social fabric which is gradually changing modern society into a sink of iniquity, and the solution is sought in a return to a pre-modern haven of innocence and stability' (McLaughlin and Halstead, 1999, p. 140; Nash, 1997, pp. 8, 17–18). The earlier charge of conservatism here reappears at a deeper level: NECE is allegedly anti-progressive in its reliance on the (re-)establishment of the (pre-)existing.

Rejoinder 4 (a) In one sense, there is no disagreement about the truth of the 'moral-declivity' thesis: moral education has declined, if not morality itself. This is the common ground from which the whole contemporary discussion of character education starts, not only that of the NECE advocates. In my estimation, the NECE engine is powered more by a moral-education-declivity thesis than a moral-declivity one. More importantly, however, (b) the books by Lickona and Kilpatrick are not textbooks for university students, let alone monographs for fellow academics (if they had been, they would, unfortunately, not have sold in the hundreds of thousands!). They are written for parents, teachers and the general public, and are part of a long tradition of moralistic writing. Books of this kind, which have appeared at regular intervals throughout the history of civilization, tend to start with a recitation of dire social problems – where it never rains but it pours – in a steadily declining world which needs to be put back on the right track. Why Lickona and Kilpatrick should have chosen this style of writing need not present much of a mystery. When fighting for the attention of readers, overstatement is more effective than understatement. I have personally been advised, when submitting a book manuscript to an American publisher, to 'make it more appealing to the reader, especially the introductory part'. I am not saying that the moralistic tone adopted by Lickona and Kilpatrick, especially in the opening chapters of their books, is merely a rhetorical trick, aimed at capturing an audience. Nevertheless, it is significant that Lickona's dire references to increased social disorder among the young play no part in his argument after the first chapter, and indeed it is difficult to envisage what changes if any he would have to make in his subsequent discussion even if it should be the case, as Nash holds, that we are going through a period of moral 'incline' rather than decline (1997, p. 35). Glum declivity moralism pervades Kilpatrick's book to a greater extent than it does Lickona's, but even his discussion does not seem to imply that improved character education at school is important only, or even essentially, because of the sad state of modern society. NECE is something that, for him, would be essential in any society under any social conditions, simply because of the way human beings are.

It should also be noted that (c) moral primitivism based on an innocence–fall–alienation–redemption model is a salient feature of the views of thinkers as otherwise disparate as Plato, Rousseau and Marx. Such primitivism, notably, does not colour the books under scrutiny here. Lickona's work is in general more historically forward-looking than backward-looking (apart from the first chapter), and Kilpatrick avowedly resents the 'idyllic imagination' which equates old and primitive with more natural and morally better (1992, pp. 213–14). Finally, (d) Lickona and Kilpatrick are, admittedly, not political revolutionaries. Yet it seems to be a gross misinterpretation of their theories to claim that they are simply pursuing a neo-conservative agenda, concerned with the maintenance of the status quo (as Purpel does, 1997). NECE suggests, generally speaking, a radical departure from existing practices of liberal education by endorsing a rich programme of character education, aimed at making the world, gradually, a better, different place. In contrast, critical postmodernism is the acme of conservatism – if we understand conservatism as aiming at the reinforcement of existing categories – with all its we-are-like-this identity politics and parochialisms (see further in Kristjánsson, 2002, s. 2.1).

Objection 5 'NECE is disturbingly authoritarian, paternalistic and self-righteous in tone and style. Its devotees orate, admonish, pontificate, ridicule, hyperbolize, cajole and accuse (Nash, 1997, p. 39) instead of arguing and teaching.'

Rejoinder 5 (a) Given the Aristotelian empirically 'vague', if 'thick', conception of the good, and NECE's short list of 'moral basics', it is difficult to justify an accusation of paternalism (see rejoinder 1c above). Besides, paternalism is counter-productive in so far as it constrains students to behave in ways which are not (yet) part of their moral make-up and, in fact, discourages, rather than encourages, them to continue in the same vein. Additionally, (b) if the complaint is that some of the writings of authors like Lickona and Kilpatrick are so polemical that their credibility is impaired, they have many accomplices among ECE theorists. Nash, for one, tends to be more strident in tone than Lickona and even seems to be rather proud of it. And again, (c) the literary genre to which Lickona and Kilpatrick are contributing as authors must be taken into account here (see 4b above and my point about the non-academic credentials of many NECE activists in Section 5.1).

Objection 6 'NECE "has failed to work out a well-grounded and systematic pedagogy" (McLaughlin and Halstead, 1999, p. 146). Its proponents are "disingenuously silent" about the didactics of NECE or overly simplistic in their faith in the "moral contagion" effect of inspiring stories (Nash, 1997, pp. 46–7). The only pedagogical arguments offered are of the anecdotal kind.'

Rejoinder 6 (a) The partners-in-crime manoeuvre comes first to mind here. The most common complaint made by students and teachers of *all* educational theories is that theorists build 'castles in the air' without regard for implementation in the classroom. Also, (b) if anything, Lickona's book should be less open to this complaint than most other treatises about character education, as two-thirds of the book concern precisely moral didactics, including such advanced techniques as cooperative learning. One of his most important statements is that values education 'is a doable job' (1991, p. 22). In general, (c) educators tend to revel in anecdotal evidence, particularly of an autobiographical nature. It would be unfair to equate 'anecdotal' across the board with 'simplistic' in this regard. And additionally, (d) both Lickona and Kilpatrick propose a multifaceted didactic programme of character education, along Aristotelian lines, which includes music, art, stories, democratic discussion and caring beyond the classroom (Lickona, 1991, pp. 68–70; Kilpatrick, 1992, p. 24). Never is it suggested that simply telling a story and driving home its 'moral' is enough. Finally, (e) evaluating the effects of character-education programmes, be they of the NECE or ECE kind, is indeed difficult. The Hawthorne and Pygmalion effects, the difference between impact (in one particular place) and general coverage, and other related problems abound (Cline and Feldmesser, 1983, pp. 66–9). I have yet to be convinced, however, that NECE theorists are less aware of these problems than other proponents of character education.

I hope that my overview of objections to NECE and possible rejoinders to them – streamlined as it necessarily was – has helped to deflect some of the challenges that NECE is considered to face. In particular, it should now be clear why I deem both a moral-declivity thesis and the purported underestimation of moral reasoning unworthy for inclusion in McLaughlin and Halstead's specifications of the essential characteristics of NECE (see Section 5.1). A more sensitive assessment of these two canonical works of the NECE movement reveals them to be more historically forward-looking than backward-looking, and duly concerned with moral reasoning as an open-minded, critical activity.

I do not find myself in agreement with every point Lickona and Kilpatrick make about proper character education; for example, I am sceptical of Lickona's stance on sexual education, which seems to go much further in the direction of narrow conservatism than is required by the 'moral basics' that he elsewhere champions. Most of the common worries about their 'conservatism' and 'narrow-mindedness', however, can be circumvented if we look closely at what they really say in their books, as opposed to what they are supposed to have said. At the same time, we should not overestimate the importance of these two works for the further development and refinement of NECE. They were, after all, written more than a decade ago, and since then much new material has appeared, within the confines of not only philosophy of education but also general moral philosophy, material that is relevant to the viability of NECE as a programme of values education, in general, and justice education, in particular.

Some Final Thoughts on Justice Education

Our considerations of the practice of justice education, embarked upon at the beginning of the present chapter, have taken us on a long journey through the ramifications of recent accounts of values education – with special emphasis on the comparison between non-expansive character education (NECE) and citizenship education – via a backward glance at Aristotle, to a rebuttal of the criticisms which are (wrongly) thought to imperil the project of NECE. Before bringing this excursion into educational matters to a close, I want to consider a final misgiving about the viability of an Aristotelian (or Aristotle-inspired) theory of emotion education, and then to compare and contrast the views of Aristotle and Hoffman on the pedagogy behind the cultivation of justice as a personal virtue.

The particular character trait in whose cultivation we are most interested in the present book is that of people's sense of desert. As we have seen in previous chapters, our sense of desert is rooted in certain desert-based emotions which are natural, 'original passions', but whose development can – as with other emotions – be fostered or stifled in moral education. Having justified the experience of these emotions in Section 4.3, the question then became that of how to foster them in the proper didactic ways, and subsequently how to accommodate them within the context of a mature sense of justice, incorporating both our sense of desert and the acknowledgement of morally justified institutional entitlements. In the present chapter, I have focused on the first, and the chronologically prior one, of those two tasks and have suggested, for that purpose, Aristotle-inspired non-expansive character education, involving a mixture of early habituation and the gradual cultivation of practical reason.

A doubt which could be raised at this point concerns habituation as a proper method for cultivating emotions such as our desert-based ones. Even if we accept the broad Aristotelian picture as adequate for a description of action habituation, we might want to question its aptness in accounting for the early development of affective dispositions. Steutel and Spiecker (2004) discuss this potential problem in some detail and consider it to rest on three premises: that (1) habituation, as a form of learning by doing, is more indicative of learning skills or crafts than of acquiring emotional dispositions (you might habituate someone to be an impeccable cleaner, but this would not guarantee pleasure felt by that person in connection with the cleaning activities); (2) habituation is about forming habits, for instance the habit of being a just arbitrator, but it is hard to grasp how performing just acts on a regular basis *qua* habit will also result in the settlement of affective dispositions such as the desert-based emotions that are, in Aristotle's view, constitutive of the virtue of justice; (3) habituation could possibly be responsible for producing various emotion-regulating virtues – such as courage, which mitigates or removes fear – that prevent us from being excessive in emotion, but not for producing those emotion virtues – such as indignation or compassion – that prevent us from being deficient in emotion.

Steutel and Spiecker themselves suggest a partial solution to this problem, namely that habituation, for Aristotle, is to be supplemented by different forms of reinforcing and punishing stimuli, meted out by a virtuous tutor, so that, for instance, the virtuous dispositions towards pain felt at good or bad fortune when undeserved and towards pleasure when deserved are cultivated by the tutor's application of pleasure and pain. However, they see this conditioning process as merely contingently related to Aristotle's core notion of habituation – as not being part of his *concept* of habituation – and conclude that it is still hard to conceive how the learning mechanism logically implied by Aristotle's habituation could, in itself, be sufficient for the growth of virtuous affective dispositions.

I agree, in essence, with Steutel and Spiecker's solution, but I do not consider it a partial solution which leaves something to be desired, but rather a definitive one. First, empirically speaking, I think these two authors overlook the effects of what de Sousa calls 'bootstrapping' (1987, p. 11). Being forced to act out an emotion, that is, to engage in actions associated with the relevant emotion, can in fact lead to its internalization. Similarly, we can, to a certain extent, defuse an emotion by inhibiting the behavioural responses that typically accompany it. Second, theoretically speaking, there is, it seems to me, no reason to believe that Aristotle ever considered the possibility of habituation without conditioning, or thought of the former as practical or conceptually conceivable without the latter. In that sense, conditioning does form part of his very concept of habituation. Indeed, to mention some of the more negative aspects of Aristotle's account, I see no escape from the somewhat dismal conclusion that Aristotle thought children first came to desire virtuous acts, and to feel virtuous emotions, by internalizing (possible) punishments through fear of *pain*, rather than through the attractions of any possible pleasures attached to the given actions or reactions (cf. Curzer, 2002); later in the habituation process, according to Aristotle, the young learn to identify virtuous activities and emotions through habituation motivated by the pain of retrospective and prospective *shame* (see ibid., p. 158) – all of this taking place before children begin to develop their own *phronesis*. One of the main reasons for Aristotle's insistence on the need for public education was in fact to guarantee that this habituation-conditioning process of motivation through fear was imposed upon every child in the community, for discouraging the development of bad habits, rather than for encouraging the formation of good ones. Children were therefore to be trained in behaviour conducive to the acquisition of moral virtue, while society's publicly enforced example operated to reinforce this behaviour. To prevent the acquisition of bad habits, Aristotle also advocated extensive censorship of all art, literature, drama and company to which children were exposed.

This brings us to another unattractive part of Aristotle's view of early habituation, namely that it is, for him, a somewhat mindless process, essentially prior to the advent of reason. There is no hint of any respectful engagement with the child during the early habituation process, no teaching through argument. Activating the child's critical reasoning abilities cannot take place before the good habits are already in place. When Sherman claims that Aristotelian habituation 'must engage the learner's critical efforts from the start' (1997, p. 79) and Reeve that 'habituation is not merely behavioral, it is also intellectual' (1998, p. 55), they are, I am afraid, engaging in wishful thinking as far as the textual evidence from Aristotle is concerned. This is why, I believe, it would be unreasonable to take on Aristotle's account of moral education in its entirety, however unwilling we are to give up our allegiance to the broader picture he paints of the process from necessary early habituation to full-blown critical thinking, and however convinced we are that what his account loses on particularities, is made up for on generalities.

It is salutary at this point to compare Aristotle's views with those of Martin Hoffman. The latter offers some pertinent comments about the nature and importance of emotion cultivation in moral education: for example, how allowing children to experience a variety of emotions, rather than protecting them, like hothouse flowers, from those emotions, is likely to expand their empathic range. This can, in the case of those emotional experiences that are missing from children's actual lives, be done, to take one example, through guided pretend playing (2000, pp. 288–90). Generally speaking, although Hoffman considers empathy to be an inherited, biologically driven response, which is at the beginning largely involuntary (see my account of biological internalization theories in Section 4.1), he strongly emphasizes the role of social learning in reinforcing and triggering empathy and the pro-social emotions to which it can give rise.

His most highly recommended method for this end is that of *induction*. When the child harms or is about to harm someone, the moral educator (parent, teacher, or whoever) should take up the victim's perspective and demonstrate how the child's behaviour harms the victim. Such inductions achieve two important things that other educational techniques do not: first, they call attention to the victim's distress and make it salient to the child, thus tapping into the child's empathic proclivity; and second, they point to the role of the child's action in causing that distress and the way in which the child is responsible for its reparation, thus creating the conditions for empathy-based guilt (ibid., pp. 150–51). Hoffman refers to this process as the creation of a transgression–induction–guilt 'script', which has motivational properties due both to its empathy and its guilt components (ibid., p. 159). The full script would then also include the parent's and victim's positive responses to the child's reparative acts, thus engendering pleasure through empathic relief and guilt reduction (ibid., p. 158).

We notice at once various similarities between Aristotle's and Hoffman's accounts of early emotion education: for instance, concerning the important role of adult intervention, the restraining function of shame or guilt (and, subsequently, satisfied shame or guilt) in motivating pro-social behaviour, and the necessity of introducing the child to a variety of emotions, including negatively evaluating ones such as compassion, from an early age in order to expand its emotive range. Hoffman, however, overcomes the two problems which mar Aristotle's account. He acknowledges the function of pleasure, as well as pain, in the early habituation (or, as Hoffman would put it, 'script-forming') process, and he recognizes the possibility of tapping into the child's reasoning abilities from the very beginning by the method of induction, through which the instructor facilitates the child's natural proclivity for empathy.

The same weaknesses as noted in my earlier exploration (in Section 4.1) of Hoffman's theory of moral development are, however, reflected in his discussion of the educational implications of his theory. What is missing in Hoffman's educational account is a guide to the use of induction in fostering a far richer set of moral emotions than simply sympathy and its psychological precursor, empathy. Instead of concentrating on the role of induction and other methods of emotion cultivation for the 'socialization of empathic morality' (ibid., pp. 287ff.), Hoffman might have told us how emotion education could also work in the case of desert-based emotions: how such education could and should be used to make the child, for instance, more prone to pain at specifically *undeserved* fortune or misfortune. Such advice would have made the subtitle of Hoffman's book, 'Implications for caring and justice', even more appropriate. The reason why he refrains from giving such advice about justice is evidently the same as I noted in Section 4.1. He thinks of justice as a set of abstract principles for the most part, principles that can only be understood and regulated intellectually, and believes that apparent violations of such principles cannot transform the child's empathic distress into empathic feelings of injustice until relatively late in the moral developmental process: perhaps not until the age of eight to ten, if – as he claims – justice primarily means reciprocity and signs of reciprocity first appear at that age. Desert-based emotions, however, generally start to have a motivating effect on children – as manifested in cries of 'That's not fair!'– from the age of two. Furthermore, it may be that Hoffman underestimates the need for direct behavioural modification; perhaps without Aristotle's conditioning approach, induction may result in mere 'passive empathy' or 'poetic compassion', where one laments the victim's undeserved misfortune from a distance without doing anything about it, even in cases where something can and should be done (cf., in a different context, Boler, 1999, pp. 156–7).

On balance, focusing specifically on the education of the desert-based emotions, Aristotle seems to neglect completely the pleasure attached to their internalization, which is strange given the fact that they seem to come naturally to children – only needing to be nurtured rather than inculcated from scratch – and to be part of our common humanity (see Sections 3.1. and 4.1). He also overlooks the possibility of engaging with children in a gradually developing dialogue on the justification of desert and desert-based emotions before the time when age and experience have given rise to their fully matured *phronesis*. Hoffman's account, on the other hand, is burdened considerably by lack of attention to the role of justice in early moral development: in seeing justice as a purely intellectual supplement to children's natural feelings of sympathy. He also seems to underestimate the necessity of 'bootstrapping' (in de Sousa's sense): of helping make children just through the enforced doing of just actions.

What we should aim for in justice education is a synthesis of the respective strengths of these two outlooks on moral education, as indicated earlier, by avoiding their respective weaknesses. One further reason for considering non-expansive character education, as presented by both Lickona/Kilpatrick and the socio-emotional learning movement, a viable method for justice education – or as I put it earlier, a 'reasonable middle-ground proposal' – is that it seems to accommodate many of the sound ideas we have encountered in Aristotle and Hoffman: to blend pleasure-conferring and critically engaged justice habituation with justice-sensitive induction into a rather promising mixture of moral tutelage.

5.3 Concluding Remarks

'Philosophy is the unusually stubborn attempt to think clearly', is one of William James's famous sayings. In this book, I have tried to bring out and clarify a number of issues relating to justice and desert-based emotions. Chapter 1 addressed the question of what kind of entity an emotion is, and from what perspective desert-based emotions are best studied; Chapter 2 focused on the topic of justice, in general, and desert and its basis, in particular; Chapter 3 engaged with the nature of desert-based emotions as a subset of reactive attitudes; Chapter 4 explored their development and justification; and the present chapter, finally, has studied their cultivation and schooling.

To recapitulate some of my principal points, I tried to drive home, in Chapter 1, the message that desert-based emotions are most fruitfully studied from an interdisciplinary perspective where disparate traditions, social-scientific and philosophical, are made to interact constructively. Chapter 2 depicted justice as an important moral virtue which, while not tantamount to the morally right, is indispensable for a flourishing human life. Justice is made up of entitlements and deserts, where the latter are sometimes weightier than, but at other times eclipsed by, the former. Desert was seen as harmony between, on the one hand, certain states of affairs and, on the other, specific moral qualities and actions of individuals that are generally held in high regard precisely because they are moral. Moral virtue thus emerged as the sole basis of desert. Chapter 3 focused on two classes of desert-based emotions, having to do with the fortunes of others and of one's own self, respectively. These were presented as paradigmatic desert-based emotions, 'purer' than many others that have been more widely discussed in the emotion literature, for example anger, which often is not, and envy, which rarely is, desert-based. Chapter 4 followed the development of desert-based emotions from the age of approximately two, when the first cries of 'That's not fair!' tend to be heard. While the empirical theories examined in this chapter lacked somewhat in conceptual rigour, it was clear at least that desert-based concerns pre-date other justice-based concerns in our lives. From these developmental excavations there followed, almost naturally, a naturalist moral justification, along utilitarian lines, of desert and desert-based emotions as not only practically and morally indispensable, but also essentially pleasure-yielding, moral concerns. Educational implications came to the fore at various levels of engagement with the emotions in question, but those implications were then worked out in some detail in the foregoing two sections of the present chapter. Non-expansive character education, concentrating on inter-human moral basics, is, I have argued, the most productive method of justice education, at least at the early stages. Citizenship education, as a form of expansive character education, may be an important supplement at later stages of schooling in Western democracies, but it cannot replace the more fundamental emphasis on the moral fine-tuning of transcultural human reactions such as our desert-based emotions.

While compassion (pain at someone's undeserved suffering) uncontroversially occupies central moral status among the desert-based emotions, the emotions that I have aimed at justifying in this book include others which have tended to receive a far less receptive hearing as moral reactions: emotions such as indignation (pain at someone's undeserved fortune) and satisfied indignation (pleasure at someone's deserved misfortune). To consider such commonly negatively evaluated emotions as fundamental to the moral life, one must, as Mason correctly noted, have become dissatisfied with the idea that 'an enlightened morality must be a gentle morality' (2003, p. 236; cf. my earlier presentation of her claim at the end of Chapter 1): dissatisfied with the indiscriminate rejection of various negatively evaluating and/or negatively evaluated emotional responses. To quote Solomon, on whose shrewd insights I have often drawn previously, there is 'nothing "negative" about indignation and outrage in the face of injustice, and there is very little that is "positive" in the love of an evil cause or person' (1995, p. 246). To rely entirely on the kindly sentiments would be an inadvisably restrictive feature of a moral outlook; those sentiments 'could not by themselves explain the enormous range or the profound depth of the many sometimes violent passions that constitute our sense of justice. We need a far richer set of moral emotions than the traditional moral sentiment theories of sympathy can provide' (ibid., p. 201). By calling attention to this 'richer set', I hope to have enriched our understanding of the real requirements of morality and helped lay to rest some of the myths to which Mason and Solomon allude.

The role of the less gentle emotions, therefore, needs to be recast and reconceived. It is all too often taken for granted that with regard to such emotions, desirable emotional change, encouraged through moral education, necessarily involves the cooling down or extinguishing of emotion. To be sure, Aristotle concedes that the good person will 'err more in the direction of deficiency' (1985, p. 105 [1126a]), and he regards inirascibility rather than (excessive) irascibility as the less destructive of the two extremes of mildness. Nevertheless, as Aristotle's discussion implies, in the case of justified indignation, increased moral understanding might make you *more* indignant than before, being more sensitive to how morally unacceptable someone's undeserved fortune is (cf. Kristjánsson, 2002, pp. 162–3). To teach morality is not just to teach kindness, sympathy and a number of prohibitions; it is to teach when and how and at whom to be justly angry or indignant, when to be satisfied at someone's deserved misfortune, and so on (cf. French, 2001, p. 111); these reactions are not merely irrational sensibilities that retard development, militate against personal happiness and undermine moral standing. Via my exploration and justification of desert-based emotions, both kindly and tough, we can glimpse an ideal of a moral society where proper pride is considered a more wholesome character trait than sheepish humility, where people of moral fibre exhibit pridefulness through modest pride (opposed, on each side, to arrogance and humility) over their attainments, as well as through expectations of proper recognition from others of those attainments – in short, a society where Aristotle's overarching moral virtue of *megalopsychia* has been actualized and accepted (see further in Kristjánsson, 2002, chs 3–5).

Across the ages, however, numerous moral objections have been pressed against the accounts of Aristotle and others who consider emotions such as indignation and satisfied indignation to be potential components of a virtue. These two emotions, for instance, are said to (a) smack of meanness, (b) express morally condemnable resentment, (c) be substitutable through other, less reprehensible, emotions or (d) be ideally disposable, were our world a better place. Responding carefully to all these objections would require a more profound fashioning of a general moral theory than the present concluding section aims or allows for, so let me simply close with a few suggestive remarks that can be extracted from the direction of my earlier discussion.

First, there need not be anything *mean* about good and honest people loathing injustice to the point that they would prefer the undeserving to be deprived of their rewards, even if it means not that the deserving would get them instead but rather that the total share of goods would be reduced (cf. Kristjánsson, 2002, s. 5.3). Second, indignation and satisfied indignation do not require *resentment of a person*. They simply require pain at the undeserved possession of goods, and pleasure when a correct balance has been restored. On the other hand, it would be quite arbitrary to say that it is good for the balance to be restored, but not good that the person in question suffer the predictable loss (see Sher, 1987, p. 39, for a related point). Third, fear, anger and compassion do not, as Nerney for one suggests, exhaust the moral force of indignation (1991, pp. 88ff.). Although one may have no reason to fear future evils that may be suffered by oneself or one's friends at the hand of the lucky unworthy, no reason to be angry because the undeserved goods were not acquired by the commission of a vicious act, and no reason to feel compassion for any victims of the lucky unworthy, one may still have a good moral reason for being upset by the very undeservingness of the good fortune in question. And finally, to be sure, moral saints will need neither indignation nor satisfied indignation – not, at least, if everyone around them is also a saint. But we do not inhabit a world of moral saints, and talk of 'an ideal of the ideally good person' totally lacking in a disposition to indignant feeling (Neblett, 1979, p. 152, emphasis omitted) is at best vacuous – at any rate, in secular terms.

All in all, nothing in the common objections levelled at indignation or satisfied indignation seems to violate the claim that a sense of desert (*nemesis*) as an emotional virtue, in Aristotle's sense, healthily reflects the moral sensibilities of people living in our world, and that such sensibilities can help – when conjoined with the proper respect for institutional entitlements – sustain a reasonable theory of justice.

References

Adams, R. (1976), 'Motive utilitarianism', *The Journal of Philosophy*, **73**, 467–81.

Anscombe, G. E. M. (1976), *Intention*, Oxford: Basil Blackwell.

Anscombe, G. E. M. (1981a), 'On brute facts', in *The Collected Philosophical Papers of G. E. M. Anscombe*, III: *Ethics, Religion and Politics*, Oxford: Basil Blackwell.

Anscombe, G. E. M. (1981b), 'Modern moral philosophy', in *The Collected Philosophical Papers of G. E. M. Anscombe*, III: *Ethics, Religion and Politics*, Oxford: Basil Blackwell.

Aristotle (1984), *Eudemian Ethics*, trans. J. Solomon, in Barnes, J. (ed.), *The Complete Works of Aristotle*, Princeton, NJ: Princeton University Press.

Aristotle (1985), *Nicomachean Ethics*, trans. T. Irwin, Indianapolis, IN: Hackett Publishing.

Aristotle (1991), *On Rhetoric*, trans. G. A. Kennedy, Oxford: Oxford University Press.

Bain, A. (1899), *The Emotions and the Will*, London: Longmans, Green, and Co.

Bandura, A. (1977), *Social Learning Theory*, Englewood Cliffs, NJ: Prentice Hall.

Barry, B. (1995), *Justice as Impartiality*, Oxford: Clarendon Press.

Batson, C. D. (2002), 'Justice motivation and moral motivation', in Ross, M. and Miller, D. T. (eds), *The Justice Motive in Everyday Life*, Cambridge: Cambridge University Press.

Bennett, W. J. (1991), 'Moral literacy and the formation of character', in Benninga, J. S. (ed.), *Moral Character and Civic Education in the Elementary School*, New York: Teachers College Press.

Ben-Ze'ev, A. (2000), *The Subtlety of Emotions*, Cambridge, MA: MIT Press.

Ben-Ze'ev, A. (2002), 'Are envy, anger, and resentment moral emotions?', *Philosophical Explorations*, **5**, 148–54.

Ben-Ze'ev, A. (2003), 'Aristotle on emotions toward the fortune of others', in Konstan, D. and Rutter, N. K. (eds), *Envy, Spite, and Jealousy: The Rivalrous Emotions in Ancient Greece*, Edinburgh: Edinburgh University Press.

Bierhoff, H. W. (2002), 'Just world, social responsibility, and helping behavior', in Ross, M. and Miller, D. T. (eds), *The Justice Motive in Everyday Life*, Cambridge: Cambridge University Press.

Birnbacher, D. (1999), 'Ethics and social science: which kind of co-operation?', *Ethical Theory and Moral Practice*, **2**, 319–36.

Blum, L. (1987), 'Compassion', in Kruschwitz, R. B. and Roberts, R. C. (eds), *The Virtues: Contemporary Essays in Moral Character*, Belmont, CA: Wadsworth.

Boler, M. (1999), *Feeling Power: Emotions and Education*, London: Routledge.

Breslau, K. (2000), 'Silicon Valley's latest craze: Schadenfreude', *Newsweek*, **136**, 64–5.

Bried, E. (2001), 'When bad things happen to good friends', *Mademoiselle*, **107**, 78–81.

Brigham, N. L., Kelso, K.A., Jackson, M. A. and Smith, R. H. (1997), 'The roles of invidious comparisons and deservingness in sympathy and Schadenfreude', *Basic and Applied Social Psychology*, **19**, 363–80.

Calhoun, C. and Solomon, R. C. (1984), 'Introduction', in Calhoun, C. and Solomon, R. C. (eds), *What Is an Emotion? Classic Readings in Philosophical Psychology*, Oxford: Oxford University Press.

Callan, E. (1988), 'The moral status of pity', *Canadian Journal of Philosophy*, **18**, 1–12.

Callan, E. (1997), *Creating Citizens: Political Education and Liberal Democracy*, Oxford: Clarendon Press.

Campbell, T. (2001), *Justice*, 2nd edn, New York: St Martin's Press.

Carr, D. (1998), 'Moral education and the objectivity of values', in Carr, D. (ed.), *Education, Knowledge and Truth: Beyond the Postmodern Impasse*, London: Routledge.

Carr, D. (2002), 'Moral education and the perils of developmentalism', *Journal of Moral Education*, **31**, 5–19.

Charlesworth, W. R. (1992), 'The child's development of the sense of justice: moral development, resources, and emotions', in Masters, R. D. and Gruter, M. (eds), *The Sense of Justice: Biological Foundations of the Law*, London: Sage.

Cheng, C.-y. (2001), 'The relationship between the justice of the state and the justice of persons', in Sterba, J. P. (ed.), *Social and Political Philosophy: Contemporary Perspectives*, New York: Routledge.

Clark, C. (1997), *Misery and Company: Sympathy in Everyday Life*, Chicago, IL: University of Chicago Press.

Cline, H. F. and Feldmesser, R. A. (1983), *Program Evaluation in Moral Education*, Princeton, NJ: Educational Testing Services.

Coker, J. C. (1992), 'On being *nemesetikos* as a mean', *Journal of Philosophical Research*, **17**, 61–92.

Cole, M. and Cole, S. R. (1996), *The Development of Children*, New York: W. H. Freeman and Co.

Connolly, W. (1983), *The Terms of Political Discourse*, 2nd edn, Oxford: Martin Robertson and Co.

Cooley, D. R. (2000), 'Readjusting utility for justice', *Journal of Philosophical Research*, **25**, 363–80.

Cooper, J. M. (1996), 'An Aristotelian theory of the emotions', in Rorty, A. O. (ed.), *Essays on Aristotle's Rhetoric*, Berkeley, CA: University of California Press.

Cornelius, R. and Fischer, A. (2002), 'Editor's column', *Emotion Researcher*, **16**, 2.

Cottom, C. (1996), 'A bold experiment in teaching values', *Educational Leadership*, **53**, 54–8.

Crouch, M. A. (1993), 'A "limited" defense of the genetic fallacy', *Metaphilosophy*, **24**, 227–40.

Cummiskey, D. (1987), 'Desert and entitlement: a Rawlsian consequentialist account', *Analysis*, **47**, 15–19.

Cupit, G. (1996), *Justice as Fittingness*, Oxford: Clarendon Press.

Curzer, H. (1995), 'Aristotle's account of the virtue of justice', *Apeiron*, **28**, 207–38.

Curzer, H. (2002), 'Aristotle's painful path to virtue', *Journal of the History of Philosophy*, **40**, 141–62.

D'Arms, J. and Jacobson, D. (2000), 'The moralistic fallacy: on the "appropriateness" of emotions', *Philosophy and Phenomenological Research*, **61**, 65–90.

D'Arms, J. and Jacobson, D. (2003), 'The significance of recalcitrant emotions (or anti-quasijudgmentalism)', in Hatzimoysis, A. (ed.), *Philosophy and the Emotions*, Cambridge: Cambridge University Press.

Dalbert, C. (1999), 'The world is more just for me than generally: about the personal belief in a just world scale's validity', *Social Justice Research*, **12**, 79–98.

Dalbert, C. and Maes, J. (2002), 'Belief in a just world as a personal resource in school', in Ross, M. and Miller, D. T. (eds), *The Justice Motive in Everyday Life*, Cambridge: Cambridge University Press.

Damon, W. (1980), 'Patterns of change in children's social reasoning: a two-year longitudinal study', *Child Development*, **51**, 1010–17.

Damon, W. (1981), 'The development of justice and self-interest during childhood', in Lerner, M. J. and Lerner, S. C. (eds), *The Justice Motive in Social Behavior: Adapting to Times of Scarcity and Change*, New York: Plenum Press.

Damon, W. (1988), *The Moral Child: Nurturing Children's Natural Moral Growth*, New York: Free Press.

Danto, A. (1985), *Narration and Knowledge*, New York: Columbia University Press.

Darley, J. (2002), 'Just punishment research on retributional justice', in Ross, M. and Miller, D. T. (eds), *The Justice Motive in Everyday Life*, Cambridge: Cambridge University Press.

De Sousa, R. (1987), *The Rationality of Emotions*, Cambridge, MA: MIT Press.

De Sousa, R. (2001), 'Moral emotions', *Ethical Theory and Moral Practice*, **4**, 109–26.

Department for Education and Skills (DfES) Web Pages on Citizenship Education (2002): http://www.dfes.gov.uk/a-z/CITIZENSHIP_EDUCATION_ba.html, retrieved 25 December.

Dunne, J. (1993), *Back to the Rough Ground: 'Phronesis' and 'Techne' in Modern Philosophy and in Aristotle*, Notre Dame, IN: University of Notre Dame Press.

Elias, M. J. et al. (1997), *Promoting Social and Emotional Learning: Guidelines for Educators*, Alexandria, VA: Association for Supervision and Curriculum Development.

Enslin, P. and White, P. (2003), 'Democratic citizenship', in Blake, N., Smeyers, P., Smith, R. and Standish, P. (eds), *The Blackwell Guide to the Philosophy of Education*, Oxford: Blackwell.

Farrell, D. M. (1989), 'Of jealousy and envy', in Graham, G. and Lafollette, H. (eds), *Person to Person*, Philadelphia, PA: Temple University Press.

Feather, N. T. (1992), 'An attributional and value analysis of deservingness in success and failure situations', *British Journal of Social Psychology*, **31**, 125–45.

Feather, N. T. (1999), *Values, Achievement, and Justice: Studies in the Psychology of Deservingness*, Dordrecht: Kluwer/Plenum.

Feather, N. T. (2002), 'Deservingness, entitlement, and reactions to outcomes', in Ross, M. and Miller, D. T. (eds), *The Justice Motive in Everyday Life*, Cambridge: Cambridge University Press.

Feather, N. T. and Sherman, R. (2002), 'Envy, resentment, *Schadenfreude*, and sympathy: reactions to deserved and undeserved achievement and subsequent failure', *Personality and Social Psychology Bulletin*, **28**, 953–61.

Feinberg, J. (1970), 'Justice and personal desert', in *Doing and Deserving: Essays in the Theory of Responsibility*, Princeton, NJ: Princeton University Press.

Feinberg, J. (1980), 'Noncomparative justice', in *Rights, Justice, and the Bounds of Liberty*, Princeton, NJ: Princeton University Press.

Feldman, F. (1992), *Confrontations with the Reaper: A Philosophical Study of the Nature and Value of Death*, Oxford: Oxford University Press.

Feldman, F. (1995a), 'Adjusting utility for justice: a consequentialist reply to the objections from justice', *Philosophy and Phenomenological Research*, **55**, 567–85.

Feldman, F. (1995b), 'Desert: reconsiderations of some received wisdom', *Mind*, **104**, 63–77.

Feldman, F. (2003a), 'Maximizing desert adjusted utility', http://www-unix.oit.umass.edu/~jvessel/Desert-Adjusted%20Utilitarianism.html, retrieved 10 September.

Feldman, F. (2003b), 'Return to Twin Peaks: on the intrinsic moral significance of equality', in Olsaretti, S. (ed.), *Desert and Justice*, Oxford: Clarendon Press.

Flew, A. (1984), 'Justice: real or social?', *Social Philosophy and Policy*, **1**, 151–71.

Foot, P. (1985), 'Utilitarianism and the virtues', *Mind*, **94**, 196–209.

Foot, P. (2001), *Natural Goodness*, Oxford: Clarendon Press.

French, P. A. (2001), *The Virtues of Vengeance*, Lawrence, KS: University Press of Kansas.

Frolich, N. and Oppenheimer, J. (1992), *Choosing Justice: An Experimental Approach to Ethical Theory*, Berkeley, CA: University of California Press.

Gallie, W. B. (1955–56), 'Essentially contestable concepts', *Proceedings of the Aristotelian Society*, **56**, 167–98.

Galston, W. A. (1980), *Justice and the Human Good*, Chicago, IL: University of Chicago Press.

Galston, W. A. (1991), *Liberal Purposes*, Cambridge: Cambridge University Press.

Gert, B. (1998), *Morality*, Oxford: Oxford University Press.

Goldie, P. (2000), *The Emotions: A Philosophical Exploration*, Oxford: Clarendon Press.

Goldie, P. (2002), 'Compassion: a natural, moral emotion', in Döring, S. A. and Mayer, V. (eds), *Die Moralität der Gefühle*: Special Issue of *Deutsche Zeitschrift für Philosophie*, Berlin: Akademie.

Goleman, D. (1995), *Emotional Intelligence*, New York: Bantam Books.

Goodstein, L. (1993), '"Declaration of a global ethic"' signed at religious parliament', *Washington Post*, 3 Sept., 3.

Gunnarsson, L. (2000), *Making Moral Sense: Beyond Habermas and Gauthier*, Cambridge: Cambridge University Press.

Gutmann, A. (1982), 'What's the use of going to school?', in Sen, A. and Williams, B. (eds), *Utilitarianism and Beyond*, Cambridge: Cambridge University Press.

Gutmann, A. (1987), *Democratic Education*, Princeton, NJ: Princeton University Press.

Hafer, C. L. (2002), 'Why we reject innocent victims', in Ross, M. and Miller, D. T. (eds), *The Justice Motive in Everyday Life*, Cambridge: Cambridge University Press.

Hafer, C. L. and Correy, B. L. (1999), 'Mediators of the relation between beliefs in a just world and emotional responses to negative outcomes', *Social Justice Research*, **12**, 189–204.

Hall, S. (2000), 'Multicultural citizens, monocultural citizenship?', in Pearce, N. and Hallgarten, J. (eds), *Tomorrow's Citizens: Critical Debates in Citizenship and Education*, London: Institute for Public Policy Research.

Hare, S. (1996), 'The paradox of moral humility', *American Philosophical Quarterly*, **33**, 235–41.

Hareli, S. (1999), 'Justice and deservingness judgments – refuting the interchangeability assumption', *New Ideas in Psychology*, **17**, 183–93.

Harris, P. L. (1989), *Children and Emotion: The Development of Psychological Understanding*, Oxford: Basil Blackwell.

Heider, F. (1958), *The Psychology of Interpersonal Relations*, New York: Wiley.

Hoffman, M. L. (2000), *Empathy and Moral Development: Implications for Caring and Justice*, Cambridge: Cambridge University Press.

Hooker, B. (2000), *Ideal Code, Real World: A Rule-Consequentialist Theory of Morality*, Oxford: Clarendon Press.

Hospers, J. (1961), *Human Conduct: An Introduction to the Problems of Ethics*, New York: Harcourt.

Huntsman, R. W. (1984), 'Children's concepts of fair sharing', *Journal of Moral Education*, **13**, 31–9.

Hurka, T. (2001), 'The common structure of virtue and desert', *Ethics*, **112**, 6–31.

Hurka, T. (2003), 'Desert: individualistic and holistic', in Olsaretti, S. (ed.), *Desert and Justice*, Oxford: Clarendon Press.

Hurley, S. (2003), *Justice, Luck, and Knowledge*, Cambridge, MA: Harvard University Press.

Hursthouse, R. (1999), *On Virtue Ethics*, Oxford: Oxford University Press.

Irwin, T. (1988), *Aristotle's First Principles*, Oxford: Oxford University Press.

Kagan, S. (2003), 'Comparative desert', in Olsaretti, S. (ed.), *Desert and Justice*, Oxford: Clarendon Press.

Karasawa, K. (1995), 'An attributional analysis of reactions to negative emotions', *Personality and Social Psychology Bulletin*, **21**, 456–67.

Karlsson, M. (2001), 'Roots of legal normativity', in Comanducci, P. and Guastini, R. (eds), *Analisi e diritto 2000: richerce di giurisprudenza analitica*, Torino: G. Giappichelli Editore.

Kiecolt-Glaser, J. K. et al. (2002), 'Emotions, morbidity, and mortality: new perspectives from psychoneuroimmunology', *Annual Review of Psychology*, **43**, 83–107.

Kilpatrick, W. (1992), *Why Johnny Can't Tell Right from Wrong: Moral Illiteracy and the Case for Character Education*, New York: Simon and Schuster.

Klement, K. C. (2002), 'When is genetic reasoning not fallacious?', *Argumentation*, **16**, 383–400.

Kohlberg, L. (1981), *Essays on Moral Development*, I–III, New York: Harper & Row.

Kohn, A. (1997), 'The trouble with character education', in Molnar, A. (ed.), *The Construction of Children's Character*, Chicago, IL: National Society for Study of Education.

Kramer, M. H. (2003), *The Quality of Freedom*, Oxford: Oxford University Press.

Krehbiel, P. J. and Cropanzano, R. (2000), 'Procedural justice, outcome favorability and emotion', *Social Justice Research*, **13**, 339–60.

Kristjánsson, K. (1996), *Social Freedom: The Responsibility View*, Cambridge: Cambridge University Press.

Kristjánsson, K. (1998a), 'Is there something wrong with "free action"?', *Journal of Theoretical Politics*, **10**, 259–73.

Kristjánsson, K. (1998b), 'Reply to Pettit and Norman', *Journal of Theoretical Politics*, **10**, 291–8.

Kristjánsson, K. (2002), *Justifying Emotions: Pride and Jealousy*, London: Routledge.

La Caze, M. (2001), 'Envy and resentment', *Philosophical Explorations*, **4**, 31–45.

La Caze, M. (2002), 'Revaluing envy and resentment', *Philosophical Explorations*, **5**, 155–8.

Lamont, J. (1994), 'The concept of desert in distributive justice', *The Philosophical Quarterly*, **44**, 45–64.

Lerner, M. J. (1981), 'The justice motive in human relations: some thoughts on what we know and need to know about justice', in Lerner, M. J. and Lerner, S. C. (eds), *The Justice Motive in Social Behavior: Adapting to Times of Scarcity and Change*, New York: Plenum Press.

Lerner, M. J. (2002), 'Pursuing the justice motive', in Ross, M. and Miller, D. T. (eds), *The Justice Motive in Everyday Life*, Cambridge: Cambridge University Press.

Lickona, T. (1991), *Educating for Character: How Our Schools Can Teach Respect and Responsibility*, New York: Bantam Books.

Liebig, S. (2001), 'Lessons from philosophy: interdisciplinary justice research and two classes of justice judgments', *Social Justice Research*, **14**, 265–86.

Lupfer, M. B. and Gingrich, B. E. (1999), 'When bad (good) things happen to good (bad) people: the impact of character appraisal and perceived controllability on judgments of deservingness', *Social Justice Research*, **12**, 165–88.

MacIntyre, A. (1984), *After Virtue*, Notre Dame, IN: University of Notre Dame Press.

Mackie, J. L. (1985), *Persons and Values. Selected Papers*, II, Oxford: Clarendon Press.

McLaughlin, T. H. (2000), 'Citizenship education in England: the Crick report and beyond', *Journal of Philosophy of Education*, **34**, 541–70.

McLaughlin, T. H. and Halstead, J. M. (1999), 'Education in character and virtue', in Halstead, J. M. and McLaughlin, T. H. (eds), *Education in Morality*, London: Routledge.

McLeod, O. (1999), 'Contemporary interpretations of desert: introduction', in Pojman, L. P. and McLeod, O. (eds), *What Do We Deserve? A Reader on Justice and Desert*, Oxford: Oxford University Press.

McLeod, O. (2003), 'On the comparative element of justice', in Olsaretti, S. (ed.), *Desert and Justice*, Oxford: Clarendon Press.

McNamee, M. (2003), '*Schadenfreude* in sport: envy, justice, and self-esteem', *Journal of the Philosophy of Sport*, **30**, 1–16.

Mason, A. (2002), 'Meritocracy, desert and the moral force of intuitions', in Bell, D. and de Shalit, A. (eds), *Forms of Justice: Critical Perspectives on David Miller's Political Philosophy*, Lanham, MD: Rowman and Littlefield.

Mason, M. (2003), 'Contempt as a moral attitude', *Ethics*, **113**, 234–72.

Masters, R. D. (1992), 'The problem of justice in contemporary legal thought', in Masters, R. D. and Gruter, M. (eds), *The Sense of Justice: Biological Foundations of the Law*, London: Sage.

Mayer, J. D. and Cobb, C. D. (2000), 'Educational policy on emotional intelligence: does it make sense?', *Educational Psychology Review*, **12**, 163–83.

Mikula, G., Scherer, K. R. and Athenstaedt, U. (1998), 'The role of injustice in the elicitation of differential emotional reactions', *Personality and Social Psychology Bulletin*, **24**, 769–83.

Mill, J. S. (1931), *Utilitarianism, Liberty, Representative Government*, London: J. M. Dent and Sons.

Miller, D. (1976), *Social Justice*, Oxford: Clarendon Press.

Miller, D. (1993), 'In defence of nationality', *Journal of Applied Philosophy*, **10**, 3–16.

Miller, D. (1999), *Principles of Social Justice*, Cambridge, MA: Harvard University Press.

Moers, M. (1930), 'Schadenfreude', *Zeitschrift für Pädagogische Psychologie und Experimentelle Pädagogik*, **31**, 126–34.

Montada, L. (2002), 'Doing justice to the justice motive', in Ross, M. and Miller, D. T. (eds), *The Justice Motive in Everyday Life*, Cambridge: Cambridge University Press.

Montada, L. and Lerner, M. J. (eds) (1998), *Responses to Victimization and Belief in a Just World*, New York: Plenum.

Montada, L. and Schneider, A. (1989), 'Justice and emotional reactions to the disadvantaged', *Social Justice Research*, **3**, 313–44.

Moore, E. (2000), 'Desert, virtue, and justice', *Social Theory and Practice*, **26**, 417–42.

Moriarty, J. (2003), 'Against the asymmetry of desert', *Noûs*, **37**, 518–36.

Muris, P. et al. (2001), 'The structure of negative emotions in adolescents', *Journal of Abnormal Child Psychology*, **29**, 331–7.

Nagel, T. (1979), *Mortal Questions*, Cambridge: Cambridge University Press.

Nash, R. J. (1997), *Answering the 'Virtuecrats': A Moral Conversation on Character Education*, New York and London: Teachers College Press.

Neblett, W. (1979), 'Indignation: a case study in the role of feelings in morals', *Metaphilosophy*, **10**, 139–52.

Nerney, G. (1991), 'Aristotle and Aquinas on indignation: from nemesis to theodicy', *Faith and Philosophy*, **8**, 81–95.

Nozick, R. (1971), *Anarchy, State, and Utopia*, Oxford: Basil Blackwell.

Nozick, R. (1972), 'Coercion', in Laslett, P., Runciman, W. G. and Skinner, Q. (eds), *Philosophy, Politics and Society*, IV, Oxford: Basil Blackwell.

Nussbaum, M. C. (1988), 'Nature, function, and capability', *Oxford Studies in Ancient Philosophy*, suppl. vol. **1**, 145–84.

Nussbaum, M. C. (1990), 'Aristotelian social democracy', in Douglass, R. B., Mara, G. M. and Richardson, H. S. (eds), *Liberalism and the Good*, London: Routledge.

Nussbaum, M. C. (1992), 'Human functioning and social justice: in defence of Aristotelian essentialism', *Political Theory*, **20**, 202–46.

Nussbaum, M. C. (1996), 'Compassion: the basic social emotion', *Social Philosophy and Policy*, **13**, 27–58.

Nussbaum, M. C. (1999), 'Virtue ethics: a misleading category?', *The Journal of Ethics*, **3**, 163–201.

Nussbaum, M. C. (2000), 'Aristotle, politics, and human capabilities: a response to Antony, Arneson, Charlesworth, and Mulgan', *Ethics*, **111**, 102–40.

Nuyen, A. T. (1997), 'Just desert', *The Journal of Value Inquiry*, **31**, 221–30.

O'Connor, D. (1988), 'Aristotelian justice as a personal virtue', *Midwest Studies in Philosophy*, **13**, 417–27.

O'Hear, A. (1981), *Education, Society and Human Nature*, London: Routledge.

Olsaretti, S. (2002), 'Desert and luck', in Bell, D. and de Shalit, A. (eds), *Forms of Justice: Critical Perspectives on David Miller's Political Philosophy*, Lanham, MD: Rowman and Littlefield.

Olsaretti, S. (2003a), 'Introduction: debating desert and justice', in Olsaretti, S. (ed.), *Desert and Justice*, Oxford: Clarendon Press.

Olsaretti, S. (2003b), 'Distributive justice and compensatory desert', in Olsaretti, S. (ed.), *Desert and Justice*, Oxford: Clarendon Press.

Ortony, A., Clore G. L. and Collins, A. (1988), *The Cognitive Structure of Emotions*, Cambridge: Cambridge University Press.

Parrott, W. G. and Smith, R. H. (1993), 'Distinguishing the experiences of envy and jealousy', *Journal of Personality and Social Psychology*, **64**, 906–20.

Pojman, L. P. (2001), 'Justice as desert', *Queensland University of Technology Law and Justice Journal*, **16**, 88–109.

Pojman, L. P. and McLeod, O. (eds) (1999), *What Do We Deserve? A Reader on Justice and Desert*, Oxford: Oxford University Press.

Portmann, J. (2000), *When Bad Things Happen to Other People*, New York: Routledge.

Pugmire, D. (1996), 'Conflicting emotions and the indivisible heart', *Philosophy*, **71**, 27–40.

Puka, B (2000), 'Inclusive moral education: a critique and integration of competing approaches', in Leicester, M., Modgil, C. and Modgil, S. (eds), *Education, Culture and Values*, IV: *Moral Education and Pluralism*, New York: Falmer Press.

Purpel, D. E. (1997), 'The politics of character education', in Molnar, A. (ed.), *The Construction of Children's Character*, Chicago, IL: National Society for Study of Education.

Rawls, J. (1963), 'The sense of justice', *Philosophical Review*, **72**, 281–305.

Rawls, J. (1973), *A Theory of Justice*, Oxford: Oxford University Press.

Rawls, J. (1993), 'The law of peoples', *Critical Inquiry*, **20**, 36–68.

Reeve, C. D. C. (1998), 'Aristotelian education', in Rorty, A. O. (ed.), *Philosophers on Education: Historical Perspectives*, London: Routledge.

Reichle, B. and Schmitt, M. (2002), 'Helping and rationalizing as alternative strategies for restoring the belief in a just world: evidence from longitudinal change analysis', in Ross, M. and Miller, D. T. (eds), *The Justice Motive in Everyday Life*, Cambridge: Cambridge University Press.

Revel, J.-F. and Ricard, M. (1998), *The Monk and the Philosopher: A Father and Son Discuss the Meaning of Life*, New York: Schocken Books.

Roberts, R. C. (1989), 'Aristotle on virtues and emotions', *Philosophical Studies*, **56**, 293–306.

Roberts, R. C. (2003), *Emotions: An Essay in Aid of Moral Psychology*, Cambridge: Cambridge University Press.

Rogers, B. (2002), 'Just deserts', *Guardian*, 19 April, 21.

Ross, M. and Miller, D. T. (eds) (2002), *The Justice Motive in Everyday Life*, Cambridge: Cambridge University Press.

Ross, W. D. (1930), *The Right and the Good*, Oxford: Clarendon Press.

Rousseau, J.-J. (1911), *Emile*, London: Everyman.

Rubin, Z. and Peplau, L. A. (1975), 'Who believes in a just world?', *Journal of Social Issues*, **31**, 65–89.

Sabbagh, C. (2001), 'A taxonomy of normative and empirically oriented theories of distributive justice', *Social Justice Research*, **14**, 237–62.

Sadurski, W. (1985), *Giving Desert its Due: Social Justice and Legal Theory*, Dordrecht: D. Reidel.

Sandel, M. (1982), *Liberalism and the Limits of Justice*, Cambridge: Cambridge University Press.

Scanlon, T. (1998), *What We Owe to Each Other*, Cambridge, MA: Harvard University Press.

Scheffler, S. (1992), 'Responsibility, reactive attitudes, and liberalism in philosophy and politics', *Philosophy and Public Affairs*, **21**, 299–323.

Scheffler, S. (2001), *Boundaries and Allegiances*, Oxford: Oxford University Press.

Scheffler, S. (2003a), 'Distributive justice and economic desert', in Olsaretti, S. (ed.), *Desert and Justice*, Oxford: Clarendon Press.

Scheffler, S. (2003b), 'Replies to Ashford, Miller and Rosen', *Philosophical Books*, **44**, 125–34.

Schoeck, H. (1969), *Envy: A Theory of Social Behaviour*, New York: Harcourt, Brace and World.

Schroeder, D. A. et al. (1995), *The Psychology of Helping and Altruism*, New York: McGraw-Hill.

Scotus, J. D. (1968), *Ordinatio*, in Wadding, L., *Johannes Duns Scotus Opera Omnia*, Hildesheim: Georg Olms.

Shaffer, D. R. (2000), *Social and Personality Development*, Belmont, CA: Wadsworth.

Sher, G. (1987), *Desert*, Princeton, NJ: Princeton University Press.

Sherman, N. (1997), *Making a Necessity of Virtue: Aristotle and Kant on Virtue*, Cambridge: Cambridge University Press.

Sherman, N. (1999), 'Character development and Aristotelian virtue,' in Carr, D. and Steutel, J. (eds), *Virtue Ethics and Moral Education*, London: Routledge.

Sigelman, C. K. and Waitzman, K. A. (1991), 'The development of distributive justice orientations: contextual influences on children's resource allocations', *Child Development*, **62**, 1367–78.

Simmons, C. H. (1981), 'Theoretical issues in the development of social justice', in Lerner, M. J. and Lerner, S. C. (eds), *The Justice Motive in Social Behavior: Adapting to Times of Scarcity and Change*, New York: Plenum Press.

Smith, R. H. (2000), 'Assimilative and contrastive emotional reactions to upward and downward social comparisons', in Suls, J. and Wheeler, L. (eds), *Handbook of Social Comparison: Theory and Research*, New York: Kluwer/Plenum.

Smith, R. H. et al. (1996), 'Envy and *Schadenfreude*', *Personality and Social Psychology Bulletin*, **22**, 158–68.

Smith, T. (1999), 'Justice as a personal virtue', *Social Theory and Practice*, **25**, 361–84.

Snow, N. E. (1991), 'Compassion', *American Philosophical Quarterly*, **28**, 195–205.

Snævarr, S. (2004), 'The metaphoric and narrative structure of emotions', paper presented at the 26th World Congress of Aesthetics, Rio de Janeiro, July.

Solomon, R. C. (1983), *The Passions*, Notre Dame, IN: University of Notre Dame Press.

Solomon, R. C. (1994), 'Sympathy and vengeance: the role of emotions in justice', in Van Goozen, S. H. M. et al. (eds), *Emotions: Essays on Emotion Theory*, Hillsdale, NJ: Lawrence Erlbaum.

Solomon, R. C. (1995), *A Passion for Justice: Emotions and the Origins of the Social Contract*, Lanham, MD: Rowman and Littlefield.

Solomon, R. C. (2001), 'Justice as a virtue', in Sterba, J. P. (ed.), *Social and Political Philosophy: Contemporary Perspectives*, New York: Routledge.

Solomon, R. C. (2002a), '"Nasty" emotions', *Emotion Researcher*, **16**, 3.

Solomon, R. C. (2002b), 'Back to basics: on the very idea of "basic emotions"', *Journal for the Theory of Social Behaviour*, **32**, 115–44.

Solomon, R. C. (2003a), 'Is pride a positive emotion?', *Emotion Researcher*, **18**, 9–10.

Solomon, R. C. (2003b), 'Emotions, thoughts and feelings: what is a "cognitive theory" of the emotions and does it neglect affectivity?', in Hatzimoysis, A. (ed.), *Philosophy and the Emotions*, Cambridge: Cambridge University Press.

Solomon, R. C. and Stone, L. D. (2002), 'On "positive" and "negative" emotions', *Journal for the Theory of Social Behaviour*, **32**, 417–35.

Stein, N. L. and Jewett, J. L. (1986), 'A conceptual analysis of the meaning of negative emotions: implications for a theory of development', in Izard, C. E. and Read, P. B. (eds), *Measuring Emotions in Infants and Children*, II, Cambridge: Cambridge University Press.

Steutel, J. and Spiecker, B. (2004), 'Cultivating sentimental dispositions through Aristotelian habituation', *Journal of Philosophy of Education*, **33**, 531–49.

Stocker, M. (with E. Hegeman) (1996), *Valuing Emotions*, Cambridge: Cambridge University Press.

Stotland, E. (1969), 'Exploratory investigations of empathy', in Berkowitz, L. (ed.), *Advances in Experimental Social Psychology*, New York: Academic Press.

Strawson, P. F. (1962), 'Freedom and resentment', *Proceedings of the British Academy*, **48**, 187–211.

Swift, A. (1995), 'Distributive justice: does it matter what the people think?', in Kluegel, J. R., Mason, D. S. and Wegener, B. (eds), *Social Justice and Political Change: Public Opinion in Capitalist and Post-Communist States*, New York: Walter de Gruyter.

Swift, A. (1999), 'Public opinion and political philosophy: the relation between social-scientific and philosophical analyses of distributive justice', *Ethical Theory and Moral Practice*, **2**, 337–63.

Tesser, A. (1991), 'Emotion in social comparison and reflection processes', in Suls, J. and Wills, T. A. (eds), *Social Comparison: Contemporary Theory and Research*, Hillsdale, NJ: Lawrence Erlbaum.

Tesser, A. and Collins, J. E. (1988), 'Emotion in social reflection and comparison situations: intuitive, systematic, and exploratory approaches', *Journal of Personality and Social Psychology*, **55**, 695–709.

Tomasi, J. (2001), *Liberalism Beyond Justice: Citizens, Society, and the Boundaries of Political Theory*, Princeton, NJ: Princeton University Press.

Tooley, J. (2000), *Reclaiming Education*, London: Cassell.

Vallentyne, P. (1995), 'Taking justice too seriously', *Utilitas*, **7**, 207–16.

Walsh, A. (2000), 'Evolutionary psychology and the origins of justice', *Justice Quarterly*, **17**, 841–63.

Walster, E., Walster, G. W. and Berscheid, E. (1978), *Equity: Theory and Research*, Boston, MA: Allyn & Bacon.

West, C. (1993), 'The new cultural politics of difference', in During, S. (ed.), *The Cultural Studies Reader*, London: Routledge.

Wiggins, D. (1987), 'The concern to survive', in *Needs, Values, Truth: Essays in the Philosophy of Value*, Oxford: Basil Blackwell.

Wilson, C. (2003), 'The role of a merit principle in distributive justice', *The Journal of Ethics*, **7**, 277–314.

Young, M. D. (1961), *Rise of Meritocracy 1870–2033: An Essay on Education and Equality*, Harmondsworth: Penguin.

Index